The Craft of
Christian Teaching

A Classroom Journey

The Craft of Christian Teaching

A Classroom Journey

by John Van Dyk

 Dordt Press

Printed in the United States of America.

dp Dordt Press
498 Fourth Avenue NE
Sioux Center, Iowa 51250

ISBN: 0-932914-46-2

doodles, diagrams, and dividers by the author

cover photos by Susan Van Dyk

*cover and layout design
by Kristi De Groot and Barb Grevengoed*

to all
who seek to teach Christianly
in their classrooms

This is a book rich in both practical ideas for teaching and insights into teaching as a Christian calling. While it is not a book on teaching theory, the discerning reader will recognize sound theoretical reflection underlying its practice-oriented approach. The author's Christian commitment is made clear in many ways, but two features stand out. One is the way in which a piety that recognizes the reality of God's presence and our dependence on him is embedded in a down-to-earth approach to the everyday issues of teaching practice. The other is that the author clearly presents himself, not as the ultimate authority, but as a fellow servant of the Lord with his readers. It is a rich resource from which novice and the most experienced teacher alike will benefit.

Stuart Fowler
Antithesis Educational Services, Melbourne, Australia
National Institute for Christian Education, Sydney, Australia

Craft is like a pair of binoculars with biblically-ground lenses—helpful equipment for surveying the landscape of pedagogy. The book exposes current views and provides alternatives built on a Christian approach to teaching. Van Dyk challenges teachers to critically examine and evaluate their teaching methods. He not only acknowledges and appreciates contributions to pedagogical insight, but also redirects and reshapes them in light of biblical perspectives. *Craft* is a useful addition to the growing collection of writings that seek to reshape education to reflect a more biblical approach. It is an excellent resource for courses on pedagogy and for staff inservicing activities. In addition, the book will be valuable for Christian school boards and/or committees as they examine issues of teaching practice.

John Vanderhoek
Executive Director
Christian Schools Development Foundation
Penticton, British Columbia

CONTENTS

PREFACE

This is a book about teaching—more specifically, about teaching as a distinctively Christian activity. Its purpose is to help teachers see more clearly that accepting Christ not only changes their personal lives, but also their teaching practice. At least, it should. In reality, being a Christian does not guarantee a Christian classroom practice. Sometimes sincere Christian teachers conduct classrooms where the Holy Spirit hardly seems welcome, although, of course, they do not do so deliberately. We all fall short. We all need to improve. Daily reflection about what we believe and deepened insight into what we do in the classroom are essential if we are to truly teach Christianly.

This book is a response to a need expressed by teachers. In the early 1980s, Dordt College initiated two new projects: (1) a series of annual education conferences, designed to address issues of direct importance to Christian elementary and secondary school teachers, and (2) the Center for Educational Services, mandated to organize and deliver inservice workshops and seminars to Christian schools. But what issues should the conference series address, and what services should the Center provide? To find good answers to these questions, a study committee undertook an extensive inquiry. My colleague, Larry Reynolds, and I conducted surveys, consulted with numerous teachers and teacher educators, and, in general, got a feel for what was going on in Christian education at that time. We discovered that teachers already have access to Christian perspectives on philosophy of education, curriculum and subject matter. But actual teaching methods and how to structure the classroom for learning were not adequately addressed. The need for inquiry into a Christian approach to pedagogy seemed overwhelmingly clear to us, so my research and thinking focused on the issue of teaching Christianly. This book is the outcome.

From the time I set foot in the classroom as a beginning high school teacher to this very day 37 years later, teaching has been a most wonderful and rewarding profession for me. Over the years, especially since I began my work as the director of the Center for Educational Services, I have increasingly come to see that teaching is also one of the most complicated of professions. Consequently, a book like this, which seeks to address teaching practice in a focused way, is a risky undertaking. Teaching is such a multifaceted activity that any book about it will inevitably leave out many aspects and important themes, and, as a result, may appear to be incomplete.

In spite of the risk, I have tried my hand at articulating what I have learned from elementary and secondary teachers, from teacher educators, and from my own experience. My book is not meant to be a conclusive answer to all questions about teaching Christianly. Rather, I see it as an introduction, much like a wading pool invites us to learn to swim. My hope is that reading this book will prompt practicing classroom teachers to reevaluate their calling and work, and to expand on and experiment with the various suggestions proposed in this book. I hope, as well, that this book will serve as a useful vehicle for staff development and a helpful resource in both graduate and undergraduate teacher education programs. For those who wish to pursue a specific topic, I have included a topical index as well as referencing notes.

The religious orientation of this book reflects the biblical perspective of Dordt College as a whole. Christian education at all levels must recognize that we live in a world created, structured, and upheld by God himself. "The earth is the Lord's and the fullness thereof" (Psalm 24:1). Sin has infected all aspects of God's good creation. But, praise the Lord, the scope of Christ's redemption is as wide as the creation itself. Christ was sent to die on the cross to reconcile all things to God the Father (Col. 1:19), to make all things new, classroom practice included. All we do—whether praying, eating or drinking, or teaching algebra or chemistry—we do to demonstrate our love for God and our neighbor. To help teachers make this biblical view more of a reality in their classrooms is the intent of this book.

Teaching is a craft, but it is also more than a craft. It is a craft in process. Teachers ply their craft as they journey together with their students. They are always "on the way." This book tries to clarify both the craft side of teaching—methods, techniques, classroom decisions, and the like—and the larger framework within which these methods and techniques are implemented. In short, the title of the book suggests that a Christian pedagogy is practiced as we—teachers and students—walk on a pathway before the face of God.

I hope this book will help Christian teachers to enhance their craft as they journey with their students.

ACKNOWLEDGMENTS

I am indebted to the many teachers who opened their classrooms to me, so I could observe, learn, and experiment in a variety of teaching situations. I owe a debt, too, to the teachers who provided feedback in the graduate courses, seminars, and workshops I have conducted throughout the world. Thanks also to the many educators with whom I discussed this material or who responded to the position papers I distributed. Without these teachers, schools, and educators, this book could not have been written.

Furthermore, I want to express my deep gratitude to the Dordt College administration and the Education Department for their strong support of both the continuing B. J. Haan Education Conferences and the Center for Educational Services. Directing both these projects enabled me to benefit in special ways from the conference activities, and provided opportunities for me to interact with schools, classrooms, and teachers.

I would be amiss if I did not single out specific people whose contributions were especially significant. I want to first mention Kim Rylaarsdam, whose editing skills helped straighten out what might have turned into abstruse language. In addition, I am indebted to Stuart Fowler who helped me talk through the more complicated issues in the book and offered insightful critique. My friend Frank De Vries, an experienced and creative teacher, read a first draft. His positive response encouraged me to stick with the project. John Vanderhoek and Lorna Van Gilst, who understand Christian education, also made helpful comments. My daughter Wendy read an original version and made detailed suggestions both for the text and for doodles. Thanks also to my daughter Tricia for a meticulous job of proofing. A special thanks to Barb Grevengoed for managing the publishing process in a cheerful, encouraging, and patient way and to Kristi De Groot for her careful work with layout and design. And finally, once again, my wife Susan stood by me with unwavering support, constant encouragement, and expertise in preparing the manuscript. Any attempt to articulate what her assistance has meant to me would be woefully inadequate.

John Van Dyk, Ph.D.
Center for Educational Services
Dordt College
Summer 2000

Teaching methods:
Tucked in the cupboard?

Lisa: Well, how is your first year of teaching going, Kristin?

Kristin: So far so good—I think. You know, Lisa, as a new teacher here I appreciate the way the principal stresses the importance of teaching Christianly. And believe me, I really want to do that. But I do wish he'd provide us with specifics. I need some practical, relevant resources that I can use in my classroom.

Lisa: Yes, I feel the same way. We've got a lot of philosophy lying about. Look on the shelf in this staff room: Wolterstorff's *Curriculum: By What Standard?*, Kienel's *Philosophy of Christian School Education*, Van Dyk's *The Beginning of Wisdom*, Edlin's *The Cause of Christian Education*; and helpful curriculum resources, too. Plenty of neat units, some good Christian textbooks, and Van Brummelen's *Steppingstones*.[1] All good stuff, to be sure. But I see little or nothing about teaching methods.

Kristin: I know what you mean. When it comes to deciding what teaching strategies to use, or how to evaluate them from a Christian perspective, we're sort of left in the dark. Why is it, do you suppose, that questions about *how* we teach are not getting truckloads of attention?

1

Teaching is no holiday cruise!

No doubt you have noticed a familiar slogan displayed in offices of teacher education professors: "No one said teaching was going to be easy!" I suspect that hardly anyone experiences the truth of this saying more keenly than the rookie teacher, freshly graduated from a teacher education program. Armed with all the latest teaching and learning theories, buoyed by confidence gained through a successful student teaching experience and a raft of recommendations, the starry-eyed novice steps into the "real classroom"—the class-room for which this fledgling teacher is now entirely responsible. Suddenly the most pressing question seems to be: "How come nobody told me about *this*? This isn't the classroom I learned about!" Almost without exception, full-time classroom teaching turns out to be a much more demanding, exhausting, and sometimes depressing task than first imagined. Why?

Well, there is, first of all, what has been called "the shock of the familiar."[2] Think of your own experience. You were in elementary and secondary classrooms as a student for at least a dozen years. You knew about teachers, textbooks, tests, and grades. You knew all about students who were remarkably proficient at disrupting the class. What was there about the classroom you did *not* know? But let's face it: until you actually taught, you did not really know what it is like to stride in front of a class of 25 or more students as a full-time teacher and take charge of their learning. As soon as you stepped into your very own classroom, the familiar twelve years or so of schooling experience began to fade into an interesting but mostly irrelevant memory.

I remember my first days as a beginning high school teacher. I naively assumed that my classes would simply be duplications of the best school days I myself had experienced as a student. I expected all my students to be eager to learn. I visualized them sitting at my feet at awed attention, impatiently waiting for the baskets full of goodies I planned to dish up. I looked forward to having the power to put an A or an F on a test. I even thought that grading papers would be oodles of fun! Alas! In no time at all I discovered that my classroom expectations were as realistic as my secret hope that some day Iowa winters will be blizzard free!

A second reality overwhelming the beginner is the unexpected busyness of a teacher's life. Fast-paced schedules, ever-burgeoning stacks of papers to correct, meetings to attend, extracurricular activities to sponsor—you're scarcely left with a minute to chase after your breath. Of course, some of this reality began to register during your student teaching experience. But student teaching was still not like the real thing: as student teacher you did not yet plan and implement a semester-long, day-after-day curriculum or take full responsibility for all of your students' learning or write detailed report cards.

Equally bewildering are the complicated student-teacher relationships. Wanting to feel accepted, you may be tempted to become too buddy-buddy with your students. The insidious "popularity syndrome" is the desire to be liked and appreciated even when it interferes with good learning or fair evaluation. A negative comment by a student can quickly destroy the self-confidence of an insecure teacher. And then you pile on top of these realities a load of additional pressures, such as the expectations of colleagues, the principal, the school board, and parents. You hardly dare ask the question: "Am I doing a good or acceptable job?" The answer can easily threaten your much-needed confidence.

Particularly demanding is the difficult task of keeping your students involved in their learning in a sustained way. Planning interesting, effective lessons on a daily basis is just plain hard, even exhausting, and sometimes discouraging work for both beginning teachers and seasoned veterans. With a nostalgic smile you may look back to the methods courses you took in college, where all sorts of tantalizing teaching strategies and learning activities were suggested and practiced. Remember all that stuff about discovery learning, simulation games, and other kinds of exciting teaching approaches? But today there is the reality of the classroom. There is Keith, for example, a kid whose specialty it is to mess up your most innovative lessons. There are the time pressures that just won't let up. How tempting it becomes to take an easy road: simply follow the teacher's manual, or just lecture and give notes, or rely on the ever-useful worksheet to keep Keith busy. The creative ideas you once contemplated can quickly fade like spring flowers in a hot summer sun.

A complication

Classroom teaching is no easy slice of banana cream pie! On the contrary, you know about all the dedication, commitment and perseverance this profession demands. Now this situation becomes even more complicated when we ask what it means to teach Christianly. Just keeping the students like live-wire Keith in line and getting them to learn is tough enough. Teaching in a distinctively Christian way points to even higher expectations. Worse, not only are there frequently contradictory opinions and theories about teaching and teaching Christianly, but bringing these theories into practice often becomes an overwhelming task. Teaching, all by itself, seems tough enough. Teaching Christianly takes us into an even more complicated ball park.

I saw these difficulties convincingly displayed in the early stages of a project on "teaching Christianly" I conducted some years ago at the Dordt College Center for Educational Services.[3] I surveyed approximately 200 teachers in the Christian schools within a 100-mile radius of our campus. Among the questions I asked were, "What, in your opinion, does it mean to teach Christianly?" and "What obstacles do you encounter in your efforts to teach Christianly?" The answers to the second question were generally quite uniform. Most teachers readily identified stumbling blocks such as lack of time, influence of television and pop culture on the students, and conflicting parental expectations. But to the question about the nature of teaching Christianly, a bewildering, even disturbing array of responses emerged. Interestingly, what seemed central to one teacher was only peripheral to another. For example, to some teachers frequent prayer and a liberal use of Bible references in the classroom are absolutely essential. To others, however, prayer and "God-talk" merely sugarcoat the curriculum with religious frosting and should be kept at a minimum. Clearly, there is no unanimity about the meaning of distinctively Christian teaching. Some of the teachers

I surveyed were brutally candid: "Don't complicate matters," they said, "by asking useless questions about teaching Christianly. Such questions have no clear answers and do little else than generate a lot of fog!"

Pedagogy: a neglected topic

But, you say, haven't Christian schools flourished since who knows when? Wouldn't we by now have come to some consensus about teaching Christianly? Very good questions! The surprising fact is that in spite of all the splendid talk about Christian education, very little attention has been paid to a Christian understanding of pedagogy, of classroom teaching strategies. The literature produced in Christian circles includes plenty of material on a Christian philosophy of education as well as an impressive array of Christian textbooks, but sustained discussion of the nature and process of teaching is as hard to find as a wild flamingo in Canada.[4]

A case in point: In the 1950s Dr. Cornelius Jaarsma, the well-known education professor at Calvin College, wrote a textbook entitled *Human Development, Learning and Teaching*.[5] This 300-page book offers an excellent Christian introduction to educational psychology. But it is instructive to note the number of pages allocated to each of the components in the title. You would think—for the sake of fairness—about a hundred pages to each one, right? Guess again! Of the 300 pages, only twelve are devoted to a description and discussion of teaching. Times have not changed since the days of Dr. Jaarsma; thorough readings on Christian pedagogy are still scarce.

I am not blaming anyone, of course. In fact, I remember how in earlier days I myself frequently delivered flowery speeches about Christian education at teachers' conferences. In the most eloquent language I could muster I would stress the importance of Christian education and the need to be distinctive. Typically, the audience would respond to my pontifications with kind applause. But I do not doubt that under their breath the teachers mumbled, "Yes, we agree with what you say, sir, but why don't you tell us how to translate all this charming talk into practical classroom walk?" Obviously, my speeches, too, missed the critical question of pedagogy as a central component of classroom practice.

You see, then, that it is not at all surprising to hear educators talk about teaching Christianly in a vague sort of way, as if it were an impressionistic painting with little definition. It is time to focus the picture and clarify the subject.

Why this neglect?

What might be some reasons for the neglect of sustained Christian reflection on pedagogy? Consider the following sentiments as likely culprits.

"Teachers are born, not made."

This is a commonly held belief. One either knows how to teach or one does not. For this reason there is much skepticism about the effectiveness of teacher education programs. Do they really help? Do they really make a difference? Can teaching actually be taught? After all, we all know of people with a "natural knack" for teaching, and we all know of others who have gone through lengthy teacher training programs but after their first year on the job are gently but firmly encouraged to look for another career—fired, in other words! Obviously, if teachers are born, not made, then any talk about how to teach is simply a waste of time.

How do you respond to this argument? It is true, of course, that good teachers have a talent for teaching, just as good musicians, engineers, and game wardens have talents for *their* respective professions. In fact, such talent is surely required. Without the requisite gifts, a career option should not be considered. If I can't tell up from down, I should not become an airline pilot. But while talent is indispensable, it is not enough. This point is as important for teaching as for piloting a commercial jetliner. Both these tasks require talent *and* much careful preparation, for both these tasks are complicated and demanding. Professional pilots and professional teachers capitalize on their gifts and talents by learning as much as they can about their craft. A trained airline captain will keep up with all the newest technological innovations to help him keep his plane on course. A gifted teacher will be eager to delve deeply into issues of child development, curricular theory, classroom management, learning styles, and pedagogical approaches in order to insure optimum learning.

A pernicious shortcoming of the "teachers are born" mentality is that it strangles a reflective spirit. If teachers are born and not made, they supposedly will get it right somehow—by trial and error—as they go along. But often they don't. I have observed this pattern on more than one occasion. A teacher may at first sight appear to be impressive and effective, but soon nagging questions arise about the why and how of the teacher's methods. More importantly, questions emerge about the compatibility of the teacher's methods and teaching Christianly. For example, I see some teachers conducting an on-task/no-nonsense efficient classroom in which much book learning may be going on but where a caring, encouraging atmosphere is entirely absent. I ask myself: Can such teaching be Christian? Or does it belong in a harsh penitentiary?

"Teaching is an art that cannot be learned."

This belief is closely related to the "teachers are made" approach. There is a long history to the question of whether teaching is an art or a science.[6] In fact, in some ways the history of reflection about teaching represents a pendulum swing between "teaching is an art" and "teaching is a science." The debate became especially lively in the mid-20th century when research increasingly assumed that it is possible to identify scientific, universal principles of effective teaching. These researchers believed that by observing, comparing, classifying, and evaluating "teacher behaviors," it would be possible to construct a standard blueprint for good teaching. Teacher education programs would merely have to make sure that student teachers understood, adopted and practiced the blueprint. While such views still hold sway over some gullible education professors, more recently the leading voices in pedagogical research have come to see that teaching is not reducible to scientific principles.[7] There is too much artistry in the act of teaching. Classrooms, learners, and teachers are just too unpredictable to permit the control of all variables.

So teaching is an art after all? If indeed it is an art pure and simple, then, of course, there is no need to discuss pedagogy at all. The rest of this book, indeed, may then be safely set aside as irrelevant drivel.

Yes, there is much artistry in good teaching. But this reality does not mean, of course, that there is no scientific basis whatsoever to be considered. A good surgeon or a good engineer is also an artist. A surgeon will pride herself in the artistry of closing a surgical incision, and an engineer will pride himself in the artistry of building a bridge. Yet such work requires careful and prolonged study and practice. It requires deep understanding of fundamental, even scientific principles. The same is true for teaching.

"How we teach is a personal matter."

Associated with the previous views is the idea that teaching is an intensely personal matter; it does not allow any universal generalizations. So any general theory of instruction will necessarily miss the point. Here, too, our response can be brief. It is true that teaching is a personal sort of thing. That's why no two teachers teach in exactly the same way. Nevertheless, there certainly are universal characteristics discernible in good teaching. For example, good teachers know about "wait time" when asking students questions, and good teachers know that lecturing for more than fifteen minutes is inappropriate at middle school levels.

The belief that teaching is a non-discussable, personal matter is less than a centimeter away from a more worrisome opinion: the notion that teaching is not only a personal, but also a private affair. "The way I teach is my business, and the way you teach is your business. As long as kids learn, questions of teaching techniques are irrelevant." This privatization of teaching prompts teachers to close their classroom doors and to cover the windows with calendars, posters, or other "Keep out!—Trespassers will be prosecuted" signs. The resulting secrecy fosters resistance to any sort of student and peer evaluations.

Such privatization is thoroughly unprofessional. I recommend that you open your classroom's doors to all visitors. Invite critical responses to what you are doing in your classroom. What's more, I recommend that all the teachers take turns having their teaching activities video-taped, shared, and discussed at staff meetings. Yes, of course, such public scrutiny will make you vulnerable! But teaching should be a team effort, a process to which we all contribute.

To be sure, teachers do have a legitimate complaint about the often less than adequate performance evaluations. For instance, you have a right to complain if your job security depends—even if only in part—on a board member popping into your classroom for about twenty minutes per year and writing a report describing your classroom as too noisy, too ineffective, too this and too that. Often such observers are not teachers themselves, and, consequently, are hardly qualified to evaluate. They may have little understanding of what to look for in good, Christian teaching. The long-standing neglect of Christian pedagogy puts all of us in the same boat: there is no consensus on the question— What is good, Christian teaching? As a result, there are no agreed-upon criteria for evaluation. So we all end up doing what seems right in our own eyes.

"A Christian teacher automatically teaches Christianly."

Here we encounter a very serious problem. The "automatic view" holds that a sincere, confessing Christian will automatically teach Christianly. For example, at an appointment interview, the school board or education committee will commonly inquire into the faith life of the candidate (including viewpoints on dance, smoking, and women's roles), but ask few questions about pedagogy or classroom teaching styles. After all, if we can be assured of the candidate's personal commitment to the Lord and his moral positions, we need not worry about his approach to the classroom, do we?

But this view is clearly mistaken. While a commitment to Jesus is, of course, absolutely essential, being a confessing Christian does not at once sanctify our thoughts and actions. Think of the early church fathers, for example, many of whom took their pagan philosophies along with them into the church once they were converted. Sometimes I see Christian teachers uncritically adopt behavioristic, pragmatistic, or other questionable practices. The assumption of the automatic theory, like the previous beliefs, eliminates the need to reflect deeply and critically about our teaching practice. The automatic theory blinds us to the power and influence of secular spirits operating in the way we teach.

"Teaching is simply a set of practical tips."

At teachers' conventions the book and materials displays are often the busiest places. Teachers constantly look for new ideas for their classrooms. Such zeal is commendable, of course. You don't want to grow stale. But teaching is not equivalent to a bag of tricks. Nor are teaching strategies simply a collection of "suggested learning activities," as they often are labeled in textbooks and curricular material. On the contrary, the choices of teaching methods are dependent on your philosophy of education and specifically on your pedagogical insight. The burden of this book is to convince you of the truth of this assertion.

"Theory and practice do not meet."

Some of your co-workers may have told you when you first walked into the school: "Forget about all that theoretical stuff your profs tried to teach you—you're in the *real* world now!" Indeed, an opinion prevails that somehow theory—especially pedagogical theory—is irrelevant and can safely be ignored. On this point we face a huge and complicated problem. The frequently perceived gap between theory and practice has a long history. It goes back all the way to the ancient Greeks, who sharply separated "knowing" from "doing."[8] To the Greeks, knowing, understood as theory, was superior to doing. This view gave rise to the long intellectualistic tradition which teaches that the mind, scientific theory, and logical thinking are the only trustworthy guides in life.

Interestingly, in our own times the superiority of theory has been replaced by an emphasis on practice. Particularly the philosophy of pragmatism has won the day, especially in the Anglo-American world. Pragmatism declares that truth is determined by action. That is, to discover whether something is true or not, all we need to do is to put it into practice to see if it works.

Now pragmatism rightly emphasizes that abstract theory without consideration for practical implementation is inadequate. But pragmatism wrongly concludes that practice determines the truth or falsity of theory. Too often our practice is so distorted that it has no claim to fame as a judge. What works is not always right.

Teachers who think that theory is irrelevant are probably tied up in the straitjacket of pragmatism. Pragmatism contributes to the neglect of indispensable critical thinking about the nature *and practice* of teaching Christianly.

"Teaching is only a function of learning."

A final reason for the neglect of pedagogy is the common idea that teaching is merely a function of learning. What does this belief mean? This view suggests that once we know how children learn we will also know how to teach them. In this view pedagogy is merely an appendix to learning theory.

Now it is, of course, essential that teachers know how children learn. All of our teaching methods must take into account child development, learning styles, and learning theory. However, simply knowing how children learn does not at all eliminate the need to reflect critically on pedagogy. As Gage pointed out many years ago, just as doctors need to know more than how the body works and farmers need to know more than how plants grow, so teachers need to know more than how children learn.[9]

A final word

So where are we? I have introduced the topic of this book—the craft of Christian teaching—by making three claims: (1) teaching is a tough job; (2) teaching Christianly is an even more difficult task; and (3) little has been done to help us understand this thing called "teaching Christianly." So what's next?

The point of this book is not to overwhelm you with complexities, and in so doing discourage you. You probably agree that in spite of all the pressures and stress, teaching is a wonderfully rewarding profession. Personally, I can't think of anything I'd rather do than teach—and not just teach, but teach Christianly. A huge challenge? Yes, of course! But a challenge that with the help of God and colleagues, parents, and even the children themselves, we can meet.

In this book I ask you to concentrate on one specific—and, perhaps, the most important—aspect of your work as a teacher: your teaching practice. My fundamental questions are these: What does teaching Christianly mean? How do we teach Christianly? True, answering these questions inevitably involves curricular contexts and learning theories. Our focus, nevertheless, will remain on pedagogy: teaching methods and classroom strategies. Before we tackle this subject in detail, however, we must consider several larger questions. Let's look at these questions.

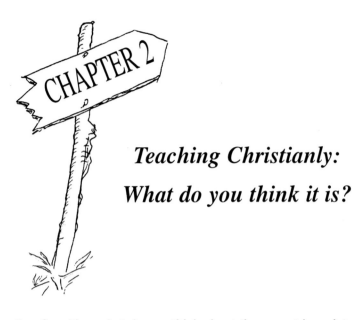

Teaching Christianly:
What do you think it is?

Jim: Say, Lisa, what do you think about these neat bracelets all the kids are wearing nowadays, you know, the WWJD bracelets? I was thinking, to ask "What would Jesus do?" might be a helpful way to understand what teaching Christianly is all about, don't you agree?

Lisa: Well, I don't know. I do know that those bracelets have become pretty popular. And they probably help the kids think in sticky situations. But I'm not sure how helpful they are for us teachers. I mean, I'm not sure how asking "What would Jesus do?" will help me decide between a worksheet or silent reading. It seems to me that it might be more useful to ask, "What would Jesus *not* do?" For example, I know that Jesus would not lose patience with livewire Keith, or reject Kelsey for failing her math test.

Jim: Hmmm—I'll have to think about that one. So you aren't sold on the WWJD formula. You don't believe it gives you a clear view of what it means to teach Christianly, right?

Lisa: Right!

Neglecting pedagogy: some consequences

Teacher conversations like the one in the scenario display the lack of directed pedagogical reflection in Christian education. This neglect results in at least three serious consequences. First, it discourages teachers from critically examining their teaching practice. In fact, some simply dismiss as unproductive the question of what teaching Christianly really means. Or they don't pose the question at all, on the assumption that they need not be concerned about it. So why allot time for reflection about something you need not be concerned about? A routine inservice here and there, and a journal article or two in the staff room should suffice, shouldn't it?

Now I don't mean to suggest that all inservice sessions are worthless. If they were, I'd be the first to quit leading workshops. Needed and missing, however, are sustained programs to help Christian teachers analyze their teaching methodology and to encourage communal self-evaluation.

A second consequence of the failure to engage in such critical reflection allows a host of subtle, unrecognized philosophies of education to stalk the Christian school, including your own classroom. Like hidden invaders, various forms of behaviorism, progressivism, perennialism, pragmatism, and a list of other -isms too long to detail creep in quietly and begin to infect the classroom practice of an unsuspecting teacher. Only an awareness of these  sneaky philosophies, revealed through careful, persistent reflection, can successfully ward them off.

Third, the neglect of classroom pedagogy has allowed a diversity of (often unspoken) opinions about the nature of teaching to flourish. There is no shared concept of what it means to teach Christianly. To each his own, as it were. Of course, you could argue that diversity of viewpoints is a wholesome phenomenon. It reflects a robust, healthy individualism, right? And doesn't the Apostle Paul somewhere talk about the Christian community as a mosaic of differences? Well, yes, in Romans 12, for example, we do indeed read about diversity of gifts, callings, and contributions. But note that Paul habitually describes diversity as differences within the bonds of unity. Though different, the parts of the body work coherently together as a whole.

Suppose I were to carry the "robust individualism" into my family life. Suppose I said to my wife: "I'll tell you what—I'll raise our children the way I see fit, and you raise them your way!" What do you think would happen? The kids would quickly learn to play one parent off against the other. The purposes of neither father nor mother would be realized. Similarly, suppose that in a church the pastor and the assistant pastor decided to be such individualists and adopt diverse, even conflicting, positions on key doctrines. Obviously the congregation would disintegrate if the leadership were in such disarray.

So it is in education. Of course, I am not advocating a stifling conformity. We are all unique individuals, each one of us endowed with special gifts. But there is a very large difference between being an *individual* and being an *individualist*. Individuals can come together to make a whole, to build and function as a community. Individualists cannot. Like stones in a jumbled rock pile, they remain isolated, loose, disconnected, and self-determining entities. Individualism leads to conflict and confrontation.

Sometimes such individualists gather around themselves a small band of followers, and thus form factions or cliques. It looks as if such factionalism was a serious problem in the early church at Corinth. Listen to what Paul says about this: "I appeal to you, brothers, in the name of our Lord Jesus Christ, that all of you agree with one another so that there may be no divisions among you and that you may be perfectly united in mind and thought."[1]

The staff of a Christian school cannot be a collection of individualists or competing factions. Rather, the staff must constitute a team, consisting of differently gifted people all working together with a *shared perspective*. Included in such a perspective is a view of teaching Christianly. When such unity of perspective ("unity of mind and thought," Paul would call it) is absent, the school is no longer a genuine, organic community, but merely an organization held together by externally imposed rules and regulations.

A diversity of opinions about teaching Christianly, operative in one and the same school system, points to confusion and possibly a lack of vision—a situation confirmed by the requests for assistance voiced by many of the teachers we have surveyed. In response to our questionnaires they would say, "I really don't know what it means to teach Christianly. Can you help me clarify?"

The role of mission statements

What about mission statements? You would think that a well-written, clearly articulated mission statement could easily control diversity of understanding within a single school system. And maybe it could. Especially helpful are educational statements that specify procedures and practices in some detail. Ecclesiastical creeds, though useful in some ways, are generally unable to prevent diverging perspectives on education. They say little or nothing about specific pedagogical styles and the curricular content to be used in a Christian school. Though they may provide a broad theological framework for churches, they cannot prevent a diversity of conflicting, even secularized perspectives to flourish within a school system.

Even well-prepared educational mission statements frequently fail to provide adequate pedagogical direction for a school. The first problem is that mission statements, even good ones, often do not function. When visiting a school, I ask the principal whether or not a mission statement is available. Often there is, but sometimes it lies buried under a pile of papers on a dust-covered shelf in the staff lounge or principal's office. Secondly, mission statements tend to be flowery and idealistic, not at all reflecting the reality of what is actually happening in the school. And, finally, they tend to be so brief that they are open to a legion of differing, even contradictory, interpretations.

Diverse conceptions of teaching Christianly

Well, you ask, what are some of the diverse conceptions of what it means to teach Christianly? Here are some of the more common approaches I have encountered:

Teaching Christianly = Adding a devotional dimension

It's the beginning of a new school day. The opening bell has rung, and you tell your students to take out their Bibles. You read a passage and ask a few questions about it. Then you have the class sing a couple of praise songs, and you conclude with a word of prayer. You instruct the students to put their Bibles away and to take out their math texts. From here on in the thought of teaching in a distinctively Christian way begins to fade from your mind.

Recognize this scenario? It locates the Christian character of teaching in classroom devotional activities, such as prayer, Bible reading, and the singing of praise songs. Usually these activities begin and end the school day. What comes in between is not all that different from what would happen in a public school. Once the prayers are said, the passage read, and the songs sung, it's business as usual, so to speak.

I call this dualistic conception "simply teaching." I mean by this that the Christian teacher, after taking care of the devotional activities, can simply follow the teacher's manual, give out the worksheets, make the assignments, and put grades on papers without much thought to these questions: How do I do these things in a distinctively Christian way? *Is* there even a Christian way? Or do all teachers—Christian, Muslim, New Age, atheist, or whatever—teach in an identical way? My point is this: while "simply teaching" is surely a kind of teaching, it is not necessarily the same thing as teaching Christianly.

The dualistic view is held by very sincere Christians. Sometimes entire schools are committed to it. Chapel exercises and Bible courses are regarded as indispensable in these schools. Take these away, and the school presumably loses its Christian character. Usually these schools also place heavy emphasis on good moral behavior. Strict discipline policies are in effect. Christian schools of this sort are understandably very popular with parents who see the public school as a den of relativism or as an amoral institution.

What is the problem with dualism? Well, consider why I use the term "dualism" in the first place. Dualism suggests two separate, independent domains. One of these domains represents the area of the sacred (the spiritual and the religious), while the other domain consists of typically secular, supposedly nonreligious ingredients. The sacred domain—prayer, devotional activity, chapel exercises, and the like—is the *Christian* component of the school's program. The curriculum, teaching, grading, bells and schedules, on the other hand, belong to the secular realm. This secular realm does not materially differ from its counterpart in public schools.

You see the problem, don't you? In the first place, dualism limits the Lordship of Christ to a supposed domain of so-called "spiritual" things. But there is no such thing as a separate realm of "spiritual things," hovering over or alongside other dimensions of life. We know and believe that Christ is Lord of all. He is the King of kings and the Lord of lords, exercising authority over every nook and cranny of life, including every aspect of school life.[2] Jesus is Lord of the curriculum, of my teaching methods, of the bells and schedules in the building, and yes, even of bus routes and budgets.

A second problem with dualism is that it leaves entire areas of the school untouched by the gospel. It supposes that subject matter is objective and neutral in character—after all, French is French and math is math, isn't it? No, it isn't! To believe that some parts of life (or the curriculum) are somehow exempt from the Lord's claims is to turn a blind eye to the significant questions of how Christians should see and teach subject matter in a Christ-honoring way.

A final problem with dualism is that it assumes a faulty interpretation of the biblical concept of "spirituality." In the Scriptures the term "spiritual" does not signify a part of life, to be distinguished from other parts such as teaching and learning. The term "devotional" refers to specific activities such as prayer, the singing of hymns, and Bible reading. But "spiritual" means "gripped and directed by the Holy Spirit." Devotional activity is spiritual activity, to be sure, but not all spiritual activity is devotional activity. The entirety of our life is to be gripped and directed by the Holy Spirit. The entirety of our life—including everything that happens in a Christian school—is to be spiritual.

Teaching Christianly = Modeling Christian behavior

Another common view sees Christian teaching as entirely a matter of setting a good example. Teaching Christianly means bringing an atmosphere of Christian love and morality into the classroom. The teacher will exhibit much care for the students, while not tolerating unacceptable behavior. Fairness, gentle firmness, a pleasant and positive demeanor, and self-confidence are some of the key characteristics to be modeled. Whenever possible, the teacher will refer to his or her faith in God.

Frequently this limited conception of teaching does not deem curricular content all that important. Subject matter is subject matter, whether taught by a Christian teacher or an atheist teacher. Consequently, this view will urge Christian teachers to seek positions in public schools. Teaching is essentially modeling, and—though with some restrictions—can be carried out in a public school as well as in a Christian school. This view of teaching Christianly fundamentally undercuts the need for separate, distinctively Christian schools.

What shall we say about this view? Modeling Christian behavior is, of course, a critically important component of teaching Christianly. It's hard to conceive of a Christian teacher who allows disrespect, cheating, swearing, and other kinds of misbehavior in the classroom. Yet, modeling is not the whole story. As a teacher you do more than set a good example. You actually teach! You design lesson plans and learning activities. You create learning situations. These, too, must be consciously subjected to the will of the Lord.

Teaching Christianly = Evangelizing students

Akin to the dualistic and modeling approaches to teaching is the notion that Christian teachers are evangelists. Their task is not, first of all, to make sure that children learn a variety of important subject matter, but to lead the children to a personal relationship with Jesus. The aim of teaching Christianly is to extract a profession of faith from the lips of the youngsters.

This approach will obviously take devotional exercises and the modeling of Christian behavior very seriously. And indeed, it is proper to hope that education will encourage children to claim Jesus as the Lord of their lives. Nevertheless, as in the previous two cases, this view of teaching tends to neglect the importance of subject matter and pedagogy. From this perspective, subject matter and pedagogy are considered only as pathways to conversion and Christian commitment.

My problem with this view is similar to what I have already suggested: it limits the Lordship of Christ and downplays our calling to be educators as well as evangelists. As a Christian teacher you are not finished when your students have become Christ-believers. On the contrary, your task has then just begun: Now it will be necessary to make clear what faith in Christ means for the learning of content and skills, for their work as students.

Teaching Christianly = Providing a Christian perspective on subject matter

Proponents of this approach—mostly strong Christian school supporters—locate the essence of teaching Christianly in communicating a Christian perspective on subject matter. They stress courses which provide the students with the equipment and skills needed to evaluate critically the spirits controlling our contemporary society. Teaching styles and strategies are often less important than a Christian curriculum. Needed most for Christian teaching, they say, are Christian textbooks. Incidentally, this view often leaves those who teach math or grammar in a quandary. It seems easier to provide a meaningful perspective on history and literature than on math and grammar.

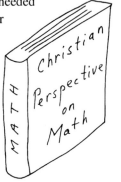

Clearly this approach takes a broader view of teaching than any of the ones I have described thus far. Nevertheless, it, too, has its limitations. One problem is that the emphasis on content perspective does not take the students far enough. It tends to be satisfied with an intellectual, academic understanding, and not pay sufficient attention to the question: How do we bring this perspective into practice? After all, a biblical view of knowledge suggests that knowledge means little if not carried over into concrete action.

Perspective without opportunity for action: I have called this position "perspectivalism." John Vanderhoek, former education coordinator of the Society of Christian Schools in British Columbia, told me of a unit he taught many years ago. The topic was "community." He taught the students everything they should know about community: its meaning, its nature, various forms of community, and the like. The students did well on the test. They gave all the right answers. The problem with all this impressive learning, John told me, was that in that classroom the students did not once actually *experience* community. For the students the concept "community," though fully understood in Christian perspective, remained an abstract concept, disconnected from the practice of daily life.

Teaching Christianly = Doing (off-campus) service projects

Still others argue that teaching Christianly is basically a matter of providing opportunities for service. Such teachers are the first to take students out of the classroom to visit shut-ins, to paint an old house, or to clean up the roadsides.

Given the current interest in service learning, this view is gaining popularity. Clearly, it seeks to overcome the limitations of "perspectivalism"; it aims to translate learning into action. My concern is this: Does this approach restrict the heart of Christian teaching to the service component? Will it see classroom learning as less important, perhaps even irrelevant? Do the off-campus activities tie into the curriculum as a whole? Or is the curriculum reduced to merely a launching pad for service projects? I know of Christian schools that stress service to such an extent that regular routine classroom activities come to be regarded as an insignificant transition to greater things. When this attitude sets in, a Christian approach to pedagogy gets short-shrift and is side-lined once again, or put out of commission altogether.

Opportunities for out-of-school service are valuable and fine. But let's be sure they will help, not hinder Christian classroom teaching.

Teaching Christianly = Enforcing tough classroom discipline and academic rigor

Once I was asked to speak to a crowd of teachers and parents of a large Christian school. I was introduced by the board chair, who decided to use the occasion for a little pep talk. "What makes our school a

Christian school," he declared, "is the excellent discipline we maintain and the high academic standards we set. We are not like the public school around the corner where kids are coddled with fun and games, where rules and regulations are snubbed, where graduates don't know how to spell their own names!"

The following day I spent some time visiting classes and talking with the teachers in this school. To my astonishment, the words of the board chair made much sense to a number of the teachers. Good classroom discipline and academic rigor—it's what our Christian schools are all about, they said.

That some educators locate the heart of Christian teaching in exercising stern discipline combined with maintaining high standards of academic rigor surprised me. I asked myself: How could anyone suggest that this is so? After all, aren't good classroom discipline and academic rigor the sorts of elements that could characterize any secular academy? Of course! It is this point exactly that makes this view so problematic. Good discipline and high expectations for learning are obviously important. But they do not define the essence of Christian teaching.

Teaching Christianly = Imprinting biblical truth on impressionable minds

This approach takes a dim view of current trends in cooperative and discovery learning. It sees group work as "pooling ignorance." Nor should students be encouraged to "discover" truth; doing so will only lead to relativism. After all, Christian teachers are teachers because they *have* the truth. Their task is to impart the truth to our youngsters. Besides, the Bible makes clear that such imprinting—translated into extensive lecturing and direct instruction—is *the* Christian way. Don't we read in Deuteronomy 6 and other Old Testament passages that we are to teach and impress the story of God's mighty acts on our children, whether we walk or sit down?

The problems with this supposed biblical view are legion—I'll mention only a few. In the first place, it assumes that the child is a passive (even empty-headed), receptive agent, with no responsibility for his or her learning: all responsibility lies in the hands of the teacher. Children are reduced to mere manipulable objects. This view is only a stone's throw from crass behaviorism. Secondly, from everything we now know about how children learn, exclusive reliance on direct instruction is quite ineffective. The Lord did not create children in the way the "imprint philosophy" suggests. On the contrary, our children are gifted, experienced, contributing image bearers of God.

Finally, it is instructive to note that Jesus himself, often regarded as the Master Teacher, rarely used this approach. If anything, his favorite way of teaching was through indirect methods, especially parables and stories. Now what is a parable? A set of clear point-1-2-3 notes? Information to be committed to memory and recited on request? Of course not. A parable is a story requiring personal interpretation. Those who heard the parables of Jesus were required to apply them to their own lives. In addition, Jesus also invited his disciples to *experience* situations which increased their knowledge. Jesus, in sum, was a firm believer in *experiential* learning.

Those who espouse the teaching=imprinting approach obviously want to take the Scriptures very seriously. But surely they should not ignore what the Gospels show us. Conclusion? Clearly, unless you are willing to set aside the example of Jesus, Christian teaching cannot be simply understood as "imprinting."

Teaching Christianly = Imitating Jesus, the Master Teacher

The brief dialogue at the beginning of this chapter prompts me to examine one more view of teaching Christianly: it is to imitate the Master Teacher. Much literature has been devoted to the teaching methods of Christ. Parable and story telling are key strategies Jesus regularly employed. Demonstration with concrete examples is another one. Christ often illustrated his points by referring to the landscape around him (as in the parable of the sower) or by placing a child in the midst of his audience. Questioning his students is still another method Jesus frequently used.

A skeptic might suggest that it is inappropriate to regard Jesus as a master teacher. After all, is a master teacher not an *effective* teacher? One who is able to make a topic crystal clear so that even the slowest of learners can understand? But let's face it: at times Jesus appeared to be quite ineffective. The Gospels frequently report that his followers either misunderstood him or did not understand him at all. Even on the core themes, such as the nature of the Kingdom and his predicted resurrection, the disciples were confused and remained in the dark for most of the time that the Lord was with them.

More important is the difficulty we face when we attempt to transfer the methods of Jesus to our own situation. For example: Jesus wrote with his finger in the sand. Does this mean we should eliminate chalkboards and overhead projectors? And what would Jesus think of the various educational issues that confront us today? How would he teach reading? By way of phonics or via a whole-language approach? Would he require manipulatives in all math teaching? What about evaluation and grading practices? Clearly, if we wish to use Jesus as an example, we need to employ so much interpretation and speculation that his real teaching methods begin to disappear behind a cloud of uncertainty. "What would Jesus do?" sounds like the sort of question that could help us make pedagogical decisions. In reality, the answers we would supply already reflect a bag full of our personal biases and (often unexamined) opinions. We easily make Jesus do what we want to do.

An evaluation

How should we evaluate these views of what it means to teach Christianly? Already I have suggested deficiencies in each one of them. Remember, however, that these approaches to teaching are *Christians'* approaches and therefore require a sympathetic treatment and discussion. They do not deserve a simple slap with the back of the hand. Wherever you see Christians struggling to understand and implement an other than purely secular approach, you need to express gratitude. I would therefore not judge any of these approaches as outright wrong, but rather as inadequate or incomplete. They tend to equate an aspect of Christian teaching with the whole of Christian teaching. To use a technical term, these approaches are *reductionistic*, rather than wrong. Wrong we should call only an unambiguously, intentionally *secular* approach, that is, a teaching practice in which God and his will are deliberately set aside. And even then we should be careful, because so often we ourselves set the Lord aside in our own lives, when we choose options and act in ways not in line with the Spirit of God.

Perhaps the difficulty you and I face is not first of all whether we as teachers espouse less than adequate views of teaching Christianly. Rather, the question is: How important to you is this issue of teaching Christianly in the first place? Are you genuinely desirous of subjecting your *entire* teaching practice, not just some aspects of it, to the will of the Lord? Do you really want to cultivate an authentic, full-orbed Christian teaching style? Or are you content to limp along?

True Christian teaching, it seems to me, requires a reinterpretation and a renewed commitment to what has too often become a cliché: to do everything to the glory of God. As professional Christian teachers, called to lead our youngsters into the pathways of wisdom, the question of teaching Christianly should be continuously before us, urging us to reflect critically on our own and others' teaching practice. It requires a willingness to expose our strategies, to open our classroom doors, and to fight our tendency towards isolation and defensiveness, so that as professional educators we can together examine what it is we are doing, how we can eliminate the inadequacies, and how as a team in a school we can enhance our Christian effectiveness.

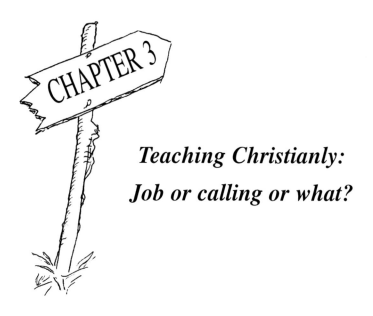

Teaching Christianly:
Job or calling or what?

Jim: I get a little tired of my neighbor telling me what a cushy job I've got. Done at 4:00 p.m., he says, and three months off in the summer! What do you say to people like that?

Lisa: Ignore them! Or get out paper and pencil and show them that the hours we work during the school year far exceed the hours he puts into his nine-to-five job!

Jim: I doubt if he would believe that, and besides, he's convinced that teaching is little more than a baby-sitting job.

Lisa: Part of the problem is that we don't explain to people that teaching isn't just a job but a "high calling," to put it in fancy terms.

Jim: Or maybe we'll just have to learn to live with putdowns and low salaries.

First things first

You are in the kitchen and you have decided to make a fine spinach soufflé—your specialty. You have put on your apron and set out the ingredients. First you crack the eggs, separate and beat them. Without egg whites, properly fluffed, no soufflé.

Reaching an understanding of teaching Christianly is a bit like preparing a spinach soufflé. You need a variety of ingredients, and some of these serve as a base, as it were, for the final product. Teaching Christianly cannot be defined by a glib one-liner or an empty slogan any more than that a splendid spinach soufflé results from tossing an egg into a bowl full of greens.

Or, to use another picture, building your understanding of teaching Christianly is like building a barn: you need footings and foundations to build on, and the work requires time, effort, and plenty of construction material. One indispensable cornerstone for building our understanding is the important theme of the calling, task, and office of the Christian teacher.

Ask yourself: Is teaching just a job, something to do to earn a living? Well, yes, you say, in a way it is. After all, you need bread and milk and spinach and eggs in your kitchen. You could even see teaching as a *good* job: It comes with long vacations, an improving wage scale, and community recognition—all pretty fair benefits, to be sure. Yet in your heart you know that these benefits are really only *fringe* benefits. For a Christian teacher, teaching is always much more than merely a job.

When students come into my education classes, I routinely ask them why they want to become teachers. In my graduate classes I ask: Why *did* you become a teacher? I am always intrigued by the answers the students give me. Their reasons vary. Many talk about their love of children or their fascination with a certain subject. Some mention the summer breaks. Still others admit that they became teachers because they simply did not know what else to do! They became teachers by default, as it were.

But when I ask all these folks to identify the one, single, most compelling reason for entering the teaching profession, I frequently hear—to my delight, I must say—that they feel *called* to be teachers.

Calling

Wow! *Called* to be a teacher! Think about that for just a minute: When you declare that you are *called*, what are you really saying? Well, obviously, to be called implies that someone has called you. Someone has talked to you. Someone said, "Hey, you! I want you to do something for me!"

Now in all likelihood, you did not hear an audible voice from the clouds, although that certainly is a possibility. More likely you became aware of a growing, deepening desire to be a teacher, and you began to recognize in yourself the various gifts needed.

I am talking, of course, about a calling from God. It was the Lord himself who called you and me to be teachers. Now let's not smugly assume that God's calling comes to just you and me, or just to teachers, or to an elite breed of "full-time Kingdom workers." The truth is, the entire human race is called. Already at the very beginning of human life, when Adam and Eve were ambling through the greenery of paradise, the voice of God came unmistakably: "Hey, you two! Take a look at where you are! You see all these trees and flowers and birds and butterflies, complete with sunshine, blue skies, and an occasional shower? I want you to help me care for this world I've made. I want you to find and to do something with all the unbelievable potential I have tucked away all over the place!"

Theologians sometimes refer to this larger task as "the cultural mandate." It is pretty clearly stated for us in Genesis 1:28: "God blessed them (i.e., the man and the woman) and said to them: 'Be fruitful and increase in number; fill the earth and subdue it.'" And a little bit later, in Genesis 2:15, we read: "The Lord God took the man and put him in the Garden of Eden to work it and to take care of it." The Garden of Eden, of course, represents nothing less than the entire universe. You and I are called to work in God's world as teachers.

Task

When little Tony is playing in the yard and hears his mother call him, he knows that she is not just practicing pronouncing his name. He knows that she wants him *to do* something. So it is with God's call to humanity. And so it is with his call to you and me. We have a task to perform: the task of teaching Christianly.

Don't miss the point: God calls us not just to teach, but to teach *Christianly*. You and I know all too well the unspeakably sad reality: sin has brought into the world tons of dark, unwashed, smelly blankets of distorted unbelief that smother and contaminate everything, obscuring the Kingdom of God. The whole creation groans under the burden of the weight of these smelly blankets, Paul explains in Romans 8:22. That includes education, curriculum, and teaching. Nothing in the entire world remains unaffected, nothing escapes the carcinogens of sin, not even the pretty bulletin boards in our classrooms or the manipulatives we use in our math lessons.

Lest we get too depressed, let me point you to the stupendous words recorded for us in Paul's letter to the Colossians: "For God was pleased to have all his fullness dwell in him (i.e., in Christ, the Word become flesh), and through him to reconcile all things, whether things on earth or things in heaven, by making peace through his blood, shed on the cross."[1] Did you catch that little but all-inclusive phrase "all things"? All things, whether on earth or in heaven, whether at your desk as you plan your next lesson or in the classroom as you teach. The incredible news is that just as sin puts its sticky fingers on everything, so Christ's redemption touches absolutely everything you do as a teacher. Teaching, like all other human activity oppressed by sin, cries out for redemption, and you, my dear reader, are called to help redeem it!

Your task, as a Christian teacher, is not simply to teach, but to teach Christianly. In response to God's calling, your work as a teacher is to be transformed into redemptive activity.

Teaching, in short, is a divine assignment and requires a holy response. When you think of "assignment," a vision of dull drudgery may come to mind. A teacher's response to God's assignment, however, should be one of enthusiasm and eagerness. If you do not feel such enthusiasm and excitement about your teaching task, you should review your sense of calling. Of course, you will have your ups and downs, your good days and bad days. Some days, in fact, will make you wonder whether becoming a teacher was really the right thing to do. Even veteran teachers regularly experience such low points. But when depression and disenchantment with teaching become a pattern that marks your attitude towards teaching, it surely is time to check your sense of calling.

One's calling and task should feel like an opportunity, a privilege. I am reminded of an insight emphasized by Professor Nicholas Wolterstorff. The cultural mandate, he argues, is not only a *mandate* or a command, but also an *invitation*. "Could it be," Wolterstorff muses in his speech at the 1992 Toronto International Educational Conference, "that where the tradition I imbibed thought it saw a mandate, we should instead have seen an invitation? On the fifth day of creation, says the writer of Genesis 1, God, after bringing into being the creatures of sky and sea, stood back, saw that it was good, and blessed all the creatures with the words 'Be fruitful and multiply. . . .'" Wolterstorff points out that these words do not so much constitute a command as a blessing, an invitation to flourish. Similarly, the *mandate* spoken to humans is an *invitation* to flourish.

To me this interpretation is fresh and liberating. The Lord *both* commands *and* invites, not unlike Tony's mother, who not only calls the boy home but invites him to come in. At least, that's how it ought to be. Unless, of course, Tony is scared of his mother. But he doesn't have to be, anymore than we need to be afraid of our Father in heaven.

So the point is this: The Lord not only *wants* you to teach, he also *invites* you to teach. And, what's more, he *equips* you to teach.

How the Lord equips you

You see, the Lord does not call you to a task that you cannot perform. Think of Moses, who objected strenuously to the Lord's request that he return to Egypt to set God's people free. "Look, Lord," Moses protested, "I've got marbles in my mouth. . . ." But God sent him anyway, along with the promise to equip him to deal with the likes of Pharaoh.

But how did you recognize your calling to be a teacher? And how does the Lord continue to equip you for teaching, now that a burning bush, a voice from heaven, and a magical stick seem to be things of the past? These are important questions, not only for undergraduate students beginning a teacher education program and who are not sure whether teaching is really for them, but also for those who, after a year or two of frustrations in the classroom, wonder whether a teaching career was the right choice.

Your calling to be a teacher is inseparably related to the ways in which the Lord equips you. How does he do so? I mention at least four ways: First, he endows you with talents. He gives you gifts. So whether you are a prospective teacher or a seasoned veteran, you must ask: What are my talents? What gifts do I have? And do these gifts qualify me to be a teacher or to continue to be a teacher? These questions are significant for anyone considering or continuing in a profession. Plumbers, mechanics, politicians, and

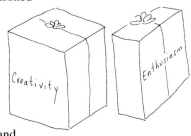

artists, too, must ask: What are my talents? Failure to ask this question easily leads to wrong choices. Failure to ask this question means failing to recognize your talents, and, consequently, failing to recognize your calling.

Second, the Lord also provides you with interests. Observe that talents and interests are not the same thing. I may have talents to be, say, a concert pianist, but my interest lies in carpentry. Or, conversely, I may be interested in becoming a carpenter but I cannot hit a nail with a hammer, so have no woodworking talent whatever. Both prospective and practicing teachers must ask: Am I *really* interested in children? Do I have a passion for the subject matter I will have to teach? Do I *like* to be in schools, in classrooms? Or would I prefer to work on a construction site or in a hospital or in a bank?

Some think that inquiring about our personal interests is inappropriate. To take interests into consideration, they believe, is really an expression of selfishness. I remember a student who came to my office tearfully confessing that he had decided to become a preacher, even though his heart lay in the theater arts. "I would love to be an actor," he confided, "but I think I must set such selfish interests aside in order to serve the Lord. If I become an actor, I will be serving only myself; but if I become a minister, I can serve God full-time." We talked for a while about the false distinction between sacred and secular, and between so-called "full-time" and "part-time" Kingdom service. False distinctions these are, of course, because *all* of our lives, 24 hours a day, are to be lived in the presence and service of God, whether as actors, ministers, sales clerks, or hair stylists. Interests, I pointed out to the distraught student, are good gifts of the Lord. You have no right to dismiss them. To disregard your interests is tantamount to saying, "Look, Lord, I know you created me in this way, but I'm just going to ignore your workmanship and make my own decisions." Interests cannot be ignored; they are powerful indicators of the direction in which the Lord is leading you.

Of course, it *is* possible that your interests turn into pure self-interest. In this case, you are not taking your interests seriously enough. If you see no other purpose for your interests than serving yourself, you may well distort your calling beyond recognition. Interests, then, cannot be the only guide. They have to come together with everything else. Your interest has to be *informed* interest. Sometimes, too, it takes time to develop your interests. In short, take your interests seriously, but treat them carefully.

In the third place, the Lord equips you for your task by the sort of personality he has bestowed on you. Let's face it—we recognize that some people are just not cut out to be teachers. At other times we say, "So and so is a born teacher: she's got the right personality." Note that our personality is distinguishable from both talents and interests. We know of people who surely have the talents to be a teacher, and may even be interested, yet will not make good teachers because of the sort of persons they are. For example, they may be good at explaining difficult concepts, but, if the truth be told, they simply enjoy computers more than people.

Finally, the Lord provides you with opportunities and confronts you with needs. He opens some doors and closes others. Be sure to stay very sensitive to the leading of the Lord, for such leading is still another way in which he prepares and equips you. Be sure to ask: Where can I serve the Lord best, given my talents, interests, and personality? Where in God's Kingdom do I see the need for the sorts of services I can provide? Could it be, Lord, that you want me to go into administration or counseling? Where do you want to place me? Consciously and persistently asking these questions gives evidence of the deep faith and trust in our Lord that must characterize your walk as a Christian teacher. Such faith and trust, in turn, suggest that you have understood the *religious* nature of your calling and task. Let's examine this point more closely.

Religion

Remember your secular textbooks in your history classes? They treat ancient Greek and other civilizations in terms of their political, social, intellectual, *and* religious structures. Such treatment makes it look as if religion is a separable component, disconnected from other areas of life. And indeed, religion is usually defined as a distinct aspect of human life, along with other dimensions such as politics, economics, art, and the like. The traditional distinction between church and state, for example, mirrors a similar distinction between religion and politics. In contrast with such traditions, you and I must unwaveringly maintain that *all* human activity, indeed, *all of life* is essentially religious in nature. Education is no exception.

But what in the world does this mean? Lest you conclude that I am merely slinging platitudinous slogans, let me be specific. To say that our lives are religious is to say that all of our activities are (1) driven by faith commitments, (2) headed in a certain direction, and (3) performed in (worshipful) service. Your work in the classroom clearly illustrates these three components.

First, your teaching is driven by what you believe, by what you consider to be important and valuable. This is true for all teaching, by the way, whether Christian, atheistic, Muslim, or whatever. The faith that drives you and me, Christian teachers, is a faith in God—not in an abstract, far-off, theologically constructed God, but in a personal Heavenly Father who loves us and cares for us, who is continuously present with us, and who invites us to make his Kingdom rule visible in the classroom. In childlike faith we see ourselves as utterly dependent on God. We trust not in our own powers, or expertise, or creativity, or charisma, or ability to get along with our students, but we trust in the Lord. In fact, we see our teaching as a collaborative affair: we teach *with* the Lord at our side, arm in arm as it were, in step with the Holy Spirit.[2] Instead of thinking "I am going to teach today" we have learned to say: "*We*—the Lord and I—will teach today." Together we will turn our classrooms into manifestations of God's Kingdom of love and righteousness and power.

Second, all teaching is headed in a certain direction. Teaching is purposeful activity. Perhaps the direction aims at exemplary citizenship, or the acquisition of an impressive set of morals, or the ability to be successful in the world. Christian teachers aim to equip their students for knowledgeable and competent discipleship.[3] We shall examine this critically important point in more detail later on.

And third, our teaching is carried out in service. Life is lived in worshipful service, either to the King of kings or to an idol. We order our lives according to the god we worship and serve. If, for example, we adopt the god of amassing material wealth as the greatest good, we will order our life and priorities for personal gain. Such an idol will control our life. A teacher would choose between jobs solely based on offered salaries. The Lord, of course, is quite upset with our habitual tendency to embrace idols. He wants us to toss them out of our lives and destroy them. He adamantly insists that we accept *Him* as the source of all meaning and value, and order our lives (including our teaching) accordingly.

Why all this chatter about religion? My point is this: your calling to be a teacher is a *religious* calling, and your teaching task is a *religious* task. The same is true for the office you as a Christian teacher hold.

Office

Recall the time when you were considering a teaching career? Let's roll an old film. You sensed the Lord calling you to a teaching task. You examined your talents and concluded—rightly, I'm sure!—that indeed you have many of the requisite skills: you relate well to children or adolescents; you are reasonably intelligent, sufficiently so to understand subject matter clearly; you have good planning and organizational skills; and so on. You also took considerable time to inquire about the status of your interests. "Yes," you told yourself, "I get excited thinking about working in a classroom. I like to sit down and plan lessons, translating subject matter into meaningful learning experiences." And yes, you were quite confident that you have the right kind of personality to be a successful teacher: kind, gentle yet firm, and diligent. Convinced of your calling you headed off to college and completed a teacher education program. After four arduous years you were declared a candidate and subsequently survived interviews.

And then it happened: You were offered a contract! Prayerfully you considered whether or not to accept. Then you made your decision and signed the contract.

What went on there? You became aware of the Lord's call. You came to realize that the Lord was calling you, inviting you, and equipping you for the teaching task. You heeded that call and accepted his invitation to work in his Kingdom as a Christian teacher. And then, finally, after years of preparation, you accepted an officially extended offer to serve as a teacher in a school.

What did you *really* do? By signing the contract did you simply accept a job offer? To be sure, the signature signified that you agreed to perform certain duties for a certain wage. More importantly, however, signing the contract symbolized that you assumed a specific, God-ordained office, a specific place in the Kingdom of God, a station, as it were, from which you could engage in redemptive educational activity.

So what is office? At bottom, office refers to a God-appointed place. It is a "locational" concept. It refers to an official position, to a place within the community of God's people. Just as the players of a soccer team occupy a variety of positions on the field, each one with a specific function, so you and I as Christian teachers are assigned to specific positions in the Lord's cadre. Each one of these positions represents an office. Each position is occupied by an "officebearer." You and I, as teachers, are "officebearers."

Sometimes you encounter very limited conceptions of office. For example, under the influence of medieval nature/grace, laity/clergy, secular/sacred distinctions, it is sometimes believed that only elders, deacons and ministers in the institutional churches are officebearers. To reinforce this idea we often "ordain" such officebearers by special acts of laying on hands and other preformulated installation rites. While the Reformation did much to undo this notion, in both Protestantism and Catholicism the idea of office has often remained limited to ecclesiastical contexts.

Such a restricted view of office is misplaced. The Lord calls each one of us to our various tasks. Each one of these tasks is associated with office. Most of us have multiple offices because we have multiple tasks: for example, I am a teacher, a husband, and a father. Each of these roles—offices, really—implies a different task, and each one of these tasks is assigned to me by the Lord. They are all religious tasks, driven by faith, headed in a certain direction, and performed in service of some kind.

One can be placed in office in various ways. A teacher assumes her office when she signs the contract. A politician is elected to office. A father becomes an officebearer through biological processes or adoption. Sometimes, as was often the case in the ancient world, the drawing of lots determined who would occupy a particular office.

It is important, too, that we recognize the significance of an office. In the early church, for example, the office of elder was regarded as particularly significant. On the other hand, the weight of responsibility that comes along with an office is sometimes not recognized. Think, for example, of young people who become parents when they are not yet ready or sufficiently mature to assume such an office. The office of teacher is especially important, since a teacher affects, for good or evil, the lives of many young people. The Apostle James reminds us of the heavy responsibility shouldered by the teacher.[4] In order to recognize and affirm the importance of the teaching office, it would not be out of place, I think, for a Christian school to conduct special induction or installation ceremonies for incoming teachers. Laying on of hands and imploring the Lord to grant his blessings would be entirely appropriate at the time new teachers begin their work. Some schools, in fact, make this a practice.

Office consciousness

It is vitally important that you recognize your office. As a Christian teacher you need to develop a sense of *office consciousness*. Such office consciousness guarantees that you will not reduce teaching to a humdrum menial task, a routine for which you receive a monthly paycheck. Office consciousness will help you to connect your work to the calling of God, and, therefore, to the work of God himself. Office consciousness equips you to see that every morning anew you enter the classroom as a place where the Kingdom of God must come to expression. Office consciousness reminds you that together with others you must strive to do his will.

Calling, task, and office: beautiful concepts that place our work as teachers in a large, Kingdom perspective. Concepts to remember as we explore what it means to teach Christianly? Yes—essential! But simply talking about office consciousness is not enough. Let's now go on to consider what it means for our daily classroom practice.

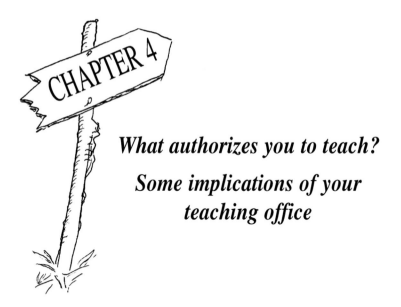

What authorizes you to teach?

Some implications of your teaching office

Lisa: Hi, Stephanie! How are you doing in Mr. Leeds' class? The same model student that you were in my class last year?

Stephanie: Hi, Ms. Lisa! Oh, I'm doing okay—I think. You know, Ms. Lisa, Mr. Leeds is a lot stricter than you were. And he doesn't ask us what we think as often as you did. Mr. Leeds likes to tell us what to do, and if we don't do it right away, he gets mad! I think he just likes to be mean to us once in a while.

Lisa: Really? Or is Mr. Leeds strict because you're such rascally kids?

Stephanie: No, Ms. Lisa, Mr. Leeds can pick on us because he's so much bigger than we are. . . . Sometimes I think he should be a police officer, not a teacher.

A scenario

It's the first school day of your first year as a teacher. Somewhat nervous and unsure you walk into your classroom. But, to your relief, the day goes fine. "Maybe teaching is not as demanding as Van Dyk said it would be," you comfort yourself.

On the second day, however, you smell trouble brewing. Keith, a young man far beyond his years in size, seems bent on testing your resolve and authority. From your position by the chalkboard you've noticed Keith whispering with the kids in the desks nearby, and by their covered giggles you deduce that interest in learning is no longer at the top of their agenda. As you turn to write, a paper clip, launched from a rubber band, comes zinging past your ear and tings against the board. You spin around, fast enough to see the rubber band disappear into Keith's desk.

A case study from a textbook on classroom management? Maybe. Scenarios like these, some much more innocent and some much more troubling, are all too real to classroom teachers at all levels. Happily, for most of us the clever tricks that students play on rookie teachers are far from serious, and, paradoxically, often lead to positive teacher-student relationships. In most of these cases, however, a central point is at issue: the authority you are to exercise in your classroom. The hidden agenda of the tricksters seems to be: What kind of a person is this new teacher? Will she become unglued? Will he be able to keep order? Can she maintain herself as an authority in this classroom? As the years pass, we get better at dealing with "Keiths." The question of authority in the classroom, however, remains a central issue, an issue that brings us right back to the idea and reality of office.

Authority

What allows me to exercise authority in my classroom? Is it because I am bigger and stronger than most of the students? Well, I suppose that sometimes size and strength may help. For example, I entered my first year of high school teaching fresh out of a logging camp in western British Columbia. Even though I had to shave off my wild, scraggly beard, surely a reputation as a big, tough lumberjack made classroom management easier for me. But did it really provide me with the authority I needed as a teacher? I doubt it very much.

So what really authorizes you to teach? Is it because you know more? Is it because you can be sure that the principal will back you up if kids like Keith should get entirely out of hand? No doubt these factors, too, play a role. But they do not legitimate your teaching authority either. Rather, our classroom authority is a direct consequence of our office. The ability to exercise authority is the first implication of the office of a teacher.

You see, authority is inseparably attached to office. This reality is true for all forms of office. My authority as a father, for example, is to be attributed to my *office* as father rather than to my size, age, or accumulated wisdom. If we disconnect authority from office and attach it to ourselves as persons, we change legitimate authority into raw power. Authority does carry power with it, of course. All authority possesses power. In fact, authority *must* possess power. In schools it is sometimes forgotten that the authorization to teach requires the *empowerment* to teach. When a school board hires a teacher and puts her in a classroom full of difficult children while at the same time withholding necessary resources, or prevents her from exercising her teaching task in freedom, the authority of her office is severely curtailed, perhaps even nullified.

At the same time, it is also obviously true that not all power is exercised within the context of legitimate authority. Power without authority—and without office consciousness—deteriorates into brute force. The political history of emperors and dictators is replete with examples. For you and me as teachers, authority in the classroom carries with it the need for office consciousness. The question of responsibility, then, brings us to the second implication of office.

Responsibility

Authority comes with the office, and the office is a God-appointed place. Defined by calling and task, classroom authority is to be exercised with responsibility. We cannot willy-nilly, arbitrarily, irresponsibly swing our weight around. There is such a thing as irresponsibly over-stepping our lines of authority.

Take the problem of Keith, for example. Suppose you had responded to his rubber band and paper clip trick by grabbing him by the scruff of the neck, hauling him off to the local courthouse, and locking him up in the clink for twenty-four hours on bread and water. Clearly such action, though conceivably justifiable, would transcend your limit of authority. After all, your calling and task are confined to teaching and classroom management. They do not include meting out jail terms.

Or, to take another example, suppose you developed an instant aversion to Keith, but took a liking to Jeanie with her light brown hair and limpid eyes. Suppose further that on a test both of them do equally well, yet you give Keith a C and Jeanie an A. Technically you have the authority to do so. After all, testing and grading are important components of your task as teacher. To function in your office of teacher you need the freedom and authority to make the necessary judgments. Yet here again, grading Keith and Jeanie according to your personal feelings rather than on the basis of their performance clearly constitutes a case of exercising your authority in an irresponsible manner.

But to whom are we officebearers responsible? Ultimately, of course, to the Lord, who has called, yes, *invited*, and appointed us to teach in the first place. But the Lord has appointed other officebearers as well, such as the principal of the school and the members of the board; teachers are responsible to them as well. Furthermore, teachers are responsible to the parents of the children, to the children themselves, and even to the subject matter they teach. To twist historical events for propaganda or other illegitimate purposes, for example, is to teach in an irresponsible way. There is, then, a complex responsibility structure encompassing the teaching task. What is important for all teachers to know is exactly what the expectations, duties, and responsibilities are. Clear, specific job descriptions help teachers responsibly exercise their authority as officebearers.

The question of sphere sovereignty

One of the subjects I taught as a high school teacher was German. One fine afternoon, after what I thought was a particularly successful day of teaching, I received a phone call from the father of one of my students. "Mr. Van Dyk," the voice on the other end barked, "I am quite unhappy about the excessive amount of homework you give in your German class! Billy has other courses to study for, you know, and kids need some time for playing sports and earning money and watching TV! I'll put it to you in plain *English*: ease up on the German, or you'll have the school board to deal with!" Well, so much for a successful day and a quiet evening! Happily, we managed to resolve the issue, thanks in part to a supportive principal.

The issue in dispute here clearly was one of "sphere sovereignty." For what is sphere sovereignty? Sphere sovereignty—"sphere authority" would be a better term—explains that the authority and responsibility of the various offices are *directly* delegated to the officebearer by the Lord Himself. For example, my authority as a teacher, placed in office, is from God, and not from the principal, school board, or Billy's father. *All* authority is from God, Paul tells us in Romans 13:1. As a teacher, endowed with the requisite competence, interests, and personality, duly appointed by the legal school authorities, I have the *freedom* to exercise my authority with responsibility.

Of course, as happened in my case, sometimes conflicts between parents and teachers arise. Parents who support Christian schools sometimes seek to settle such conflicts on the basis of a supposed *in loco parentis* ("in the place of the parents") principle. Presumably the teacher simply takes over from the parent, and, consequently, the teacher's authority is subservient to parental authority. Sphere sovereignty, however, suggests that the *in loco parentis* principle is problematic. While it is true that parents have the responsibility to see to it that their children are nurtured in the Lord, they do not necessarily delegate the authority of teaching to the teacher, any more than parents *delegate* the authority to the medical profession when their children require surgery. A parent has no more authority over a teacher's lesson plan than over a surgeon's decision of which scalpel to use. Competent teachers and competent surgeons are officebearers in the educational and medical arenas, and their offices come with their own peculiar authority and responsibility assigned by God. Of course, a parent can *withdraw* a child from the authority of a teacher or a surgeon. And yes, incompetence or arbitrary use of power on the part of teacher or surgeon must be addressed, but then through proper channels, not by merely pitting one's authority over against that of another.

Ironically, when we view the teachers or the school as *in loco parentis*, we support the argument for the claim that schools *can* and *should* take over all duties from the parents. The *in loco parentis* principle suggests that the authority and responsibility of the school are not fundamentally different from the authority and responsibility of the family. And if there is no difference, schools should be able to do whatever parents do. Surely we agree that while schools are in fact increasingly taking over parenting duties—due to the continuing breakdown of the family—they *ought* not to do so. They are neither designed nor intended for that.

Servanthood

As an officebearer, endowed with authority and responsibility, you are to carry out your teaching task in self-effacing servanthood. Here again, office consciousness is vitally important. Without such consciousness, you might believe that you are doing just fine as long as your work gives you a sense of personal satisfaction. Or you might see your profession as an opportunity to express your desire to be a leader, or to be in charge, or to feel important. Such thoughts are essentially self-serving. Rather, the great commandment "Love God and your neighbor"—which, according to Paul in Galatians 5 translates into "Serve God and your neighbor"—must be the guideline for you and me as Christian teachers. Consequently, all the classroom teaching decisions we make must be made in response to the question: How will this serve the Lord? And how will this serve the young people in my care?

This is not an easy matter. Yes, it is easy to say "I teach to serve the Lord," but in actuality we often teach in a self-serving way. Think, for example, of how defensive we teachers tend to be, how difficult it is for us sometimes to accept and make use of legitimate critique, and how quickly we blame our students for their failures rather than ourselves for our poor teaching technique. Think also of the times when you found it impossible to really love one of your students, or when you wished that kids like Keith would transfer to another school. The daily practice of selfless, loving servanthood is a difficult goal to achieve. In a sense we never achieve it. But we need to work at it all the time. As teachers we must take time regularly to reflect on the extent to which we successfully exercise servanthood.

It may be helpful for you to think of servanthood in teaching as a special kind of ministry. What does ministry mean? Usually we think of it as helping those who are hurting, and thereby reduce ministry to a healing ministry. Teaching could be defined as an "equipping ministry." Such ministry surely includes healing: as a teacher you must meet needs and heal hurts; you must forgive and encourage. But you must also celebrate your students' gifts and equip them for service. In so doing you are ministering to them. That is, you attend to their needs and gifts; enable them to recognize their own calling, task, and office; and thereby help them develop their desire and ability to function as knowledgeable and competent disciples of the Lord.

Religion once more

Tomorrow you plan to teach an exciting lesson on photosynthesis. You have articulated some goals and objectives, and the learning activities are in place. Now you put down your pencil for just a little while, and lean back in your chair. In a moment of reflection you become aware once again of the privileges and joys of being a teacher. You *know*, and are thankful, that the Lord has called you, invited you, to be a teacher. You know you made the right decision when, by signing your contract, you accepted the school's offer to teach there. In short, you are aware of your office. You experience office consciousness. Yes, and more—as officebearer you see yourself as a Kingdom worker, aggressively confronting distortions and seeking to bring the healing redemption of Christ to your classroom, in your lessons and units, and in everything you do with your students.

These reflections bring you back to your lesson on photosynthesis. Aware of your office, you recall how critically important it is to recognize the *religious* underpinnings of your lesson on photosynthesis. You recall that the expression "religious underpinnings" means that your teaching activity is driven by a faith commitment, headed in a certain direction, and performed in service. So you ask yourself: What faith drives my lesson on photosynthesis? Is it really my faith in God as creator and sustainer of the universe? Or will I unwittingly include remnants of a faith in natural law and scientific analysis as the final arbiters of truth? And in what direction is my lesson going? You review your goals and objectives once more. Do they include goals aimed at awe and wonder, at students deepening their love for and commitment to the Lord? Or will you be satisfied if your students can merely recall the technical specifics of photosynthesis on a forthcoming test? And finally, you ask: Does this lesson really *minister* to my kids? Does it meet the needs and celebrate the gifts of all my students? Will it help them grow as loving servants of the Lord? Am I teaching this lesson as "a work of service"?[1]

Now you may think that these ruminations are contrived and represent a superfluous whittling away of your precious time. Don't be fooled! They are absolutely indispensable to your work as a Christian teacher. The reality is that if you do not continuously recognize the religious character of your teaching, you run grave risks. First, you risk losing sight of the Christian faith that governs your teaching, thereby becoming vulnerable to the incursion of other faiths and perspectives. Second, you may lose your sense of direction. Derailed by unwanted philosophical influences, you may end up going where you really should not go. Your lesson on photosynthesis may land, for example, in a morass of scientific facts that keep your students from experiencing the presence of God. And, last, missing the religious character of your lessons may blind you to your calling to be a servant, so that you forget to minister to your students. Your lesson may turn out to be merely a self-satisfying affair or do little more than meet requirements imposed by standardized tests.

A final word

A consideration of the craft of Christian teaching must begin with understanding the role of religion and the idea of office. Office, in turn, always directs our attention to the Kingdom of God. Office consciousness helps us see that Christian teaching is Kingdom activity. This means that Christian teaching takes place *within* the Kingdom. The Kingdom, after all, is the territory ruled by the King. This includes, of course, the entire creation, for there is no part of reality anywhere about which the Lord has nothing to say or over which he has no authority. Your classroom is Kingdom territory.

But, of course, because of human sin the Kingdom of God has been obscured. It is our task to make it visible again. In response to the question, Where is the Kingdom of God? we might say that it is everywhere, but it becomes visible wherever the will of the Lord is done. Now God's will applies to every nook and cranny of life, including life in the classroom. Office consciousness, therefore, will encourage us to see our task as Kingdom activity and encourage us to ask the hard questions about every aspect of classroom work: How does my curriculum reflect God's will? How does my classroom management reflect God's will? How do my lesson plans, my goals and objectives, and my teaching strategies respond to the will of the Lord? Office consciousness enables us to seek the Kingdom first.

The will of God is for a Kingdom of righteousness and love, a place where shalom, joy, and delight reign. Seeking this Kingdom first must come to daily expression in your classroom. Throughout the teaching day, you must uncover and exhibit this Kingdom. You begin with tone-setting, meaningful devotions linked to the learning activities of the day. The Kingdom becomes visible through caring relationships between you as the teacher and the students, and between student and student. When Marci has a bad day and can't concentrate on the multiplication of fractions, the Kingdom becomes visible when you encourage her with patience, persistence, and understanding. The Kingdom of peace becomes visible in social studies class as you observe how Julia, without prompting, quietly supports Jeffrey's attempts to make the outline you have assigned. The Kingdom becomes more visible still when you make it a point to recognize Julia's servanthood. The Kingdom of shalom appears when, upon discovering that Ashley has written a nasty note to Kim picturing her as a waddling, ugly duckling, you solve the conflict with gentle but firm admonition instead of harsh punishment. You offer Ashley the opportunity to heal the rift by placing her together with Kim in a group activity.

In all these ways—some seemingly insignificant or addressed in unobtrusive, incidental fashion—the Kingdom of God emerges and radiates its power in a weak, groveling world. All components of your teaching activity must point to the Kingdom: "See, the Kingdom is here, and here, and here." Christian teaching, in other words, is a signpost of the Kingdom. It is "rock-piling activity." Just as the Israelites were to build a heap of stones to remind them of the crossing over the Jordan,[2] so the work of the Christian teacher is a continuous reminder of God's redemption.

Christian teachers must be much in prayer. Every day anew you must ask the Lord to keep you conscious of your special calling, task, and office. Office consciousness, indeed, requires a close walk with God, a "keeping in step with the Spirit."[3] While I have already mentioned it earlier, I cannot overstress this point, for the realities of life in the classroom tend to peripheralize office consciousness. The demands and the stress of teaching quickly crowd the idea of office and its implications out of our consciousness.

I recommend that Christian teachers surround themselves with reminders. A little note taped on your desk with words such as "Remember your office!" may be helpful. Or perhaps a rock pile of sorts. Such reminders should be frequently changed, to keep them fresh and functional.

But, you ask—perhaps a bit frustrated—I still don't know what you mean by teaching Christianly. True, I have not yet offered a complete description. But whatever the final description may be, one point is clear: teaching Christianly requires a living, vibrant office consciousness. A second ingredient is a clear sense of purpose. I invite you to read on.

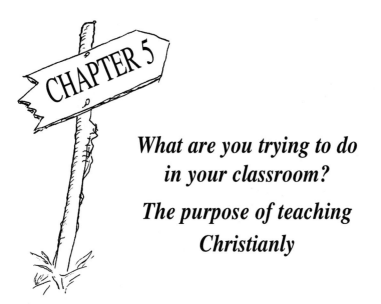

CHAPTER 5

What are you trying to do in your classroom?
The purpose of teaching Christianly

Claire: I still think this school doesn't pay enough attention to academic excellence. There's too much warm-fuzzy stuff around here! How will these kids ever succeed if we don't get them ready for the real world?

Lisa: Well, yes, we do need to prepare our students for the real world. But don't you think there is more to the real world than academics?

Claire: Of course there is! But if we don't emphasize a disciplined study of core subject matter, all the other lofty talk about discipleship and kingdom service won't amount to a bowl of peanuts.

A controversial question

Picture a teacher walking into a classroom. She says to the students, "Okay, sixth-graders, rummage around in your textbooks for a while, or browse through the magazines in the back corner, and see if you can find something to learn. You may take the whole day, if you like!" How would you evaluate such teaching? Well, you will say, it sounds suspiciously like the open classroom of yesteryear: no structure, no specific goals, no clear direction.

Aside from the question of whether or not it represents an open-classroom philosophy, clearly there is something problematic about this teaching approach. Your teaching, like everything else you do, cannot be aimless. It has direction. It goes somewhere. It strives for certain outcomes.

I can think of at least three reasons why your classroom teaching always aims at specific—though possibly not always clearly specified—goals. The first is that teaching is religious activity, and, as we saw, all religious activity is headed somewhere. A second reason is that what you do in your classroom you do within a school, and schools have a mission, either explicit or implicit. As one of its teachers, you must translate the school's institutional mission into specific classroom goals and objectives. Normally your unit plans and lesson plans articulate such goals and objectives. The third reason is that aimless teaching is by its very nature a contradictory concept. Teaching always seeks to bring about learning. Of course, what *kind* of learning we aim for may be a subject of debate. But teaching that leads to nothing does not seem to be teaching at all.

Well, what *should* be the purpose of teaching? Proposals abound, but consensus is rare. Even among Christian educators, consensus is sometimes as easy to spot as seaweed in the Arizona desert. Academic rigor and excellence leading to high achievement is a commonly mentioned goal. Another is preparing young people for the job market. Or for participation in the American way of life. Or to train for democratic citizenship. Or to enable our graduates to enjoy the good life. Or . . . and on and on and on.

Goals and objectives

The debate about what schools should accomplish is certainly not a brand-new phenomenon. During the past half century or so, educators have spent much time thinking about goals and objectives. The standard lesson plan you use today, for example, is still very much in line with what Ralph Tyler proposed nearly fifty years ago: first state what you want to achieve in your classroom, then plan how to reach your goals, and finally evaluate the extent to which you have succeeded in meeting them.[1]

But how are you to determine your goals and objectives? What should you try to accomplish in your classroom? Tyler himself suggests a number of useful criteria.[2] For example, he urges teachers to take the general social milieu into account. If he were alive today, Tyler would no doubt point to the current demand for technologically skilled people. "Be sure to include technological goals in your lesson plans," he would tell you.

You must also take the developmental levels of your students into account as you consider your objectives. Understanding square roots, for example, would be an inappropriate goal in a lesson plan for a second-grade class. Resources, too, will affect the sorts of goals you can reach. Without a zoo nearby, it will be difficult to get the kids to enjoy petting a penguin. And, of course, there are the institutional goals. They can't help but play a controlling role in your specific lesson plans. If your school as a whole aims to develop critical thinking skills, your principal and the parents will not appreciate lesson plans which call only for memorization and regurgitation of facts.

In the 1950s and 1960s behaviorists sweet-talked educators into believing that learning amounts to little more than "observable and measurable changes in behavior." They said that only when your students display a desired change of behavior can you be sure that learning has occurred. So your classroom objectives should be formulated as "behavioral objectives" or "performance objectives" to be prescribed in detail and rigorously tested. Textbook definitions of behavioral objectives go something like this: "A behavioral (or performance) objective is a description of an intended and measurable or observable outcome of teaching/learning activity."[3] For example, a science teacher might write

The Craft of Christian Teaching

the following performance objective: "Given a list of 35 chemical elements, the students will be able to recall and write the valences of at least 30." Effective, purposeful, and productive teaching, the behaviorists argued, depends on the use of such performance objectives.

Before you applaud and haul out pencil and paper to start writing your performance objectives for tomorrow's lessons, tune in to the voice of the widely respected critic, Elliot Eisner. Excessive dependence on performance objectives is bad news, says Eisner.[4] For one thing, such objectives overemphasize predictable outcomes. You know in advance that all your students will be able to write the valences of at least 30 elements. So you will teach strictly to ensure this (measurable) outcome. But where will this leave the teachable moments, the unexpected tangents, and student creativity, all of which might lead to unintended but valuable learning? Performance objectives will scarcely allow for such possibilities.

Probably the most serious criticism Eisner launches is that excessive—or worse, exclusive—reliance on performance objectives blinds teachers to other, non-measurable, aspects of teaching and learning. By their very nature, performance objectives exclude subtle goals such as enjoyment, appreciation, attitudes, and commitments. Since they are difficult to assess, such goals, the behaviorists will tell you, should not play a significant role in your lesson planning. Better yet, avoid them altogether.

Note that Eisner does not reject performance objectives altogether. Rather, he encourages us to pay more attention to what he calls "expressive objectives." An "expressive objective," unlike a performance objective, does not specify a specific learning outcome to be measured. Rather, it describes an "educational encounter," and thus may be different for different students. For example, "The students will learn to interpret Mark Twain's *Huckleberry Finn*" is an expressive objective. Such an objective allows for a variety of interpretations. It encourages diversity of outcome, not a stifling conformity, as performance objectives tend to do. Expressive objectives, therefore, take into account the individuality of the students, and pay attention to differing gifts and needs. Behavioral objectives, in contrast, promote "educational egalitarianism," a point of view which assumes that all students are basically alike, ought to be able to meet similar objectives, and can be evaluated by the same criteria.

A heavy dose of behavioral objectives, in short, torpedoes our confession that children are unique image bearers of God. Reliance on such objectives, in fact, makes teaching Christianly virtually impossible, as we shall see.

Goal taxonomies

So, you say, Eisner helps me see that there are different types of objectives. But I still don't know what they should aim for. What learning outcomes should my objectives—whether performance, expressive, or whatever—work toward? Who will help me do *that*?

Well, let's begin by turning to Benjamin Bloom's celebrated "taxonomy of educational goals."[5] Bloom asked three questions: What should your students know? What sorts of feelings and beliefs should they harbor? And what should they be able to perform physically? Bloom translated these three questions into three sets of goals: goals in the "cognitive," "affective," and "psychomotor" domains. Bloom himself elaborated the cognitive domain, while leaving the specifications of the affective and psychomotor to others.

The cognitive domain, Bloom proposed, consists of a series of progressively complex levels of goals. The basic level is simply to teach the ability to memorize and recall factual information. Next is the level of comprehension. Students must not only be able to recall, they must also be able to demonstrate comprehension by, for example, explaining or paraphrasing a point. The higher levels in the cognitive domain describe ability to apply, analyze, synthesize, and, finally, evaluate.

I suggest you extricate Bloom's taxonomy from the piles of college class notes undoubtedly stashed away somewhere on your shelves. Look again at the six levels in the cognitive domain. Now ask yourself some hard questions. Do your teaching strategies take your students through all six levels of this cognitive domain? Do you routinely ask higher-level questions, not merely questions about facts? Do you require José to apply the insights you teach to a variety of situations? Do you encourage Tim to analyze a problem? Do you invite Marci to offer some well-reasoned judgments? Or are you the kind of teacher who is satisfied with teaching and learning at the basic level of Bloom's taxonomy only—facts, memorization, recall, and regurgitation?

Bloom's taxonomy, then, can help you rethink what you want to accomplish in your classroom. The levels in his cognitive domain provide the beginnings of a handy checklist. His total taxonomy reminds us to take the affective and psychomotor domains into account. Bloom, therefore, helps offset a reductionistic intellectualism that sees goals of education as limited to academic areas of study. And finally, Bloom's taxonomy, especially his cognitive domain, may help you sequence your instruction. You could begin a unit with factual information (the basic levels) and progress upwards, as it were, through the hierarchy to the advanced levels of synthesis and evaluation by requiring your students to engage in increasingly sophisticated studies. For example, suppose you teach a unit on Charlemagne. You would make sure, of course, that your students know the essential details of his life and accomplishments. Now work your way "upwards" through Bloom's cognitive domain. Ask the students to paraphrase the story to ensure comprehension. Invite them to apply their understanding by creating a skit or writing a play. Ask "what if" questions about Charlemagne's career in order to provide opportunities to analyze and synthesize. And finally, require your students, on the basis of evidence and sound argumentation, to evaluate Charlemagne's decisions.

In spite of the positives, Bloom's taxonomy exhibits serious short-comings. I will mention four of them. First, the taxonomy suggests that intellectual matters are distinct from "affective" matters, as if knowledge is unrelated to faith and feelings. The separation between the cognitive and the affective suggests that knowledge is an independent body of content. Thus it fosters the old positivistic idea that knowledge is objective and unaffected by presuppositions, prejudices, and religious beliefs. Bloom's taxonomy fosters a dualism. But from our Christian, holistic perspective, we cannot relegate and confine religious issues, beliefs, and commitments, along with the call to be Christian in all areas of life, to a nebulous area called the "affective."

Secondly, Bloom's understanding of "cognitive" looks too limited.

By "cognitive" he appears to mean what Howard Gardner would call the "logical and the lingual intelligences."[6] But there is much more to cognition than logic and language. Humans know in many different ways. This broader understanding of knowledge is ignored by Bloom.

Thirdly, the domains proposed by Bloom are very difficult to distinguish clearly. This blurriness makes it difficult to write objectives clearly. And no wonder: in reality what Bloom calls the cognitive and the affective constitute one seamless fabric. Life is of one piece. Our thinking, knowing, believing, and feeling are all inseparably interwoven.

And finally, Bloom's taxonomy, though going beyond the cognitive, is still too narrow. It does not include social skills or communication skills, and, in general, neglects creativity. It does not fully address the "whole child." There is much more to a child than the three dimensions Bloom proposes. Your goals for Christian teaching must be considerably broader than those suggested by Bloom.

The Christian response

Imagine that you are the principal of a Christian school. You want your teachers to write goals and objectives that reflect a basic biblical perspective. Would you just insist on performance objectives categorized according to Bloom's classification? Of course not. What you would do first is consider the goal taxonomies advanced by Christian educators. You could begin by reviewing, for example, what Henry Beversluis, working on behalf of Christian Schools International (CSI), suggested.[7]

Like Bloom, Beversluis proposed a three-category classification of goals: the intellectual, decisional, and creative. No doubt you would sense at once that Beversluis's "intellectual" closely resembles the "cognitive" of Bloom's taxonomy. The decisional domain suggests that students must be confronted by choices: they need to be taught to make the right decisions, an important goal indeed. But what exactly Beversluis meant by the third domain, the creative, will likely remain somewhat of a puzzle to you. It looks as if the intent was to provide educational opportunities that help students reach their full potential. But how such potential is to be distinguished from the intellectual and decisional domains is not very clear. More recently, CSI has added a fourth category, namely, the emotional, to make sure that factors such as self-esteem and self-confidence are not neglected.

Next, you might take a look at the work of Donald Oppewal, long-time education professor at Calvin College.[8] Oppewal provides us with an interesting translation of the CSI taxonomy. He proposes a three-phased "three C's taxonomy": curriculum and instruction should lead students (1) to consider, (2) to choose, and (3) to commit. Oppewal explains, "The first phase, the consider phase, lends itself best to the intellectual dimension, the choose phase lends itself to the decisional dimension, while the culmination in the commit phase lends itself to the creative dimension of learning goals."

Not convinced, you examine yet another Christian goal taxonomy, the one suggested by Nicholas Wolterstorff.[9] Schools, he said, should aim at three types of learning: knowledge, competencies, and tendencies. Our graduates, he argued, should be familiar with a wide range of content (knowledge), equipped with a wide array of skills (competencies), and firmly set on the road towards discipleship (tendencies). Curriculum writing in some CSI districts follows Wolterstorff's taxonomy.

To complete your survey, you turn to Harro Van Brummelen.[10] Van Brummelen expresses appreciation for the various attempts to spell out specific goals for Christian schools. Nevertheless, he remains fundamentally critical of the proposals just reviewed. Like Bloom's taxonomy, the CSI taxonomies introduce too sharp a distinction between the intellectual and the other domains. Such a distinction makes it look as if knowledge is a separate, objective category, unrelated to the affective or tendency or decisional dimension. Van Brummelen believes that the proposed taxonomies "are still rooted in a dualistic view of life that assumes a neutral body of knowledge exists to which we can add a moral or affective or decisional dimension."[11] Note that in response to such critique CSI has made efforts to make clear that the intellectual dimension is to lead to the decisional and creative dimensions.

Van Brummelen goes on to suggest a more holistic, integral taxonomy. Rather than work with three distinct categories, he designed a hierarchical taxonomy. The ultimate goal of Christian education, he says, is responsible (more recently: responsive) discipleship. But such discipleship cannot come about without the right disposition (the tendencies of Wolterstorff) leading to commitment. These dispositions, in turn, must flow from the more basic curricular and instructional goals. Van Brummelen suggests at least three types of goals at this basic level: knowledge-that (content), knowledge-how (skills), and creative, problem-solving goals.

Van Brummelen's model constitutes a significant contribution, it seems to me. Responsible discipleship—to which I shall return in a moment—clearly must be the overarching, ultimate goal of our Christian educational efforts. If we train only for marketable skills, academic excellence, and good moral behavior but neglect the higher purpose of Christian discipleship, we lose our distinctiveness as Christian educators. After all, many public schools and secular universities teach marketable skills and academic expertise, as well as encourage good moral behavior.

The ultimate goal of Christian teaching

Question: Do we really need complicated goal taxonomies in order to avoid reductionistic traps? Perhaps not. I propose—more simply— that the purpose of your Christian teaching activity should address two levels of goals: (1) an "ultimate" goal, and (2) a set of intermediate, subservient "goal areas." A word about each of these levels.

The ultimate goal of all Christian teaching should be to lead your students into knowledgeable and competent discipleship. This goal should be the central, controlling goal, not only for you as an individual teacher, but for the entire institution in which you serve. To be reminded of this goal, I recommend you place a paraphrase of Ephesians 4:11-12 on your desk: "I am called to be a teacher in order to equip God's people for works of service."

Observe that Paul's expression "works of service" is shorthand for knowledgeable and competent discipleship. In a sense, all Christian institutions, not just Christian schools, should aim to practice discipleship. Nevertheless, the focus is different in different institutions. In the home, children are led into a trusting and emotionally secure kind of discipleship. In the church the focus falls on worship, faith, and fellowship. The Christian school, however, aims at *knowledgeable and competent* discipleship. Think about it: to function as a disciple in today's complex world plainly requires a good deal of knowledge and a wide range of skills.

I take the adjectives *knowledgeable* and *competent* to express in contemporary language what the Old and New Testaments describe as "wisdom." What is wisdom? Psalm 111 summarizes it for us: "The fear of the Lord is the beginning of wisdom: a good understanding have all those who do his commandments." Wisdom, then, cannot be understood apart from the desire to do God's will. Abstract, disconnected, unrelated knowledge is not really knowledge at all. Ultimately such knowledge is foolishness.[12]

Wisdom and discipleship belong together like the two wings of a bird: Lose one and the other becomes useless. But what exactly is discipleship? Simply put, discipleship is the correlation between hearing and doing. The Scriptures actually picture all of human life in these terms: we are to hear the Word of the Lord and to do it. Hearing without doing means little or nothing.[13]

Note that the correlation between hearing and doing differs from the traditional Greek distinction between knowing and doing. To the Greeks, given as they were to a worship of the intellect, knowing is the superior, controlling dimension. This view led to elitism: those who work with their minds are seen as more noble than those who labor with their hands. But the Scripture knows nothing of such a distinction. In biblical perspective, knowing is itself a form of doing, a response to hearing. Hearing and doing together form the essence of wisdom.[14]

Discipleship, then, requires first of all a hearing of the will of God. "Hearing" does not mean that we merely understand the language of God's commandments. It involves nothing less than experiencing God's presence in our lives. Often in our schools, because of intellectualism, our students learn much *about* God without ever actually experientially encountering Him. When we aim for discipleship as an educational goal, we aim to create situations in our classroom in which our students actually experience the authoritative, yet comforting presence of God.

In response to such hearing you must teach your students to *do*. What kind of doing am I talking about? The doing here refers to loving servanthood. Love God and neighbor means *serve* God and neighbor.[15] Outside of this central command nothing is really significant. Apart from this summary of the law, everything will be distorted. If your teaching is to be Christian teaching, whatever subject matter and skills you work with must ultimately contribute to the children's ability to serve.

A note about servanthood: Servanthood consists of two dimensions. The first is stewardship or caretaking (care giving). We are to take care of ourselves, of one another, and of the entire creation around us. Your classroom should be a place where such stewardship is demonstrated and modeled and practiced. Stewardship is actually built into the creation, but distorted by sin. We were created to be caretakers. If we had not sinned, we would still function as good and productive stewards, normatively responding to the great command "Dress and keep the Garden." But now that sin has come into the world, an additional dimension of servanthood becomes necessary: healing, reconciliation, and peace-making. Distortion and brokenness are everywhere: in our personal lives, in our relationships with one another, and in the creation itself. Discipleship now requires that we set about to heal such brokenness, wherever we encounter it. Ask yourself: Is your classroom a place where such servanthood is demonstrated and practiced?

By means of "goal areas"

I am persuaded that this overarching goal of knowledgeable and competent discipleship should set the stage for all your other goals and objectives. Rather than return to the traditional taxonomies, consider a number of "goal areas." I suggest you work with the following goal areas, which, taken together, will nudge your teaching efforts in the right direction and help you meet the overarching goal.

- *Content/skills:* This goal area comprises what we traditionally call the academic requirements of the standard curriculum. Obviously this area constitutes a very large part of your goal statements. Your students must master many skills—including the so-called "basics"—and develop insight into an ever-expanding range of subject matter. They must be able to recall, survey, define, describe, explain, and articulate all sorts of important matters.

- *Critical thinking skills:* This goal area is closely related to the one we just considered, since it focuses on one of the important skills all students must learn, namely, the skill of critical thinking. As Christians living in a confused world, your students must be able to reason cogently, distinguish sharply, analyze thoroughly, and judge rightly. Now, you could easily subsume this area under the previous one, especially if you are willing to include critical thinking among the "basics." You can't go wrong by singling out this goal area and giving it special emphasis. Your teaching should not get bogged down in a myopic reduction of education to merely the transmission of content. So don't hesitate to place the goal of critical thinking high on your agenda of objectives to be achieved.

  What do critical thinking objectives look like? Take another look at your lesson plans, then write objectives using verbs such as analyze, evaluate, compare and contrast, justify. For example, "My students will be able to compare lifestyles in Southeast Asia and Mexico."

- *Psychomotor or physical dimensions:* Let's face it: You and I as teachers have a tendency to limit our teaching to cerebral and intellectual affairs, thereby neglecting the need for students to be involved in hands-on learning. They need opportunities to build and construct and to be physically active, especially in classes where there is heavy emphasis on "seat work." So consider objectives such as the following: "My students will construct, build, manipulate, experiment, or manufacture."

- *Creativity:* Our fourth area focuses on creative abilities. All of our students have creative and imaginative gifts. All teachers need to include in their unit plans goals and objectives that aim at the development of children's imagination and their artistic and dramatic powers. Too often, I fear, genuine creativity is encouraged only in art and music classes.

- *Feelings/emotions:* How students feel has everything to do with how they learn. The recent writings of Daniel Goleman power-fully underscore this point.[16] As Christians we confess a holistic anthropology: our children are integral, unified beings. If we aim, for example, to make our lessons enjoyable, our students will learn better. So be sure to include in your plan a goal such as this: the students will enjoy this lesson. Once you accept enjoyment in learning as a legitimate goal, you set the stage for more creative and effective teaching. Other objectives in this goal area might relate to emotions such as righteous anger and joyful celebration. In teaching a unit about rain forests, for example, one goal should be to awaken in the students a holy anger. They should be upset when they encounter the greed, exploitation, and injustice people display in the wanton destruction of God's good creation. Such righteous anger should lead to a resolve to do something about the problem. It should lead to action.

- *Discipleship skills:* This goal area is designed to promote the skills required to meet the overarching goal of knowledgeable and competent discipleship. Our unit and lesson plans should include objectives aimed at developing patience, a willingness to listen to and respect one another, and an eagerness to encourage and to assist. In short, your planning should seek to equip your students to exhibit the fruit of the Spirit. As Christian teachers you and I do want our children to learn these skills, yet we seldom explicitly state them as specific goals.

Not all of these goal areas can be specifically pursued in every lesson. But over the course of an entire unit all six goal areas should be addressed.

Some teachers will object to including all of these goal areas in their units on the grounds that they cannot always assess whether or not students have reached such goals. How can you assess whether or not your students actually enjoy your lessons? How do you know whether a sense of righteous anger has really been aroused? Worse, how do you assign grades for such areas? But such objections reflect a behavioristic spirit. They assume that you should teach only what you can assess.

Christian teachers should reject such behaviorism. And in fact they do. Christian teachers know that, for example, modeling a Christian life style is important because students learn from such modeling. Teachers can easily distinguish between students who pick up on such modeling and those who don't. No formal assessment procedures are necessary here. And so it is with much of our teaching, as Eisner has reminded us.

I suggest that you look again at your current unit plans and ask whether objectives belonging to each of the six goal areas are indeed addressed somewhere along the line. Ask yourself: besides planning to teach facts and develop skills, am I teaching my students to analyze, to evaluate, and to explore the connections of one day's learning to the next? Do I provide opportunities for hands-on learning and physical activity in my classes, even when at first these may seem inappropriate— or have I concluded that such activity has a place in early elementary grades only? Do I encourage creativity in my classroom? Do I promote self-confidence, good feelings, an absence of fear, and both appropriate laughter and appropriate indignation? Am I busy teaching my students the servanthood skills needed to function as knowledgeable and competent disciples of the Lord?

The fluidity of these goals should also be readily apparent. They do not represent distinct, separate domains. Rather, they represent facets of your teaching task. Nor are they carved in stone. In fact, they can easily be reconfigured in accordance with institutional priorities and local needs. No doubt there are additional goal areas as well.

The suggested goal areas provide you with a checklist. They help you identify what you are stressing and what you are neglecting. They provide you with a corrective of your vision, especially when they reveal that your teaching is heavily skewed towards one or two goal areas.

What is the purpose of Christian teaching? To equip our students for works of service. That is, to enable them to function as knowledgeable and competent disciples of the Lord, exercising their Kingdom tasks by hearing the will of the Lord and implementing it wherever they find themselves. Your goal is to teach your students to walk in the ways of wisdom. Go to it![17]

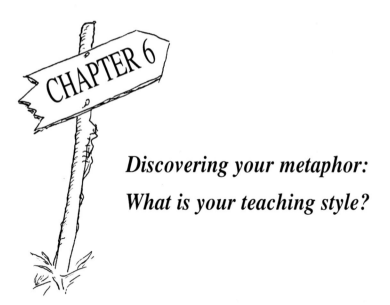

CHAPTER 6

Discovering your metaphor:
What is your teaching style?

Lisa: Hi, Stephanie! You haven't gone home yet?

Stephanie: Not yet, Ms. Lisa. I wonder, are you busy right now? Could I talk with you a minute?

Lisa: Sure, Stephanie. What's bothering you?

Stephanie: It's Mr. Leeds. I'm doing the best I can in his class, but he keeps barking at us. He must think he's running an army or something. I can't stand people always hollering at me. I wish I had you for a teacher again.

Metaphors of teaching and classrooms

Recently, in my curriculum and instruction class, I asked my students to describe in a single word the style of one of their elementary or high school teachers. The suggestions were not slow in coming. "My teacher was a bear," one student reported. "Not mine," another declared, "mine was a clown!" Others saw their teachers as a drill sergeant, a tease, a spy, a preacher, a robot, or a judge. Still other students were more complimentary: they suggested metaphors such as a mother, a friend, or an older sister or brother.

Metaphors of this sort are a shortcut to describe a dominant teaching style. The metaphor captures one or two essential features of a teacher's style. It is exactly this point, of course, that makes metaphors of teaching reductionistic and unreliable. One or two words do not begin to describe the complexity of your teaching style. Nevertheless, the use of metaphors is quite serviceable in trying to understand your style. They prompt self-reflection. Ask yourself how your students will think of you and describe you ten years from now. How do you want to be remembered as a teacher?

Each metaphor can be expanded into a more detailed description. The metaphor of a drill sergeant, for example, suggests a teacher who is authoritarian, loud, inflexible, insensitive, and aggressive. The metaphor of a mother, on the other hand, points to a teacher who is tender, loving, caring, sacrificing, and occasionally strict and demanding. One future teacher in my curriculum class thought of herself as a tree: deep roots securely anchored in the knowledge of a Christian perspective on life, spreading branches to keep the class comfortable, twigs and leaves hiding a multitude of interesting creatures to learn about. To amplify metaphors in this way is surely a useful, reflective exercise. You might take a moment to find a metaphor that you think identifies your teaching style and expand it into a series of descriptive adjectives. Or, if you dare, ask your students to do this for you.

Not only your teaching style, but also your classroom atmosphere can often be captured in a metaphor. For example, if "drill sergeant" describes your teaching style, your classroom is likely to resemble a "boot camp." If the students see you as a clown, they probably perceive your entire classroom setting as a circus. If your metaphor is "coach," your classroom may well echo a locker room atmosphere or a ballpark. I have visited classrooms that unmistakably reminded me of a zoo. At other times I thought I had walked into a pressure cooker!

Lastly, metaphors can catch the way you view your students. Are they animals to be tamed? Empty vessels to be filled? Savages to be civilized? Objects to be manipulated? Clay to be molded? Flowers to be cultivated? Or what? You probably think of them as "image bearers"—another metaphor! If so, what does "image bearer" really mean to you? And how does your understanding of "image" affect your teaching and your classroom management procedures?

Positive and negative metaphors

As the examples solicited from the students show, metaphors may refer to either positive or negative teaching styles. To have you described as a drill sergeant or clown and your classroom as a boot camp or circus certainly is not flattering. These and similar negative metaphors describe teaching styles and classroom climates to be avoided, especially if they are consistently applicable. Such styles surely are to be avoided if you want to teach Christianly. There may be times in the classroom when it is quite appropriate to appear as a drill sergeant. But if the students see you first of all, and almost always, as a drill sergeant, the metaphor becomes undesirable.

Military metaphors are commonly used to describe schools and classrooms in a presumably realistic, but often subtly negative way. Schools are depicted as "war zones," the classroom is a "battlefield," teachers are "in the trenches," students are "troops," and authority relations are "a chain of command." Sometimes this language is heard in Christian educational circles as well. Ask yourself: Are these metaphors appropriate and helpful? True, there are occasions when even the best of schools may resemble a battle zone. But when such metaphors become patterns, we should be concerned. A Christian school should not be a war zone but a place where the love of Christ permeates all activities and relationships, where patience, kindness, and gentleness prevail. Military metaphors gloss over what may be a serious distortion.

True, the Apostle Paul himself employs military metaphors to describe the Christian life. He talks about breastplates and helmets and other kinds of battle gear.[1] But the military language used in the Bible assumes a different kind of war zone. Paul is talking about the cosmic conflict between evil and good, between sin and redemption. The apostle encourages us to do battle with all varieties of evil wherever we meet them. To engage in this battle requires all sorts of "military" hardware: the breastplate of righteousness, a shield of faith, the helmet of salvation, and the sword of the Spirit.

Military metaphors applied to education, however, normally depict quite a different situation. They suggest conflict and battle *within* classrooms and school communities. They describe unhealthy, adversarial, tension-ridden relationships among students, between students and teachers, and between teachers and administrators. Such discord and disunity should not be present in a Christian school. Classrooms and schools should be communities where educators work in harmony and concord to face the foe. And what is the foe? Not the teachers, the students, the principal, or the parents, but the spirits of the age that militate against your best efforts to teach Christianly.

Happily, there are positive metaphors to be cultivated. Metaphors such as friend or older brother often reflect styles quite compatible with teaching Christianly: they frequently echo various biblical metaphors applicable to the Christian life as a whole. Friendship and brotherhood are fully in harmony with biblical metaphors such as "the fruit of the Spirit," "the body of Christ," and "walking in the truth." Ask yourself: Do these positive metaphors match up with my teaching style? With my classroom as a whole?

Common secular metaphors

A dominant cluster of metaphors still widely promoted in the teaching profession sees the teacher as an expert, a decision-maker, a manager, or a scientific technician. These metaphors have functioned as main themes of the so-called "effective teaching" movement, representing an approach to teaching commonly taught and fostered in university teacher education programs. "Effective teaching" came to be the battle cry prompted by educational research, especially by studies conducted in the 1950s and 1960s. Researchers carefully documented the "behaviors" of presumed master teachers in an attempt to identify those traits, characteristics, competencies, and actions that appeared to lead to successful learning.[2]

Recently the effective teaching approach, along with its expert/decision-maker/manager/scientific technician metaphors, has come under increasing critique.[3] From your Christian point of view, too, these metaphors are to be carefully evaluated. Can you see the negative implications in each one of these metaphors? The teacher as expert suggests that the students are "dumb," so that their experience and insights do not need to be taken seriously. The teacher as decision-maker and manager implies that students can be passively manipulated and need not be consulted. And if we see a teacher as a scientific technician (one whose teaching practice consists of little more than the application of research results), we diminish the personal, human, and unpredictable elements in teaching.

In reaction to the scientific and effective teaching approach, philosophies proposing alternative schooling have emerged.[4] These tend to be heavily "child-oriented" and are fond of using metaphors such as gardener and nurse. The child is like a plant, ready to grow and blossom naturally, as long as it receives the requisite amount of light, warmth, and water. So the teacher must prepare an environment in which the children can come to full fruition. Or the child is viewed as basically healthy but easily laid up with an infection or two. So, like a nurse, the teacher must provide wholesome conditions and occasional medication to help the child recover and flourish. Should a child, for example, display a mean streak, gentle correction may be required.

Other examples of metaphors

Many educational philosophies espouse favorite metaphors. Suppose you were a loyal perennialist whose main aim is to transmit the classical wisdom of the ages. What would be an appropriate metaphor? You would see yourself pouring buckets of knowledge into empty heads (or depositing funds into an empty bank account, to use Paulo Freire's metaphor).[5] Enamored by such a transmission approach you might find the metaphor of drill sergeant quite attractive. If, on the other hand, you were a staunch progressivist, you would view yourself as a facilitator and coach. Asking educators to state their favorite teaching metaphor often pointedly reveals their philosophical orientation.

Christians, too, use various metaphors. Henry Nouwen, for example, speaks of teaching as either a violent or redemptive process.[6] This is a very powerful metaphor. To recognize that teachers can teach in a violent way—by unilateral, alienating, and competitive classroom strategies—should give pause for reflection and add weight to the Apostle James' warning that teachers will be more heavily judged than others. Parker Palmer proposes that teaching is to create a space within which truth can emerge.[7] Such a metaphor is very suggestive and prompts us to envision a classroom quite different from a circus or boot camp.

Still other metaphors deserve discussion. Recently Alfonso Montuori described the ideal classroom as analogous to a jazz band.[8] A classroom and jazz band are similar, he said, with respect to creativity, learning, collaboration, and social organization. In such a classroom, teacher and students are attuned to each other and improvise, as it were, their way through the curriculum. Kieran Egan proposes to see teaching as story telling.[9] He has developed ways of translating  curricular materials into the stories to be told, complete with plot, suspense, and resolution. Alan Tom describes teaching as a moral craft.[10] This approach has led Harro Van Brummelen to see teaching as a religious craft.[11] Teaching is a craft in that it involves both technical know-how and personal intuition. But the teaching craft is not merely moral, Van Brummelen reminds us: it is also religious.

In his recent book *The Courage to Teach* Parker Palmer amplifies the metaphor applicable to his own teaching style. After explaining what a good classroom should look like—a "space where teacher and students can communally inquire after truth"—he describes his metaphor as follows:

> I can illustrate both the risk and the payoff by exploring my own metaphor. It came to me twenty-plus years ago, under conditions long forgotten: when I am teaching at my best, I am like a sheepdog—not the large, shaggy, lovable kind, but the all-business Border collies one sees working the flocks in sheep country.
>
> I once saw such dogs at work in Scotland's rocky fields, and that may be where the image took root in me, though teaching was far from my mind at that time. But as I unfolded the meaning of my metaphor. . . I began to understand how the image of the sheepdog offers some clues to my identity and integrity as a teacher.
>
> In my imagination . . . the sheepdog has four vital functions. It maintains a space where the sheep can graze and feed themselves; it holds the sheep together in that space, constantly bringing back strays; it protects the boundaries of that space to keep dangerous predators out; and when the grazing ground is depleted, it moves with the sheep to another space where they can get the food they need.[12]

Metaphors, in sum, provide important avenues for teachers to explore their classroom approaches.

A metaphor for teaching Christianly

I introduce the concept of teaching Christianly by using two metaphors, namely, the teacher as craftsperson and the teacher as guide.

Craftsperson

On this point I follow Alan Tom and Harro Van Brummelen. What is a craft? Think of the medieval cobblers. Theirs was a craft: they made standard shoes, yet imprinted their personal stamp. I know of a scholar who could look at a medieval shoe and tell you where it was made and by whom. The shoe was a shoe like all shoes, yet it could be unmistakably iden-tified as a personal product. A surgeon, too, is a craftsperson. No two surgeons make incisions in exactly the same way, yet they follow scientifically established rules.

A craft, then, has two dimensions: (1) a universal dimension, consisting of common elements that all good craftspersons know about and practice; and (2) a personal dimension that allows craftspersons to bring their personal, intuitive characteristics to their task. In this way we may consider teaching, like the work of the cobbler and the surgeon, as a craft: (1) there is the universal element that all good teachers know about (often discovered by educational research); and (2) there are the personal, intuitive elements, the personality and gifts of the individual teacher which make every teacher unique.

If you want to teach Christianly, see yourself as a craftsperson. You need to know, on the one hand, the basic technical skills all good teachers practice. These were probably taught in your teacher education program. These basic skills involve understanding how children learn, how to translate subject matter into pedagogical content knowledge,[13] and the basic rules for effective classroom management. On the other hand, you must reflect keenly on the special, personal gifts you want to bring to your teaching practice. You need to recognize and capitalize on your special strengths and minimize your weaknesses. Be sure to develop your own personal metaphor and style, and not slavishly imitate the model of, for example, your idolized second-grade teacher.

Most importantly, always aim to subject both the universal and personal dimensions of your teaching craft to the will of God. How do you do this? By continual study, discussion, reflection, meditation, Bible reading, and prayer. Since the universal dimension is often suggested by educational research, you and I as professional teachers need to know about such research and be able to evaluate it from a Christian perspective. Such analysis and evaluation require an articulated Christian philosophy of education to be used as a touchstone.

Our personal elements, too, must be scrutinized in the light of God's Word. Self-reflection of this sort is not an easy matter, something we can do in a few spare minutes here and there. We need to encourage and promote meaningful staff development designed to help teachers come to grips with these important types of evaluations. Urge your principal and colleagues to foster self-reflection, mutual classroom observation, and meaningful inservice programs. Encourage the leadership in your school to provide more time for these kinds of indispensable activities.

Guide

As a Christian teacher you are not merely a craftsperson, but also a guide. In order to clarify this metaphor fully, we should expand it to include the entire classroom. What metaphor can we use to describe a Christian classroom situation? I suggest that you see yourself and your students as a company of travelers on a journey, of *viatores*, as the medievals used to think of themselves, as "fellow-travelers on the way."[14] Sometimes we speak of the Christian life as a pilgrimage, and of Christians as pilgrims. I suspect "travelers" may be a better term: pilgrims focus too much on getting to a place other than where they are right now. Travelers, however—if they are anything like me!—take the current terrain into account; they stop to observe the birds and to identify the wildflowers along the way.

Seeing the classroom as a company of travelers on an adventurous journey implies a number of important themes. First, the journey surely is to lead to a destination. The *viatores* are not aimlessly wandering about. Although there are detours and byways, the travelers are nevertheless going somewhere. Consequently, as a Christian teacher journeying with your students, you must frequently stop to ask: How far have we traveled today? Are we closer to our destination than we were yesterday? How can we make progress tomorrow? Do I have the right destination in view? Is my compass set correctly? Is my classroom company of travelers heading towards the attainment of knowledgeable and competent discipleship?

Secondly, the journey leads through a terrain. For your classroom company, this terrain comprises much of the curriculum. There is the lay of the land to be taken into account. Sometimes the road is smooth; at other times it looks as if you are traveling through a construction zone. What is clear, however, is that in order to advance on the journey someone must have a map and be able to negotiate the terrain. Someone must know exactly where to travel and how to overcome or circumvent the various roadblocks you will inevitably encounter. These needs bring us to the third theme: someone in the company of travelers must function as the guide. You guessed it: you, the teacher, are this guide.

As the teacher you must function as a knowledgeable (knowing the map) and competent (able to negotiate the terrain) guide. Knowledge of the map further implies that you know the destination. If I want to go fishing in the wilds of northern Ontario, I hire a guide to lead me to the proper destination: the place where the fish are. If, after a few hours of navigating through the rivers and lakes, the guide were to say: "Well, I suggest we try it here! I have no idea where we are or where the lunkers might be, but this looks as if it might be a good spot," I would be justifiably annoyed and tempted to dismiss the guide. For this guide is no guide: he does not know where to guide me.

Note, then, that guiding, if it is to be guiding, is purposeful. It must have direction. I cannot overstress this point. You cannot really be an authentically Christian teacher, I believe, if you do not frequently stop to ask: Are we on the right path? Are we heading towards the destination? Are we continuously aiming at knowledgeable and competent discipleship?

Note also that you are not with your students on a life-long journey. We teachers have students in our class for only a little while, a year or so, and then we start a new journey with a new group. So the destination we are to reach is not in the far distant future, but relatively close by. Having students for only a short time underlines the importance of a school agreeing on the destination and each teacher guiding a leg of the trip. Parents, too, must be clear about and agree on the destination.

A final word

In order to relate the two metaphors of craftsperson and guide, we need to return to what we saw a moment ago, namely, that a guide must be knowledgeable and competent. Indeed, guiding itself can be considered a craft. It, too, exhibits both a universal and a personal dimension: there are the things all good guides must know and be able to do, but they do them in their own particular, personal way. The guiding, in other words, is not a willy-nilly roaming about. On the contrary, it is to be conducted in craftsmanship fashion, based on sound knowledge and governed by appropriate personal intuition.

In the following chapters I shall relate this metaphor to a more specific description of teaching as guiding, unfolding, and enabling. As a teacher you guide your students towards a destination, that is, to meet the educational purposes described in the previous chapter. You do so by way of unfolding the lay of the land, the terrain to be traversed, the various skills and content to be learned. In guiding and unfolding you enable your students to function as knowledgeable and competent disciples of the Lord. Let's look more closely at this portrait.

Teaching Christianly:
Sketching the portrait

Alex: Boy, did I have trouble today! The kids just seemed bent on wasting their time. It's so frustrating—I feel out of control!

Lisa: Well, time on task doesn't always have to drive your classroom, does it?

Alex: Time on task is a basic Christian principle, Lisa. Redeem the time, the Scripture teaches us. Nose to the grindstone, I always say. That's the only way kids will learn to be productive and efficient.

Lisa: I'm not so sure, Alex. What about Nicole? She's a student who needs a more relaxed atmosphere if she is to flourish. Time on task could paralyze her and kill her curiosity.

Teaching: What is it?

Ready for a quiz? Here are three questions. See if you can answer them correctly. Be sure you are able to support your responses with cogent arguments!

1. What does the word "teaching" mean?

2. What is the essential difference between teaching activity and other kinds of human activity?

3. What is the difference between teaching and training?

For extra credit, let's toss in another assignment:

Clearly differentiate between the following terms: teaching, instruction, informing, tutoring, drilling, indoctrination, schooling, and education in general.

Well, how did you do? Obviously not a snap quiz, you will agree. Answering questions like these is no cinch. Educators and philosophers have debated them for centuries. One wise guy suggested that if you can't *do* something, you *teach* it![1] Among the more serious definitions proffered, two have stood an extended test of time. One of these sturdy suggestions maintains that at its core teaching means "to transmit or impart knowledge." The other one views teaching as tantamount to "training others to perform certain skills" (such as reading, writing, thinking critically, and solving problems).

Sixty years ago serious scientific investigation into the question of just what teaching is began its still unfinished career.[2] The research interests ranged from defining the essential nature of teaching to describing the effective teacher's characteristics, competencies, and classroom behavior. Included in the inquiries were issues such as the relationship between teaching and learning. For example, a major question was this: Does teaching imply learning? Have we really taught if our students have not learned? In other words, is teaching to be

$$teaching \overset{?\ ?}{\Longrightarrow} learning$$

defined in terms of its outcome? The goal of much of this research was to figure out just what it is that distinguishes an effective from an ineffective teacher. But we shall lay these fascinating puzzles aside. A book on the history of pedagogy would surely be helpful at this point. I may write it some day.

Three ways

No matter what your definition, you can teach in at least three different ways. Let's look first at Mr. S. Mr. S is a teacher who walks into the classroom in the morning, confidently teaches all day long, and leaves the school at 4:30. A dedicated teacher, you say? Yes, but there is a problem. You see, at no time during the entire day does Mr. S give any thought to what the Lord might have to say about what he is doing in his classroom. Mr. S, in fact, believes that the question about the Lord and his will has no relevance whatever. Mr. S's teaching, in sum, is essentially secular teaching. Secular teaching is teaching that simply ignores the Lord and sets aside what the Lord desires. Clearly this way of teaching is no option for you.

Now picture our second teacher, Ms. D. Ms. D teaches ninth-graders in a Christian high school. She opens the day with her customary prayer and devotions. She even asks for prayer requests. But as soon as the Bible is closed and the praise books put away, Ms. D reverts to teaching subject

$8:30 - 8:45$

prayer/ Bible

$8:45 - 2:45$

math – lang –
science –
soc st - PE

$2:45 - 3:00$

Bible/ prayer

matter in a way virtually identical to a nonchristian teacher in a public school. This type of teaching I call "simply teaching." As we saw in an earlier chapter, "simply teaching" suggests a dualistic approach. The "Christian" aspect of teaching is confined to a time of devotional activity, usually reserved for the beginning and the end of the school day. The rest of class time is simply business as usual.

But there is a third way. It is the way of genuine Christian teaching, the sort of teaching that this book is all about. This is the way of teaching that emerges from a philosophy of education grounded in a holistic, life-encompassing biblical worldview. Of course, no matter how you see it, your worldview determines both your definition of teaching and your classroom practice. Mr. S, for example, assumes a world in which God is irrelevant. Ms. D, on the other hand, is probably a Bible-believing Christian, but she espouses a philosophy that divides life into two clearly demarcated realms: a realm of the sacred, to be practiced at the beginning and end of the school day, and a realm of the secular, comprising the subject matter she teaches.

Teaching and worldview

Let's take a closer look at how your world-and-life view affects both your definition of teaching and your understanding of how you should teach. Now remember, your worldview is not limited to sweeping generalities about God and humankind, or to a set of theological truths. As a teacher, your worldview controls what you believe not only about the big picture, but also about subject matter, about children, and about the purposes of your efforts in the classroom.

Take, as an illustration, Mrs. P, a true-blue perennialist teacher. Somewhere in your teacher education program, I'm sure, you learned about perennialism, an educational philosophy with a long tradition. In line with perennialism, Mrs. P sees the world as a pretty stable place. "Nothing new under the sun" is her motto. Change and development are merely alterations of a perennial state of affairs. On this assumption it follows that the subject matter to be taught in schools must surely reflect the unchanging wisdom of the classical authors. Mrs. P endorses a curriculum heavily focused on the "great books" of the Western liberal arts tradition. What was good for the ancients, Mrs. P contends, is good for today's youngsters. And what are youngsters? According to Mrs. P they come empty-handed—really empty-headed—to the teacher, to be filled with the wisdom of the ages. So what is the purpose of education? It is to have our students acquire this wisdom. Note that these themes pretty well determine how we are to view teaching. Teaching, from this perennialist perspective, can be defined as the transmission of information. Teachers function as intermediaries between the great classical past and the empty heads confronting them in the classroom.[3]

Clearly, if we are to describe teaching Christianly, we need to become explicitly conscious of our underlying worldview, then check whether or not our own definitions of teaching are in sync with our educational philosophy. Contrast an authentically Christian worldview with Mrs. P's perennialist position. A biblical view does not take off from notions of an unchanging world of classical wisdom. On the contrary, illuminated by the Word and Spirit, we begin with a vision of God's good creation, dynamic and wonderfully complex. Against the backdrop of the Lord's brilliant, breathtaking handiwork the Scriptures describe human sin that brought about a suffering and groaning of the entire creation waiting for redemption. The Scriptures open our eyes and ears to the work of Jesus Christ by telling the greatest story of all, a story of reconciliation of all things.[4] The Scriptures assure us that knowledge is not primarily a matter of the liberal arts or of scientific inquiry, but a profound understanding of what the world is like, of who we are, and of what we are to do as agents of his reconciliation. Our children are not empty containers as Mrs. P would have us believe, but unique, gifted, contributing image bearers of the Lord, precious in his sight and to be treated with the utmost respect. Consequently, the purpose of our classroom efforts cannot simply be the transmission of classical intellectual insight, but, rather, the whole-person equipping of our children for knowledgeable and competent discipleship in a hurting world.

Definition of classroom teaching

In keeping with this briefly stated philosophy of education, I propose to define teaching as follows: Teaching is multidimensional formative activity consisting of guiding, unfolding, and enabling. Note that this definition includes three key concepts: multidimensional, formative, and guiding/unfolding/enabling. I want to examine each one of these themes in more detail. The first two I shall explore in this chapter, the third one in the next.

The Craft of Christian Teaching

Multidimensional

Teaching activity is extremely complex. Nevertheless, upon examination we can discern a variety of dimensions.[5] You might think of these dimensions as functions. Each one of these functions—like the rest of life—has a normative character. That is, each one of these dimensions *should* appear in your teaching activity in a normative way. "Normative" here means "according to the will and invitation of the Lord." Of course, exactly what the will of the Lord is in each case is not always easy to determine. Such determination requires continuous prayer, a close walk with the Spirit of God, and much communal reflection and discussion.

Just as each function of the teaching act should exhibit a normative character, so it is possible for it to come to expression in an anti-normative, disobedient, and distorted way. When you observe such distortions in the classroom, you intuitively sense that something is wrong. You sense that such "anti-normativity" is not according to the intent of the Lord, that it is not an appropriate response to the way God designed his creation and to the way he invites us to live.

But enough of these abstractions! Let's survey a number of these functions as they occur in our daily classroom practice and identify both their normative and anti-normative expressions.

Faith

All teaching carries the message of what the teacher believes. In fact, this aspect can be regarded as the direction-setting function. As we noted when we discussed the religious character of teaching, our faith determines the way we order and conduct our lives. Our faith is a direct expression of our heart commitment: what lives in our hearts will come out in all of our lives' activities. As the ancient sage declared: "Out of the heart are the issues of life."[6] So how should our faith direct us in a normative way? You know the answer as well as I do: We are to be committed to the Lord as the King of kings and Lord of lords, which means that we not only *acknowledge* that Christ is Lord of every part of our teaching practice, but that we also earnestly seek to *align* the entirety of our classroom work with God's will. What we *believe* about God and the world and humankind will shape our curricular and instructional decisions.

It is easy for this aspect to assume an anti-normative direction. Think, for example, of Ms. D's dualistic, "simply teaching" approach. Think of Mrs. P's faith in the unassailable value of classical wisdom. Or, like Mr. S, we can take a virtually secular approach to our teaching practice.

Trust

Teaching Christianly requires the cultivation of trust relationships in our classroom. Students will not learn well from teachers they do not trust. The establishment and maintenance of trust relations is a normative response to this aspect. Such trust relations must exist between student and teacher, student and student, student and principal, and between all of these and the Lord. Such trust implies that we will not fail or forsake one another. It means that we can share our problems and difficulties in confidence.

Unfortunately, in some classrooms this aspect comes to anti-normative expressions. Sometimes we encounter situations in which the students do not trust the teacher—thinking that the teacher is out to "get them." Too often students do not trust each other. Sometimes whole classrooms exude a climate of mistrust and suspicion, resulting in serious discipline problems. Harsh discipline might squelch these problems, but such an approach simply fortifies the anti-normativity of an essentially unwholesome and unchristian situation.

Fairness

When I ask high school students to list the characteristics of their best and their worst teachers, the notion of fairness quickly enters the discussion. This aspect of your teaching shows itself in a normative way when you treat the students fairly in every respect. That is, you must be fair in the assignments given, in the evaluation of a student's work, and in the exercise of discipline. Students are usually quite perceptive on this point. They quickly sense when a teacher shows favoritism or is inconsistent.

Fairness does not necessarily mean that you give each student an equal amount of attention. Doing so may look fair, but in actuality be quite unfair. Some students need more attention than others. Fairness cannot be determined on the basis of a mathematical formula. True justice is always tempered by mercy and by keen sensitivity to the needs of the students.

Creativity and imaginativity

Is teaching an art or a science? This question reflects another age-old debate.[7] We may connect this debate, perhaps somewhat roughly, to our earlier discussion of teaching as a craft. In a sense, the scientific character of teaching can be associated with the universal craft dimension, while the artistic side is especially present in the personal flavor a teacher brings to her work.

Your teaching should reflect a playful, imaginative spirit.[8] Your lessons should be creatively designed. The classroom environment itself should display an aesthetically pleasing and stimulating character, conducive to learning. It is interesting that, in general, elementary teachers pay much more attention to classroom environment than do secondary teachers. Even different subject areas appear to affect the teacher's aesthetic imaginativity. I know of computer classrooms that look barren and sterile, reflecting a cold-hearted unfeeling technology. I also see such classes decorated with green plants and an aquarium in the corner, to remind students that technology cannot be divorced from a living, breathing creation.

When our teaching becomes dull, stale, or mechanical, we respond anti-normatively to our calling to be imaginative teachers. Similarly, when we ignore the classroom setting, we fail to do justice to the aesthetic aspect of our teaching task.

Pacing

This function focuses on good stewardship versus wastefulness of time and resources. Do you conduct your lessons with appropriate efficiency or are you wasting precious time? Do you provide sufficient time for the students to be able to do their best work, or do you short-change them one way or another by rushing them along, worried you might not have time to "cover the material"?

This dimension of teaching can confront us with serious difficulties. For one thing, many teachers are responsible for altogether too many students. In facing a classroom with more than 30 students, a teacher often feels she has no choice but to teach to the median ability level, thereby boring the high achievers into listlessness and losing the low achievers altogether. As we shall see in chapter 16, there are appropriate ways of dealing with this situation. In general, however, in large classes it is difficult to respond normatively to the stewardship dimension of our task.

An important question is, What really does it mean to waste time in the classroom? Here again, your philosophy of education will have an impact. The "effective teaching" movement, referred to earlier, adopts the metaphor of the teacher as a manager, thereby attributing a business-like character to the classroom. According to this philosophy, the teacher must start teaching promptly at the beginning of the hour and continue to the last second. The students are to get out their books and do their work in a quick, no-nonsense, business-like fashion. "Time on task" is a priority in this approach. Off-task behavior is regarded as a serious sin.

As a Christian teacher you should be highly suspicious of this approach. The classroom is not a business organization. Many students have learning styles that require a relaxed, unhurried environment in order for them to learn. "Time on task" for them may well be the worst, possibly even the most unfair treatment they can receive from a teacher. Parker Palmer, who argues that teaching is "to provide a space," suggests that we introduce extended periods of silence into our classrooms.[9] Such silence—doing nothing—may at times be the most productive way of conducting a lesson!

Good/normative pacing practices require much experience and a sensitivity to the needs of students. No hard and fast rules apply.

Social relations

This dimension of your classroom practice is particularly important since it provides one of the basic building blocks needed to forge community in your classroom. Community is a large, rich concept which we shall consider later on. In the present context I limit my remarks to interpersonal relationships.

A normative response to the social aspect of teaching consists of encouraging your students to bond together, to establish close friendships, and in general to relate to one another in a helpful, positive, and encouraging way. Problems emerge when you see your students begin to exclude one another and form cliques and factions. A particular concern is the negative peer pressure that plays such a significant role in the lives of your students. As a Christian teacher you should be thoroughly familiar with child and adolescent psychology, and understand the social forces at work in your classroom. Aim to expand your ability to turn negative peer pressure into positive interpersonal relationships. For example, a teacher told me the following story: "A six-year-old boy recently taught me that to hold my thumb and index finger in the shape of an 'L' at someone is to label him or her as a Loser. I had a golden opportunity to challenge his thinking about the value of each human being made in the image of the Creator, and to foster positive interpersonal relationships."

Communication

Much of your teaching makes use of language. I need not remind you that we are to use language with clarity and precision. As in all social practices, relationships break down when communication breaks down. Obscurity and vagueness should be avoided.

Using clear and precise, grammatically correct and stylistically acceptable language provides a good model for your students. When you misspell words on the chalkboard or neglect good usage, your students will learn to believe that sloppy, even mistaken language is acceptable. You also model to students that words have power and connotations. For example, by using gender-inclusive language you communicate that both males and females *count* and are taken into *account*. In our times good use of language is frequently under attack, so it is important to take this aspect of your teaching task seriously.

Planning and appraisal

This theme comes to expression in the careful planning of units and lessons, in the organized sequence of learning activities, and in the exhibition of clear thinking in our classrooms. "Winging it" and fuzzy analysis hurt our effectiveness as Christian teachers.

Of course, not everything you do in the classroom must always be carefully planned in advance. Such an assumption would nudge you into the direction of technicism, an approach that fosters the belief that science and technology are the keys to ordering our lives. Much of the "effective teaching" movement, referred to earlier, has been built on this assumption. When teaching is reduced to merely technical know-how with little room for spontaneity, we torpedo the full, rich meaning of teaching Christianly. But being flexible is no excuse for sloppy planning. You need to invest time and energy into matching the best pedagogy to each subject at hand. And do not neglect to take time to reflect on your teaching. Consider keeping a journal in which, at the end of the day, you write a few remarks about what went well and what could be improved. Above all, reflect on the extent to which you have worked for the goal of knowledgeable and competent discipleship.

Feelings

Because of a tradition of Platonic intellectualism, feelings and emotions are frequently suppressed in our classrooms. Don't hesitate to encourage the expression of emotions. In the classroom there are times to be joyful, to be sad, and to be righteously angry. Such expression of emotions ought to be carefully cultivated. The Lord created us as emotional creatures. It is an affront to Him to act as if this aspect is of no concern, or worse, is nonexistent. Teachers can be effective models if they judiciously demonstrate how they themselves deal with their feelings.

The emotional dimension is also displayed normatively or anti-normatively in the sensitivity teachers exhibit towards their students. Neither a cold, harsh demeanor nor a flippant, anything-goes attitude has a place in the Christian classroom.

Finally, we sense the importance of the emotional aspect when we recognize that your feelings affect your teaching. I don't know of another profession in which the way you feel so profoundly affects your work as in teaching. For this reason it is necessary that teachers remain emotionally healthy and physically fit. If a teacher "doesn't have it all together," the children in the classroom will suffer. As a community, the staff, principal, and parents can encourage each other and support each other on difficult days.

Some other aspects

Liveliness and intensity are qualities requiring your attention. Your classroom should be a lively place, not a dull, stale holding pen. When students complain that the class is boring, do not glibly dismiss such critique as ignorant, irresponsible drivel. Rather, don't hesitate to ask yourself some hard questions: Is my teaching "alive"? Do I present my material in as dynamic, enthusiastic, and spirited a way as I can muster? Of course, it is unreasonable to expect that every day and all day you are at your vibrant and energetic best. Life is not that way. Nevertheless, liveliness and enthusiasm are qualities that can be cultivated, I believe.

Finally, I mention what we may describe as "context dimensions" of classroom teaching. I have in mind not only the location where teaching takes place, that is, appropriate surroundings and adequate facilities, but also an appropriate curricular and institutional context. Teaching Christianly requires a compatible curriculum, supportive colleagues, and a constituency that shares the vision of the school. Contexts like these don't automatically happen. Through effective and prayerful leadership they need to be carefully nurtured.

Formative

The second key component in my definition of teaching is the concept "formative."[10] Can we identify some essential characteristic that sets our teaching apart from other multidimensional things we might do, such as praying, painting pictures, running a business, or playing a ball game?

The use of the term "formative" rings a bell for most teachers, for often it is thought that teachers "form," "mold," or "shape" their students—preferably in the image of the teacher—as if teachers are potters and students are clay. Such a metaphor is probably too strong, however, since in reality we cannot form or mold anyone. Only the Word and Spirit can do this. Recall Paul's remark about himself planting, Apollos watering, but God giving the increase.[11] Formative, then, does not mean "forming," but merely "to exercise a formative influence." It suggests activity intended to bring about change and development. While the "formative" is a dimension of every kind of human activity, in teaching it takes on a central role. It points to the essential change we seek to achieve through our teaching, namely, learning.

The idea of the formative cannot be understood apart from its link to the purpose of teaching. Whatever we take to be our educational aim will determine what sort of forming we are talking about. I have argued that the goal of Christian teaching is to equip for knowledgeable and competent discipleship. The formative, therefore, in our sense of the word means to exercise an influence which sets the students on a pathway towards discipleship.

I do not mean to suggest that the "formative" leads to predetermined ends. We must avoid the idea that our students can be manipulated, that they are merely objects to be subjected to the technical expertise of teachers. If anything, our "forming" should be equipping our students to be self-directive, in accordance with God's will.

The formative nature of teaching displays once again the awesome responsibility you and I assume when we enter our classrooms. Teaching can never be merely fun and games, or the telling of interesting stories, or the drilling in various skills. Yes, these certainly are legitimate ways to teach. But remember: all forms of teaching will inevitably exercise a formative influence on your students. The overriding and sobering question is: *What sort* of formative influence?

Formative activity comes to expression in the third component of teaching, namely, the functions of guiding, unfolding, and enabling. To these I now turn.

Teaching Christianly:
Sharpening the image

Ken: I hear there's talk about getting a second Bible teacher in this school system. Great!

Lisa: No kidding! Well, it's about time! We can stand plenty of Bible study. Why do *you* think it's a good idea, Ken?

Ken: You know how the principal is always harping on every one of us to turn our students into sweet little Christian disciples. Well, I barely have time just to cover the stuff I have to teach. An extra Bible teacher will help take some of this discipleship load off our backs!

Lisa: I was afraid you'd say that.

The metaphor again

In a previous chapter I described classroom teaching as "a journey together." I spoke of three key themes emerging from this metaphor: first, there is the guiding/leading/direction-setting function; second, the "pathway we travel," such as a wide or narrow road, detours, and so on; and third, the destination, the place where we want to end up. Now picture yourself in your classroom. Can you see yourself as a guide? I mean, are you consciously aware of the fact that every time you walk into your classroom your students will be encouraged to head in a certain direction? What direction have you chosen, and how do you intend to get your students there? What pathways will you follow? What would you like them to see on the way? And where do you want your students to be by the time they leave you at the end of the term?

I propose that you view yourself as a guide, leading your students through curricular territory and enabling them to be the sort of persons the Lord wants them to be. These three themes translate into the concepts guiding, unfolding, and enabling.

Guiding

As a teacher you guide the teaching/learning process in your classroom. I prefer the term "guiding" to "leading," because "guiding" allows for more self-directedness and responsibility, qualities we need to cultivate in our students. "Leading" reminds me too much of "leading a bull by the nose," a situation which offers the bull little choice and where he's often digging his hooves into the ground in protest. Guiding can be translated as "nudging this way, not that way, this way, not that way." It consists of both a gentle pressing in a certain direction and an enticing invitation to come along.

Guiding, then, can be understood as the direction-setting aspect of teaching. It both points to and urges the students along towards the destination, that is, towards the high goal of equipping for knowledgeable and competent discipleship. In your classroom guiding happens through the following means:

Modeling

Modeling, setting an example, is a vitally important guiding function. When you model a certain lifestyle and behavior, you are in reality saying, "Follow my example, walk in the ways in which I am walking." Research has shown how effective such modeling is.[1] Often it is the single most important formative influence a teacher has on a student.

In the summer sessions I conduct, I frequently invite the participants to write a story about their successes (or failures) as teachers. They may share their stories or keep them confidential if they wish. I have been struck by how often the positive effect of modeling appears as a theme in the success stories. I recall a gripping story by a high school teacher in British Columbia who wrote about a boy who had been abused and was heading for a life of crime. The turning point for the boy came when he told his teacher: "I want to be like you!" The rest is history. Many teachers can recount similar experiences, but are often too modest to talk about them. Modeling is a subtle but powerful way of nudging students in the right direction.

What should be modeled? A Christian lifestyle, of course, especially the fruit of the Spirit, as described by Paul in Galatians 5. Love, joy, peace, patience, kindness, goodness, faithfulness, gentleness, and self-control are all virtues to be exercised in the classroom. At the same time you and I recognize that we are humans—imperfect and struggling with sin in our own lives. This reality, too, we ought to model. Our students must understand that we, too, are weak and frail. They need to see how we cope with feelings of failure and inadequacy. Consequently, we should not hesitate to create classroom conditions in which we share our joy and our pain with one another. Sometimes we teachers want to appear as even-keeled, self-controlled experts. But such attempts introduce a phoniness that most students easily see through. They create an unwholesome distance between teacher and students. They interfere with authentic Christian teaching.

Modeling is the type of guiding that plays an especially crucial role for Christian teachers in the public school. Sometimes modeling is the only expression of teaching Christianly legally permitted in the public school classroom.

Motivation

In my seminars for student teachers, I ask what problems they encountered in their teaching. Invariably the "unmotivated student" ranks high on the list of items to be considered. We then spend time reviewing the factors that prevent students from being motivated and the strategies we can use to motivate them. Again, these are matters for educational psychology, but as in the case of discipline, it may be helpful to look at motivation as a guiding function. Motivation is necessary in order to guide the student into the right direction. It is difficult to guide someone who doesn't want to go where you want him to go. So the study of what motivates students is important.

You can see why we would call motivation a form of guiding. When I motivate a student, I am setting that student on a path where I can continue to guide him. Motivation, then, refers to the initial steps on the right path.

Particularly important are some of the approaches taught in teacher education courses. Terms like "anticipatory set" and "focusing event" should be regularly reviewed. How I start the day or the lesson may have everything to do with how the day proceeds. The beginning of the very first lesson can sometimes determine the extent to which you will be able to guide your students for the rest of the term.

Discipline

This is not the place to engage in a lengthy discussion about the kind of discipline Christian teachers should exercise in the classroom. Educational psychology courses usually survey and evaluate the various options available. Suffice it to remind you that as much as possible discipline should prevent misbehavior rather than correct it, and restore your students rather than punish them.

It may be useful to see the exercise of discipline as a guiding function. Discipline should always nudge: I want you to go this way, not that way. Disciplinary measures will be faulty if they fail to redirect the child towards the ultimate destination of discipleship. Be sure to consider carefully and prayerfully your management decisions on the basis of a fair evaluation of the situation and with great sensitivity to the needs of the child involved.

Don't overlook the connection between exercising discipline and modeling. The way in which you discipline speaks volumes. Angry words, sarcasm, unjust punishment, and attempts to "get back at" the student or to "get even" are counterproductive. They teach the child that, for example, losing one's cool is okay. The issue of modeling plays a major role in the debate about whether or not teachers should be permitted to administer corporal punishment. Students may be tempted to imitate such action and come to believe that violence is acceptable in conflict situations.

Devotions

Too often classroom devotions are merely tacked on to the day's work. They tend to become routine and meaningless. I hear both teachers and students murmur about the effectiveness—or lack thereof—of the opening devotions at the start of the school day. What can we do? If devotions are as important as most of us believe they are, we should pay more attention to doing them right. It is a good plan for a team of creative teachers to come together in the summer to hammer out some fresh devotional strategies.

To start with, I suggest that devotions can best be considered a guiding activity. It is nudging activity. It should be designed to set the tone, indeed, the direction for the entire day. And by the end of the day, when there is opportunity for concluding devotions, it will be helpful to reflect on the key question inherent in all of guiding: Did we head in the right direction today? Even if it looks as if we detoured, can we still see that we are on the right track?

In order to function as effective guidance, devotions should not be abstract or detached. They should concretely relate both to the lives of the children and the work to be done. Linkage to curriculum should also be an important criterion to consider in planning devotional activity. There should be a smooth, uninterrupted transition from devotional activity to the regular learning activities. I know of one fourth-grade teacher who introduced a unit on the senses with a devotional activity that required the students to assume that the Lord is deaf: How can we

The Craft of Christian Teaching

show that we love him when he can't hear us? The students suggested they kneel, raise their hands, and make beckoning gestures. One child proposed that the class shout "real loud," in the hope of penetrating God's ear drums. Linking devotions to curriculum does not always have to be this complicated or dramatic. In a unit on neighbors, for example, the teacher could simply use the Good Samaritan story.

Encouragement

The Apostle Paul frequently admonished the early Christians to encourage one another. We all need encouragement. If we do not receive words of affirmation, we soon begin to question the value of our work, if not our lives. Teachers, too, must pay special attention to this need in children. Ask yourself, "Am I encouraging my students?"

Encouragement is clearly a guiding function because it is a form of nudging. It acknowledges that children are on the right road. When I encourage a student, I am in essence saying: "You are on the right track! Keep moving in the same direction!" Such encouragement can be given in two types of situations: for tasks accomplished ("Thoughtful answer, Hanna!"), and for tasks to be carried out ("Come on, Steve, you can do it!").

For encouragement to be effective it needs to be genuine and deserved. It is easy for a teacher to use expressions like "good job!" or "right on!" ad nauseam, to the extent that they lose all their meaning and, in fact, make it more difficult for the children to experience true encouragement. Be sure to encourage your students as specifically as possible, so that they know what exactly you are promoting. For example, instead of saying "Good listening, José," you guide more effectively with "José, when you looked at Kyra while she was talking, you showed that you cared about what she was saying."

Facilitating/structuring

These terms refer to the ways in which we organize and present our lessons. I will address this topic when we turn our attention to specific teaching strategies, that is, to specific ways of structuring the classroom for learning, but for now we need to recognize structuring as an important guiding function.[2]

When you structure the classroom for learning, you are setting the stage for your students to head in a certain direction and nudging them along. Ask yourself: Do my teaching strategies—no matter what the grade level or subject matter—move my class along towards the overarching goal and the various goal areas discussed in chapter 5? Or are they short-sighted, aimed only at immediate learning outcomes, and detached from concerns about the meaning of teaching Christianly?

An awareness of your role as a guide is indispensable to teaching Christianly. Take time—or make time—to cultivate this awareness. Surround yourself with reminders. Use pictures of a woodsman guiding the pioneers, or arrows pointing in different directions, or simply write the word "GUIDE" across your desk.

Unfolding

We can define this term as follows: "To open up to the children what as yet they do not know or cannot do." To use the metaphor of the journey again, unfolding refers to the terrain to be traversed, to be understood, and to be navigated. All of this requires knowledge and skills. It requires a curriculum.

Unfolding the curriculum is a bit like unfolding a map. Initially we see only a small section of the map. But as we unfold the map further, we see more and more, until we can finally see the lay of the land—the big picture. So it is with curricular content. In the early grades children learn to see some basic elements of mathematics, language, and social studies. As they proceed through the grade levels, they see more and more. Teachers continually open up the map to wider and more comprehensive vistas, all the while encouraging the students to perceive more detail and understand increasing complexity.

A key component of unfolding is disclosing. The teacher reveals the ways in which the students are to travel through the terrain. As we shall see, there is a tendency for disclosing to be linked to direct instruction— the teacher doing all of the work. For that reason it is important to sense that teaching Christianly describes the type of teaching in which both teacher and students communally engage in unfolding activities, that is, both teacher and students open up the curricular content. I shall explore this process in subsequent chapters. Unfolding, then, includes disclosing but goes beyond disclosure.

What is to be unfolded? Asking this question lands us smack in the middle of an unending curricular debate: What knowledge is worth teaching? What skills are worth learning? We can only answer this question satisfactorily if we first ask still another question: What do our children need to know and what must they be able to do if they are to function as knowledgeable and competent disciples of the Lord in our complex world? Or, to relate this question to a previous chapter: What curricular content will best serve to meet the overarching goal and the various goal areas of Christian teaching?

No doubt our students must learn to understand and to evaluate the world and human life in it. The great biblical themes of creation, fall, and redemption surely must play the governing role. Our students must sense God's design and intentions for this world. They must also see how sin has distorted God's good creation and obscured the Kingdom of the Lord. Following up on such insight, our children are to be taught the ways to be redemptively busy, exercising their discipleship in servanthood, stewardship, and peacemaking.

Putting it this way once again shows the inadequacy of a still too common preoccupation with factual content. The learning of facts without the larger context of creation, fall, and redemption renders much teaching hollow and meaningless. Teaching facts without perspective is largely a waste of time.

Perspective again

When we speak of unfolding, then, we speak of a Christian perspective on subject matter. Many Christian schools stress such perspective and regard it as the distinctive feature of their program. We do need to be concerned, however, about "perspectivalism," the view that imparting a Christian perspective makes our teaching fully Christian. True, it is hard to see how we can teach Christianly without providing a Christian perspective. This partnership is precisely what makes teaching in a public school so problematic. Genuine unfolding, in terms of creation, fall, and redemption, is prohibited by law in the public school, and thus limits the ways of teaching Christianly to modeling and other forms of guiding.

Nevertheless, I do believe that teaching for perspective, though indispensable, is not sufficient. It is quite possible for students to be able to articulate a right perspective and yet live disobedient lives. Unfolding must go beyond perspective to include a willingness to serve the Lord. For that reason, teachers in Christian schools must do everything possible to provide opportunities for the students to put the perspective into practice. We are dealing with the lingering bugaboo of intellectualism once again. Knowing without doing is not really knowing. All knowledge, to be true knowledge, must lead to committed action. So be sure to include in your unfolding activity plenty of opportunity for designing "redemptive action steps." Once your students recognize something is wrong, challenge them: what do they intend to do about it?

Interestingly, meaningful unfolding activity leads to the "unfolding" of the children themselves. It encourages the children to blossom as true disciples, equipped to do the Lord's work. At this point unfolding begins to merge with enabling, a dimension of teaching Christianly to which we will return momentarily.

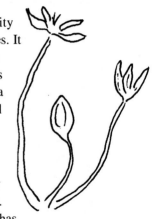

Relevance

Unfolding curricular content should obviously be aimed at appropriate development levels. Currently the term "developmentally appropriate" has come in vogue. I appreciate this term. For too long a subject-centered type of perennialistic education has neglected to ask questions about the children on whom all this content is foisted. In my classroom observations I still see teachers missing their children because the stuff they are teaching does not match where the children are developmentally.

I suggest we add to "developmentally appropriate" the notion of "experientially appropriate." Occasionally I spend time interviewing high school students. I remember one young man who had just come out of a chemistry class. Clearly he was not bubbling with enthusiasm about what he was learning there. I asked him: "Tell me, why are you learning this stuff?" He sighed and said: "Honestly, I have no idea. And I bet the teacher doesn't know either!" Few teachers have not heard a child ask: "Why do we have to learn this?" How do you answer this question?

Below are some common responses. Check the ones you have used:

___ You will need it for college!

___ This stuff is important.

___ Some day you will understand . . .

___ Every educated person should know this!

___ Because it will be on the test!

___ Because I say so!

___ Don't ask dumb questions!

I believe that we teachers too easily dismiss inquiries about relevance. I encourage you to take the question "Why do I have to learn this?" very, very seriously. If you cannot answer the question, or you've used one of the answers above, you need to review your unfolding practices. Your unfolding of content and skills should be "experientially appropriate." That is, unfolding should be characterized by connectedness; the stuff that we teach should be connected to the children's prior experience, to their present situation, and to their future lives. If you cannot make such connections, raise doubts about the necessity of your lesson content.

Some subject areas are more difficult to "connect" than others. Literature seems easy, because it deals with issues commonly experienced by everyone. But what about math? Yet, math too can be made much more experiential than is often the case. Mathematical operations should be related to the children's concrete experience, to what they already know, to what they can already do, and specifically to how what they are learning can make a difference in their lives. Manipulatives and real-life examples are obviously indispensable to establish connectedness. Nor should the larger picture be neglected: mathematics should be taught as human activity engaged in for good or for evil. Mathematics is used to make both medicines and bombs. Connectedness will sharply reduce the number of cases of "math anxiety."

Enabling

Finally, a look at the third component of the trio guiding/unfolding/enabling. What is enabling?[3] In essence it means "equipping the children for works of service." It refers to the ultimate outcome of teaching Christianly.

Enabling can best be seen as a characteristic of guiding and unfolding. Our guiding and unfolding are to be enabling, not disabling, in nature. Enabling is therefore not a separate function, something we do in addition to guiding and unfolding. Enabling must hover as a continuous presence over all of our guiding and unfolding activities. The question to be continuously asked is this: Will my guiding and unfolding *enable* or *disable* my students for discipleship?

You can see why the concept of enabling is to be explicitly noted as a key component of teaching Christianly. Frequently our teaching gets enmeshed in purposes other than equipping for discipleship. Often our teaching enables, but not for Christian servanthood. Think of the many ways we teach the serving of self, or of money, or of success, and the like. Such teaching occurs under the guise of Christian virtue through the use of honor rolls, unhealthy and often unmatched competition, mass teaching, standardized evaluation and grading practices, and individualistic classrooms.

We are dealing here with a major problem in our Christian schools: the contradictory character of so much of our teaching. On the one hand we preach love and gentleness, yet promote a "may the best man win" mentality. We say that we are to esteem others higher than ourselves, yet foster competition that easily leads to self-glorification. We confess that each one of our students is a unique image bearer of God, yet we continue to structure our schools and classrooms for stifling conformity. While we use enabling talk, we continue with disabling practices. I recognize that these words may be interpreted as harsh criticism. My concern is this: do we really mean it when we say we want to "do all things to the glory of God"?

To stress the enabling function of teaching Christianly is no luxury or idle, religious talk. It is at the enabling level where we reach the heart of what it means to teach Christianly. Once we neglect this component, or give it only lip service, we leave ourselves open to all sorts of philosophies that contradict and curtail and derail the overarching goal of teaching Christianly.

Enabling must be a concern of every teacher in every classroom. Sometimes I hear teachers say: "I teach math—I have no time for enabling: I have to cover the textbook. Besides, we have Bible teachers and counselors who take primary responsibility for the religious purposes of the school." But such talk ought not to be heard in a Christian school. It is the responsibility of every single teacher, no matter what the subject matter or the grade level, to guide and unfold in an enabling way.

Enabling must also be a concern of every day, not something to be relegated to long-term programs. Your students are to be disciples today, not just on some date in the far future in "the real world." The classroom today *is* the real world. Today is the day for servanthood. Remember, too, that the student in your class today may not be there tomorrow. If an accident should suddenly snuff out the life of one of your students, will you be able to say: I have done my best trying to enable that child for each day of his short life?

Finally, we need to recognize that ultimately we cannot fully enable anyone. Enabling is ultimately the work of the Holy Spirit and the Word of God. Sometimes teachers think that for that reason we need not concern ourselves with enabling. After all, you can lead a horse to water but you cannot make it drink. But is this true? I would think we can make the horse thirsty by making it run around and around the water hole! So it is in our classrooms. We can do much to encourage an enabling climate. We must create classroom conditions inviting to the Holy Spirit. We do this in part by normative responses to the various dimensions of teaching, as described in the previous chapter. A classroom in which there is fear, tension, anger, suspicion, or unfairness cannot be an enabling place. No guiding and unfolding of the enabling kind can go on there. It is a place where the Holy Spirit is not welcome.

Enabling, then, requires that you expressly invite the Spirit of God to be present in your classroom. Consider a banner outside of your classroom door saying: "Holy Spirit, you are welcome in this classroom. Please enter and do your enabling work. We hope that you will find the conditions in our classroom to your liking." Such a banner will help you rethink your classroom decisions and your teaching practices. It will set you on the road to teaching Christianly.

CHAPTER 9

Where in the world are you teaching?

The context of teaching Christianly

Jim: I know that our classrooms should not be quarantined, but this is ridiculous! Just this afternoon alone, since the noon hour, my class was interrupted—I counted!—seven times! Four times an intercom message—none for me or for my class. Twice some people walked in without an invitation and started to wander about, and then the fire drill. Do you know how much time I lost, Lisa?

Lisa: That just goes to show you, Jim, that your classroom isn't a hermetically sealed sterilized cubicle floating about in outer space. But I agree, there are altogether too many unnecessary interruptions. What bugs me is that these interruptions have an uncanny habit of popping in at a teachable moment or just at the point when Keith is finally paying attention!

Jim: So what can we do to maintain some semblance of classroom privacy—so we can teach—and protect ourselves from all that interfering stuff that bumbles its way into our classrooms?

Lisa: Well, for starters we might raise the issue at the next staff meeting.

A web

Guiding, unfolding, and enabling do not occur in a vacuum, as if suspended in space. On the contrary, teaching Christianly proceeds within a complicated, intertwined context. Classroom activity is not a separate, self-contained, detached entity, but an intertwined whole hooked into a much larger web. What kind of web? Let's see if we can unravel some of the tangles.

Three worlds

As a teacher you work in three worlds simultaneously. Most immediately, there is the world of your classroom: your neatly organized desk; the students—including kids like Keith who, without trying, demand much of your attention and energy; your lesson plans—carefully crafted, of course; the bulletin boards; the overhead projector; the bookcase in the corner; and the like. I shall single out this "world" for closer examination in a moment.

Your classroom exists in a larger world, the world called the school. I think of the building itself: its hallways, the playground, the principal's office, the staff room, and so on. This world directly affects what you do in your classroom. Consider, for example, the institutional goals of the school in which you work. Its mission will set the tone and direction for much of what you do in your classroom. Or think of the schedules and the bells, or of the numerous interruptions like the ones Jim complained about.

The world of the school, encompassing the world of the classroom, is itself very much impacted by the largest world of all, the ambient world enfolding the school. This world constitutes the ultimate environment, the broadest context in which you do your classroom teaching. This larger world includes the parents and their expectations, government regulations, TV, videos, and pop culture, as well as the

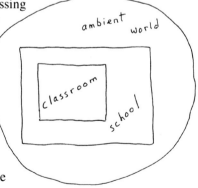

social backgrounds that affect your students, their behavior, and their ability to learn. Not to be overlooked, meanwhile, are the many philosophical spirits that lurk in our society, ready to infiltrate and silently overpower your classroom. These spirits are especially seductive and effective when the enabling aspect of your teaching is neglected. In a later chapter we shall spend some time unmasking the most pernicious of these evil spirits.

Working in three intertwined worlds at once obviously complicates your task: since you cannot cleanly divorce your classroom practice from what is happening in your school and in society at large, your reflections cannot be restricted to just your classroom work. You also need to think about the interplay between your teaching, the school you work for, and the bigger world beyond playground and parking areas. Your Christian antennae must be attuned to a broad range of issues affecting your efforts to teach Christianly.

I realize that I am suggesting an overwhelming task. I hear you ask, with a measure of controlled annoyance, "Where in the world am I going to find the time and energy to examine and analyze what is happening and what should happen not only in my classroom, but in the rest of creation as well?" The temptation, of course, is to ignore the bigger picture and to stay behind your desk. How do you prevent caving in to such a temptation? The answer is, you need to hold hands with your colleagues, the principal, the board, and the parents. Blessed with a profuse abundance of gifts and insights, the entire school society must earnestly, vigorously, and prayerfully pursue the will of the Lord for education. To do so, we must encourage one another daily, as the Scriptures repeatedly tell us.[1]

Classroom components

The intertwinement of the three worlds does not mean, of course, that a concentrated, focused investigation of the classroom as classroom is ruled out. Just as we can examine the jet engines of a Boeing 747 in isolation from its wings and fuselage, so we can look inside the classroom and ask what's going on there.

My specific concern at this point, then, is not the school as an institution or the problems in the world at large. Rather, I want to focus your attention on the classroom itself, the place where you are to teach Christianly.

Even a cursory look at a classroom and its inhabitants reveals a number of distinguishable components. We may designate them as the who, the whom, the what, the why, the where, and the how of teaching. Some of these elements I have already discussed in previous chapters. Especially the why we have considered in detail. So I limit myself to a quick survey.

The who of teaching

When I visit a classroom, one of the first entities to strike my attention is the teacher as a person. There can be no meaningful, sustained classroom teaching without a real live teacher. Already we have investigated the importance of seeing the teacher as an officebearer, endowed with talents, personality, authority, and responsibility. Who I am as a teacher, and the extent to which I possess a measure of office consciousness, will have much to do with my ability to teach Christianly.

To get at the *who* of teaching, I must ask myself some tough questions: Do I, a Christian teacher, reflect the sort of godliness depicted in the Scriptures? Am I a prayerful, loving person, gentle and patient, displaying all the other fruits of the Holy Spirit? Am I passionately devoted to Christ, eager to do his will and to promote his Kingdom? Do I exhibit the skills of leadership, management, and the various competencies required for good teaching, such as knowledge of subject matter and ability to prepare and implement effective lessons? Continual self-evaluation on all these points is indispensable if I truly want to teach Christianly.

The whom of teaching

The second thing I note when I enter a classroom is the students. Often there are too many of them for the space available! Nevertheless, they form an indispensable component of the classroom: if there were no students in your classroom, what would you do?

Recall the metaphors of the classroom we considered. How I see the students will have everything to do with how I teach. So more hard questions come at me with inescapable persistence: Do I really see the kids—even rascally kids like Keith—as image bearers? Do I see Jesus in them? Do I view them as my fellow travelers, joyfully wandering through the curricular terrain on the way to knowledgeable and competent discipleship?

To enhance our understanding of the kids we teach, knowledge of educational psychology is indispensable. Educational psychology is a field of investigation keenly interested in the nature of the students, how they develop and grow, and, especially important, how they learn. While this is an area of much debate and conflicting research, there can be no doubt that Christian teachers should remain updated on the latest theories about learning styles. I suggest we keep posted on, at the very least, the following research areas:

- *Child development:* What can we expect from children at various stages of growth? Our interest should not be confined to intellectual development; physical, emotional, social, moral, and faith development are all important aspects to be considered as well.

- *The more traditional learning style theories:* Good work has been done in identifying differing learning styles and their characteristics. Though far from perfect, the conclusions suggested by experts like Bernice McCarthy and Anthony Gregorc are worth listening to.[2] Harro Van Brummelen has adapted McCarthy's work in his own four-stage lesson plan procedures.[3] In addition, research on environmental factors, such as conducted by Rita and Kenneth Dunn, is helpful for realizing that the learning environment is much more important than previously believed.[4] Factors such as light, warmth, and sound, for example, can make a big difference in the learning of our students. A change in lighting can significantly affect a child's ability to read.

- *The multiple intelligences theory of Howard Gardner:* Gardner has proposed that students are smart in at least eight different ways.[5] I suspect that there are many more. In any case, his approach offers a more diverse set of categories than the quadrant models of McCarthy and Gregorc. The literature on this theory is rapidly expanding. While we can't read everything, we should be familiar with at least the basics of this material.

I do not mean to advocate an eclectic approach, a mere dabbling in various, often diverse or even contradictory, theories. Clearly what we need is a coherent Christian understanding of how learning takes place. But in the absence of such an overarching, generally accepted framework, the best we can do is to examine what research offers and make every effort to reinterpret its results within an explicitly articulated Christian framework. On this point much work awaits the Christian educational community.

The what of teaching

This component brings us back to curricular issues. A teacher always teaches someone something. But what that "something" is, or should be, remains a subject for debate. How we answer the question depends on our philosophy of education, on our priorities and value systems, on our understanding of content and skills and of knowledge itself, and on what we consider to be the goals of education. Whatever the content you must teach, try to unfold it in the way suggested in an earlier chapter: show how it reflects God's norms, how humans have perverted it, and what redemptive action steps are necessary to make things right again. And don't forget about "connectedness"! Remember, if you can't answer the question "Why do we have to learn this stuff?" it's time for some disciplined reflection, and probably some thoroughgoing revisions as well!

The where of teaching

The where and the how of teaching will occupy our interest in the remainder of this book. Both of these topics concretely address the environment in which you work and the strategies you use to teach Christianly. We begin our explorations with the "where" of teaching.

What sort of classroom environment and atmosphere allow you to teach Christianly? In order to respond meaningfully to this question, you need to consider at least four ways in which you can organize your classroom.[6]

The individualistic classroom

This is the common classroom we find in North America, a continent dedicated to individualism. In such a classroom each student is responsible directly to the teacher and not to anyone else. The students are concerned only about their own learning, not about the learning of others in the class. In short, in an individualistic classroom the learning of one student does not affect the learning of anyone else. Mareesha's problems, for example, make no difference to any of the other students. Did Mareesha fail? Well, that's too bad. But she is sort of dumb anyway, right? So her failure is to be expected, and should not trouble any one of the other students in the classroom. Similarly, should Steve succeed after numerous tries, well, ho-hum, what difference does that make to any of the other students in the classroom? None whatsoever. Every student is on his or her own.

Note that in such an individualistic classroom, community can only be a platitudinous buzzword. There is no place for mutual and communal caring. The individualistic classroom is a place where there is no room for discipleship skills such as helping, caring, encouraging, and mutual weeping, mutual coping, and mutual rejoicing. Such skills are simply irrelevant. They have nothing to do with the classroom teaching/learning situation.

The competitive classroom

In this second type of classroom the learning of one student does affect the learning of the others, but in a negative way. That is, Steve's success now depends on Mareesha's failure. The more Mareesha fails, the more success Steve will experience. Grading on the curve is a good example of this type of competition. Such grading determines in advance that some will succeed only if others fail.

Watch out! This sort of competition can emerge in subtle forms. Picture a teacher who regularly engages in classroom questioning—a technique we shall consider in a later chapter. When the teacher asks a question, all the students (especially in the early elementary grades) vigorously vie with one another for recognition and approval. Both Mareesha and Steve, for example, raise their hands, eager to respond with the correct answer to the teacher's question. But Steve inwardly hopes that Mareesha's answer will be wrong; an incorrect answer will allow him to give the *correct* response, and thereby give him a better chance to shine. Group work in such a competitive classroom is destined to fail: individual students, especially those with ambitious or aggressive tendencies, are not willing to risk the chance of having their work identified with classmates who supposedly achieve less than they do.

The competitive classroom builds on the individualistic classroom. In fact, the competitive classroom is impossible without the foundation of an individualistic classroom. For this reason you need to constantly monitor the extent to which you inadvertently foster individualism in your classroom. There is only a small step between an individualistic and a competitive classroom. A competitive classroom makes it doubly difficult for you to teach Christianly.

"Simply group work"

When I come into a school for purposes of classroom observation, I routinely ask the principal if there are teachers who use authentic cooperative learning. Invariably the principal will respond by pointing to a number of the staff who presumably use this approach regularly and effectively. Upon entering their classrooms, what do I see? Well, yes, I see students in groups sitting around tables, diligently cooperating on their assignments. But are they really? A closer look frequently reveals that in each group there is one student who does all the work while the others simply "hitchhike" or "ride coattails." Or I see individual students, seated in close proximity, doing their work independently, scarcely interacting with their classmates at all. This situation I call "simply group work." The assignments are structured in such a way that, appearances notwithstanding, no real cooperation is required.

Simply group work occurs most frequently as a change of pace in a normally individualistic or competitive classroom. It is a deceptive strategy, for it makes it appear as if, at times, there is real community in the classroom. In fact, simply group work hides individualism or competition under a cloak of collaboration.

The collaborative classroom

The fourth way is the right way. I believe that the collaborative classroom is the required context for teaching Christianly. In other words, it is the type of structure we Christian teachers should aim to establish and maintain. The theme of community is strong, even dominant, in the Scriptures. In both the Old and New Testaments, God's people are depicted as belonging together, bound together in common mutual service to the Lord and to each other. In the Old Testament the Hebrew nation represented such a community. In the New Testament this community is extended to include the Gentiles as well, leading to a new, larger, universal community called the Body of Christ.

There are many things in the Scripture that puzzle us. Many themes, on the other hand, are as clear as the lenses in a brand-new pair of glasses. One of these unmistakable biblical givens is the calling to be one body, to be a community, to be members of one another, to serve one another, and to be co-laborers with Christ.[7] Unhappily, the Body of Christ is often reserved for ecclesiastical structures. Often it is thought that community and fellowship belong only in the institutional church. Community presumably becomes visible when Christian churchgoers gather together in the sanctuary on Sunday. Then as soon as they walk out of the church, they can enter into their individualistic ways again. This sort of dualism still clings to many Christian believers. I remember a student visiting me in my office not so long ago. He described his home and church life. "My father is a business man," he explained. "On Sundays he's in church, holding hands with his Christian brothers and sisters singing 'Blest be the tie that binds,' and then on Monday he's back at it, going after the almighty buck in his world of cutthroat competition."

The New Testament word for "church" (*ekklesia*) literally means "those who are called out." The e*kklesia* of the first centuries referred not to a group of people getting together to sing the sacred songs of Sunday, but to a society within the larger, pagan, Greco-Roman society. The church refers in the first place to the people of God, communally working and serving in *all* areas of life: in the instituted Christian church, in the Christian home, in Christian education, as well as in the political and economic arenas. Sadly, individualism has come to control most of the areas outside the Sunday church.[8]

Our classrooms, I am persuaded, must be expressions of the Body of Christ. There is no reason to suppose that the Body of Christ excludes the children in our classrooms.[9] On the contrary, our classrooms are to breathe the presence of the Holy Spirit who calls us all, young and old, to be his people, united in love and purpose, whether in church, home, or school. Our classrooms are to be communal, redemptive workshops in reciprocal and mutual enabling.

Characteristics of the collaborative classroom

What characterizes a collaborative classroom? How can you distinguish it from an individualistic or competitive classroom, or from a simply group work situation? The following are some of the chief features:

- The learning of one student is *related* to the learning of all the other students. If Mareesha fails, all the other students feel the pain. If she succeeds, especially after many honest attempts, all share in the joy. In a collaborative classroom, students take pains to be aware of their classmates' successes and struggles. Together they celebrate achievement, together they cope with hurt. They laugh together, they carry the burdens together.[10]
- The students are *responsible* for each other's learning. When Mareesha fails there is not only communal pain, but also a communal effort to help her succeed. If Mareesha fails, in a sense all the other

students fail. So Mareesha isn't left to struggle by herself, with just the help of the teacher.

- There is a palpable sense of "our classroom" in which every student experiences a sense of belonging. Too often the classroom is really the teacher's domain, into which the children are invited to come learn for a while. A collaborative classroom conveys quite a different invitation: Come join us, for we belong together in this classroom. At the high school level, where the curriculum is fragmented and students move about from class to class, such a sense of ownership is difficult to achieve. Much can be done, however, if there is adequate space and time for "homerooms." We need to encourage a change in the structure of the secondary schools. (It's about time! High schools today have changed very little from what they were 100 years ago!). Longer class periods and an integrated curriculum

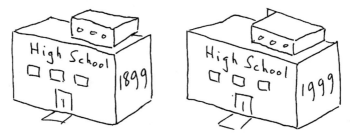

would be helpful to the development of collaborative classrooms in secondary schools. Let's not forget: if students in a class do not develop a sense of belonging, they will break up and bond in mutually hostile cliques and peer groups.

- The collaborative classroom provides a secure, safe, accepting, mutually supportive atmosphere. Individualistic and competitive classrooms usually exude pervasive fears: fear of failure, fear of the teacher, fear of one another.[11] But love casts out fear. In a classroom suffused with fear, the Holy Spirit cannot work. Safety, of course, has become a number one concern of many schools. Violence, guns, drugs, and numerous other forms of criminality have introduced unprecedented fear into classrooms. In many of our schools, however, such physical violence is not the problem. The real problem is students who respect neither classmates nor teachers, or teachers who turn their classrooms into bastions of fear and competition. Such violence, not perceived by metal detectors, may be more worrisome than the risk of guns and knives.

- Gifts, talents, interests, and differences are mutually encouraged and celebrated. Here again, the contrast between a collaborative classroom and individualistic and competitive classrooms is stark. In competitive classrooms differences are regarded as threats, not as reasons for mutual encouragement and class celebration. In the collaborative classroom, on the other hand, cultural diversity, different learning styles, and differences in talents are regarded as gifts, not as problems.
- The collaborative classroom provides a context for developing and practicing discipleship skills. It encourages practicing the sorts of knowledgeable and competent servanthood skills required if the students are to be equipped to function in the world. Specifically, I think of skills such as listening to each other, encouraging each other, helping each other, deeming the classmate higher than oneself, and the like.
- Finally, the collaborative classroom exhibits the Body of Christ. Teacher and students form a community that visibly belongs to the Lord, eager to serve as his disciples. As such the Christian collaborative classroom is a testimony to God's grace. This sort of classroom represents a rock pile along the Jordan, a symbol of the trustworthy leading of the Lord.

Prerequisites

If you have been trained in an individualistic tradition, establishing a collaborative classroom will look like a daunting task. And indeed, doing so requires a fundamental shift in attitude towards the classroom. This shift touches at least the following four areas:

- *Shift in paradigm.* The current paradigm calls for the teacher to teach and the student to learn. The collaborative classroom invites us to see the teacher as learner as well, and the students as teachers. Teaching and learning become a collaborative, rather than a unilateral activity. This, $teacher \rightleftarrows student$ of course, does not mean a return to a warmed-over Deweyan democracy. The teacher remains *the teacher*, a special officebearer endowed with authority and responsibility, as we have seen. The teacher remains the guide. Important to recall at this point is the distinction between "leading" and "guiding." Guiding encourages a good deal more self-direction and personal responsibility than does leading.

- *Change in metaphor.* Closely related to the previous point, changing the metaphor specifically concerns changing our teaching styles in the classroom. In the collaborative classroom we discard metaphors—such as drill sergeant or commander-in-chief—that support unilateral or authoritarian teacher-student relationships, and cultivate instead a vision of teaching as a journey, traveling together through our Father's world.

- *Recognition of the limitations of the teacher.* Traditional views of effective teaching promote the metaphor of the teacher as the all-knowing expert and unerring judge. The children are assumed to be empty-headed. The teacher knows it all. This attitude is so deeply ingrained that teachers sometimes hesitate to admit to the class that they do not know the answer to a student's question. To confess ignorance is often a painful, even embarrassing experience for a teacher. But why should this be so? Think again of modeling: We need to model how we cope with our weaknesses and failures. Doing so requires that we publicly recognize our limitations and shortcomings. Incidentally, some studies suggest that teachers who readily admit they don't know everything create a much healthier classroom atmosphere than do those who pretend to be polyglots and wizards.[12]

- *Renewed desire and commitment to celebrate the worth, gifts, knowledge, and experience of the learners.* The collaborative class-room, I have claimed, is a place in which everyone seeks to identify, work with, and celebrate all the many talents and experiences the students bring along with them. But doing this is not always such a simple task. It takes effort and dedicated perseverance, but the rewards are many. Many first-grade teachers, for example, are frequently astounded at the wisdom of some of these little kids. Teachers who are open to learn from the children are often pleasantly surprised by their insights. Such experiences renew our commitment to take into account the experience of the students as we—both the teacher and the students—work together on the construction of effective teaching/learning situations.

An important distinction

Be sure to distinguish between the collaborative classroom and cooperative learning. The collaborative classroom is the larger context in which cooperative learning can be useful. Cooperative learning—a strategy to be examined in detail in a later chapter—is but one of the many instructional methods you can use in the collaborative classroom. A collaborative classroom does not require continuous cooperative learning strategies. Direct instruction is just as important as cooperative learning or as any other teaching method.

A final word

In this chapter we have surveyed the context of teaching Christianly. We have looked at the three worlds, identified the elements that make up a classroom situation, and explored the idea of a collaborative classroom. Now I move on to consider an inevitable question: How do you go about establishing such a classroom? Let's take a look.

CHAPTER 10

Getting where you want to be: Establishing the collaborative classroom

Randy: I'm afraid I'm going to give up on all this collaborative stuff, Lisa! Yesterday I sent a letter home with the kids explaining my plans to give the students some choice in the amount of homework they should do, and to share more in the way we run the classroom. Well, something broke loose, Lisa, and I'll let you guess what it was!

Lisa: Why, what happened, Randy? I thought you merely suggested that the kids share with you their home obligations, so you could tailor-make the assignments more reasonably. What you were proposing looked innocent enough to me. And besides, giving students more voice in the classroom will help teach them responsibility, won't it?

Randy: Well, yes, I thought so. But a parent called me and pretty well ended my teaching career, or so it seemed. "Aren't teachers paid to teach?" she wanted to know. "Aren't you the experts, while the youngsters are inexperienced, innocent, and ignorant? Shouldn't students be drilled in basic skills? This wishy-washy collaborative stuff is the reason why so many kids aren't learning a thing nowadays!" And so on and so forth.

Lisa: Wow! Maybe we'll have to be more diplomatic in our communications?

A concern

Randy's story suggests that the collaborative classroom, like learning to speak the native language in a foreign land, can be scary and uncomfortable, even intimidating, to both teachers and parents. After all, aren't teachers paid to teach, as the parent fumed in the scenario above? Shouldn't children obediently listen to the teacher and do as they are told?

These questions are important and need to be addressed. Parents do have a legitimate worry about whether or not their children are learning, for it looks as if the present school systems—at least in North America—are creaking and cracking. We hear the unending media reports bewailing the failures of public education: many students are not learning (especially in comparison to other countries) and many high school graduates are dismally uninformed and illiterate. The question is, What is the problem? Are collaborative classrooms at fault? This cause seems unlikely, because, honestly now, for the last twenty years or so schools have hardly been shining models of meaningful collaboration.[1]

A view of education that places a premium on stern discipline, a drilling in the basics, and a rigid academic core curriculum requires critical evaluation. Too often this kind of approach fails to recognize the wealth of experience and knowledge our children bring into our classrooms. It assumes that teachers know everything and that students know nothing—or, at least, not much. Such a view prevents our children from learning to take responsibility for their own lives, and shuts down possibilities for genuine collaboration.

Establishing a collaborative classroom

What kind of magic does it take to brew a collaborative classroom into existence? Is it a genuine, achievable possibility, or an idealistic pipe dream, promoted by fanciful educators who have lost touch with the real world?

The answer is simple and straightforward: *Of course* it is possible! How do I know? Because I have seen such classrooms with my own eyes. I have seen them in the United States, in Canada, in Australia, and in Korea. True, none of these classrooms, I suspect, meet all the criteria fully, but then, can perfection be found in our world? The important point is this: Don't allow skeptics to dissuade you from pursuing the ideal.

Some basic principles

Obviously, the ability to establish a collaborative classroom depends much on what kind of person you are and what kinds of relationships you can build. If by nature you are an insecure teacher and you think that the kids are sneaky and out to get you, or if you are very self-centered and desire to project an image of power or expertise in your classroom, the collaborative classroom quickly dissolves as an option. If you are unwilling to listen to your students, or assume that they are not really worth listening to, close this book right now and turn to a Louis L'Amour novel instead. Review the prerequisites articulated at the end of the previous chapter. Are you really willing to change the classroom paradigm?

Assuming that you are the kind of teacher who really does have the welfare of students uppermost in mind, and assuming that you really do want to see Jesus in all of them, what sorts of things can you do to get the collaborative classroom under way? I begin with a consideration of "the first-step approach."

First step

What is the "first-step approach"? I use this term as shorthand for "inviting the students to participate in establishing and maintaining a collaborative classroom." Perhaps the easiest way to understand the term is to contrast it with the more commonly practiced "plummet-right-in approach." When "plummeting in," a teacher typically begins his classwork at the beginning of the term by announcing: "Okay, kids, here is the stuff I am going to teach you, and this is what you will have to learn this term— whether you like it or not! Here is the grading scale that I will use. And as far as the rules are concerned, they're posted on the wall. Do you see them? Obey them and we will get along. Break them and you will be in

RULES / RULES
1. Be quiet!
2. Do as I say!
3. Don't ask!
4. Name on board twice and you're OUT!
Note: Principal's office is around the corner!

serious trouble!" Such is the "plummet-right-in" approach. It is a jump, because there is a first step—extending an invitation to participate—which has not been taken. The plummet-right-in approach prevents, at the outset, the establishment of a collaborative classroom, since the students from the very beginning are silenced. From that point on, there is place only for unilateral, teacher-controlled instruction. The students can only function as recipients and responders. There is no room for student initiatives, and little or no opportunity to learn responsibility. The plummet-right-in approach lays the foundation for a classroom geared to foster passivity, boredom, and a learning for grades only.

For most teachers, the "first step" is really nothing new. I see elementary teachers appoint classroom helpers, middle school teachers ask students to help evaluate and improve each other's compositions, and high school teachers invite their students to help write test questions. All these practices reflect a first-step approach.

Some components

Randy is a teacher who has learned—in spite of occasional worries expressed by some parents—to frame a collaborative classroom. To do so, he basically implements a two-pronged plan. First, he decides—every year anew—to commit himself to engage in extensive inventory work at the beginning of the term, to discover just who his students really are. He wants to learn as much as he can about them. He wants to know what makes them tick. The more he knows about his students, the better he is able to design appropriate classroom activities. The second prong of Randy's plan is to give his students, as far as is feasible, a voice in the way the classroom is to be conducted. Let's examine Randy's approach more closely.

Inventory

The first prong of the "first step" is to engage in extensive inventory work at the beginning of the term. Who are your students? What kind of persons are they? What are their gifts? What are their needs? Their interests? Their experiences? Of course, I do not mean to suggest that it is possible to find out all you need to know in the first week or two after school opens. Your students, like the rest of us, are unbelievably complex creatures. Not even a lifetime would be enough to really get to know them. Only the Lord fully knows us. Nevertheless, it makes a difference whether or not you consciously decide on a program of inventory work. If your attitude is simply one of "covering the subject matter" or making sure the specified grade level outcomes are achieved, the goal of a collaborative classroom will fade away into unreality. Committing yourself to knowing your students, no matter how imperfectly, will make the collaborative classroom a possibility.

Since Randy is an elementary school teacher, he has a better shot at successful inventory work than do his colleagues who work in the high school. No doubt, extensive inventory work is a difficult task at the secondary level, where teachers commonly teach five or six different classes per day, and thus must work with more than 100 students. Nevertheless, there may be solutions to the problem of conducting a meaningful high school inventory. For example, students could be assigned to homeroom teachers who become responsible for a group of students during their entire four-year career. Adopting a block system with longer and fewer class periods per day offers another alternative.

What should be inventoried, and how might you go about it? I suggest you explore the following broad, rough (somewhat overlapping) categories:

- *Life's experiences before entering the classroom:* We no longer live in times of the one-room schoolhouse, when the teacher knew all the families in the community. Teachers now must make a special effort to become sensitive to the background of each student. Some suggestions: home visits, parent questionnaires (to help assess values and priorities in the home, as well as parental goals and expectations), student questionnaires, journals, conferences and conversations, and the like. Schools might be encouraged both to require teachers to do this sort of inventory work *and* provide opportunities for it (for example, by arranging family picnics or summer activities well in advance of class time). A word of caution here: When you use surveys and questionnaires, be mindful of right-to-privacy laws. Always make the completing of a survey a voluntary activity. Always acquaint the parents with your intent.

Avoid every appearance of prying or seeking to enter a person's privacy.

- *Personality/character:* Try to become closely acquainted with each one of your students as a person. What interests does she have? What priorities does he set? In short, what kind of persons are they? How do you as a teacher react to each one of your students? To whom are you attracted? By whom are you repelled? Why? Here you will need some keen observation skills, as well as the ability to draw out the students and engage in critical self-reflection.

- *Gifts and needs:* To identify gifts and needs requires the previous two steps as prerequisites. Only when you see a student as a whole developing person will it make sense to talk about gifts and needs. In a later chapter, when we explore ways of celebrating gifts and meeting the needs of all our students, we shall examine this point in greater detail. For now, I suggest that you include in your inventory work the following questions:

  - What is the relationship between the student and the Lord? Are there faith needs?

  - How does the student relate to her parents, siblings, and peers? What social problems does he carry along into the classroom? What social skills does he possess? Or lack?

  - What physical strengths and weaknesses play a role? Is there impairment of sight, hearing, or speech?

  - What self-concept does the student have? What fears and hopes govern the student's life? What gifts or needs of self-confidence do you see?

  - What kind of a learner is the student? What environmental factors affect the student's learning? What areas of strength and weakness in learning does the student display?

  - What "academic" gifts or needs does the student exhibit? What are his or her reading, writing, thinking, computing, and communication skills?

How do you determine such gifts and needs? Perhaps you could devote at least two weeks at the beginning of each term to engaging the students in a variety of activities designed to determine just where they are in each one of these categories. These activities could include having the students write essays, respond to certain types of literature, construct artwork and other hands-on products, play games, simulate situations, demonstrate skills, evaluate music, and the like. You might be able to work these activities into, or, at least, attune them to the standard curriculum. In addition, aim to interact as much as you can with students on playgrounds, at picnics, on field trips, and during other out-of-class situations in order to observe and interpret important clues.

Be careful with the cumulative files. While they can provide you with essential information, they may also prejudice you. Some students are labeled—or mislabeled—as learning disabled or stuck with behavioral problems or doomed to failure from kindergarten on. Escaping from such labels frequently turns out to be an impossible task.

Involving the students in classroom procedures

The first prong of Randy's two-pronged plan is to do inventory work. But, of course, he will not be satisfied by simply being able to report what his students' hobbies are. He aims for a larger goal, the second prong: to build a community in which students will be taking responsibility for their own and each other's learning. To do this, it will be necessary for him to get the students to know each other as well. Of course, many of them do. Yet, in many classrooms some of the students remain strangers to one another, or relate only in external, superficial ways. To make sure the students get to know one another, Randy plans to use a number of cooperative learning strategies. But since cooperative learning is a specific teaching strategy, I want to postpone describing ways of using it to a later chapter.

Besides having the kids get to know each other, Randy plans to invite them to participate in determining what a collaborative classroom should look like. From the very beginning he wants his students to know what such a classroom is like and what the expectations are to be. But he will present such expectations in a first-step, not a plummet-right-in manner. Randy invites the students to contribute to the description of the classroom. He asks his students to decide, right along with him, what sort of expectations should be set.

Randy usually gets the job done by way of a class discussion or a brainstorming session. What kinds of behaviors will make this a good class? Which should be avoided? What can we expect from each other? What can the students expect from the teacher? What can the teacher expect from the students? What sorts of rules do we need to function as a safe, helpful, encouraging, and fun class?

Sometimes Randy finds that his students don't take his offer seriously. Such students are primed to expect the teacher to make all of the decisions. They are programmed to follow orders. In such cases, Randy exercises patience. Gently but persistently he tries to persuade them that he really does want them to have a voice in what goes on in his classroom. Of course, Randy does have the option of falling back on his authority. He can always say, "Okay, if you don't want to take my invitation seriously, you give me no choice but to make the decision myself." However, before it comes to that point, Randy does everything possible to convince the students of their obligation to participate. In some cases he finds that time will have to pass before the trust relations between himself and the children are sufficiently strong to allow the sort of participation he is looking for.

Randy also invites his students to participate in the determination of the classroom setting, such as seating arrangement and environment. He knows that some elementary teachers complete colorful bulletin boards in their classrooms before the first day of school on the grounds that they wish to make their classroom as inviting and friendly as possible. Randy always leaves substantial space on bulletin boards for student participation. A collaborative classroom, he believes, is a classroom that exudes a sense of "our classroom," not just the teacher's classroom.

Randy is on the right track. He habitually and persistently works at getting his kids involved. He gives them a voice. He provides them with a sense of ownership and of responsibility for their own and each other's learning. He instills a feeling of "we don't want to let each other down" among his students.[2]

Additional suggestions

I already referred to the practice of appointing "teacher's helpers." Here the possibilities are limited only by your imagination. I know of teachers who find a classroom job for every one of their students. Such jobs range from collecting milk money, keeping attendance, erasing the chalkboard, changing the calendar, checking the paper supply, and keeping sections of the room neat to feeding the fish in the aquarium and preparing the VCR equipment.

Other areas for "first-step" participation are the curriculum and evaluation. Giving the students curricular choices, as well as freedom to follow up on interests, are good ways to encourage genuine learning. One first-grade teacher offers the kids a choice between first learning to count money or first learning to tell time. A third-grade student suggests a relevant field trip and the teacher follows up on that suggestion. And in a weather unit, students listen to the weather report each morning on a local radio station. One student says, "I'd like to meet that announcer and ask him how he knows what to say." Together the class plans a brief field trip to the station, brainstorming for questions and selecting the best ones. A middle school teacher I worked with offered the students a choice in the sequencing of topics in life and physical sciences.

Evaluation procedures, too, should involve the students. Ask for student input on constructing rubrics, on designing portfolios, and on what constitutes passing and failure or fair evaluation procedures. Invite them to frame review, test, and evaluation instruments. These activities contribute to a good collaborative classroom.

One English teacher I worked with for a semester in an Iowa high school decided to use the first-step approach. We spent several class periods having the students discuss grading procedures. The time was at the height of the farm crisis, when land values had dropped and many farms were in danger of being foreclosed. A number of the students in the class came from such farms: they had to work day and night to help keep the operation afloat. They had little or no time for out-of-class homework. In view of this situation, the students came to agree that it would be okay for some students to get an A for reading only five books, while others might earn only a B for reading as many as ten. In other words, the students understood that they were different and found themselves in various circumstances, so that blanket grading or class-wide criteria for evaluation were not necessarily appropriate.

First-step approach: its Christian character

The first-step approach is fully compatible with teaching Christianly. The following characteristics should help make this clear:

- It treats students as gifted and responsible image bearers of God. The students are not simply empty-headed dunderheads or mechanical puppets. They are the Lord's special creatures, called to unwrap their gifts and to bring their insights to expression. In addition, by treating the students in this way, the teacher acknowledges that he or she, too, is a fallible human being with limitations.

- The first-step approach takes sin seriously in individual lives. The inventory work brings to light problems and distortions in the lives of the students to be reckoned with as the teachers and the students embark on their journey together. Taking sin seriously in this manner is more meaningful than simply reaffirming the principle of total depravity. Sin is indeed a tragic and powerful reality. There is a huge difference, however, between simply declaring children to be sinful (and, consequently, introducing a harsh penal code into the class-room) and seeking to discover just how the ravages of sin affect them. Merely pontificating about sin prevents us from coming to terms with sin, from meeting it head-on, from engaging in authentic redemptive activity. I am often struck by our willingness to accept the sinful status quo in our world. I hear teachers say, "My students must learn how to be good competitors and good winners or losers because that is what they will encounter in the 'real' world." To me this is like saying, "We better have the kids become familiar with pornography, for, after all, they are likely to encounter it in the 'real' world." As Alfie Kohn once said, "Just because there are carcinogens in the world, is it right to expose our students in our schools to them?"[3]

- The first-step approach provides an opportunity to exemplify the Body of Christ: the students work together on their classroom responsibilities. From such collaboration emerges a sense of "we-ness" that replaces a "me-by-myself-against-the-world" mentality.

- It teaches responsibility: students are given responsibility for such procedures as classroom rules or seating arrangements and for curricular decisions. Of course, as indicated, the teacher has the authority to take over if the children are unable to handle the responsibility.

- It encourages discipleship skills of mutual love, esteem, and care. The students will have to listen to and care for each other as they participate in the determination of classroom procedures. The example above of the Iowa farm kids helps make this clear.

- And finally, the first-step approach gives students ownership of their learning. Such ownership encourages responsibility and increases a desire to unfold gifts and address weaknesses.

The first-step approach: is it realistic?

A nagging question remains: Is all this collaborative activity realistic? I tried to respond to this question earlier in the chapter when I reported that with my own eyes I have observed what I would surely call successful collaborative classrooms. I know that our classrooms are frequently populated with difficult children. Sometimes just one child can wreck our best intentions. Sometimes we have a classroom that virtually drives us to despair. So we must face a reality: Since classrooms are different and since classroom dynamics differ from year to year and from grade to grade, the possibilities of establishing what we really want our classroom to be vary from year to year and from grade to grade. Nevertheless, I continue to offer the following advice: Don't give up, not on any one of your students, and not on any one of your classes.

Remember the difference between "what *ought* to be the case" (a truly collaborative classroom) and "what often *is* the case" (a difficult class). Don't accept the "what is the case" as an inevitable, immutable situation. Continue to try to change the "what is" into "what ought to be." At times you will be pleasantly surprised.

As always, be much in prayer, not only for every one of your students, but also for your class as a whole. Remember and believe the words of Psalm 133: "See how pleasant and good it is when brothers and sisters live together in harmony! There the Lord will command his blessing!"

CHAPTER 11

What is this thing called "teaching strategy"?

A closer look at the how of teaching

Jim: I'm not so sure all this talk about "teaching strategies" is helpful, Lisa! I think that as long as you know what you want the kids to learn, and as long as you have a pretty good perspective on the stuff you're teaching, it doesn't matter all that much *how* you teach.

Lisa: Oh, I think it *does* matter. Won't the kids learn differently if, say, they just take notes from the teacher than if they discuss the content among themselves? Haven't you yourself sat in a class where you realized that once you talked to a fellow student, you suddenly understood quite clearly what the teacher was trying to teach you? And what about the hands-on stuff? Don't science and math teachers always say that kids haven't learned something until they do it?

Jim: Hmm . . . I guess I need to be convinced. Let's see what Van Dyk has to say about all this.

A first look

Back in your college days you learned that a high-grade unit or lesson plan must include a number of key components. Just as a jetliner needs, among other things, two wings, a tail, and several engines to make it fly, so your lesson plans need objectives, content to be taught, teaching and learning activities, and evaluation procedures. Components like these never go out of style, no matter what lesson plan format you end up using. They need your continued professional attention—whether or not your principal asks to see your weekly lesson plans.

But a funny thing happened on the way to the classroom: the teaching strategies somehow slid off the wagon. And they *continue* to receive short shrift. For example, I still see many packaged curricular units in which teaching strategies and learning activities are treated as peripheral, tacked-on "suggestions" or "tips," or even as just a "basket of tricks." Typically, textbook units lay out the content to be taught—usually without a discussion about appropriate teaching methods—then add "suggested activities." Often these suggestions merely spotlight follow-up practice or application or extension and enrichment activities. Like a random hodgepodge of yard-sale merchandise scattered over the lawn, these teaching tips are usually presented as a loose, eclectic collection of activities, divorced from a coherent, consistent framework.

Paradoxically, the learning activities and tips, though haphazardly suggested, do have something in common: They are all *practical!* The common denominator underlying almost all suggestions consists of one, single criterion: *they work.* The suggested activities help students digest the content or learn the skill you are trying to teach.

The need to be practical

At the next teachers' convention you attend, spend some time at the display tables put up by the publishing companies. But instead of looking at the books, observe the customers. Watch how teachers sniff through the mounds of materials invitingly decked out for them. What are the teachers looking for? Well, they look for resources, of course. But what do these resources do? They provide new ideas and new tips that work. They supply practical stuff to help make teaching more effective and interesting. The teachers hunt for useful things they can take with them into their classrooms to brighten up what sometimes threatens to become a dull routine.

Similarly, at staff development workshops, teachers soon tune out if they perceive that the material presented has little or no application to what they are doing in their classrooms. They want to hear "practical suggestions," pointers that will help them teach. They look for useful teaching strategies that work.

How should we judge this attitude? Snicker and sneer and call it "utilitarian recipe hunting"? Should we point a finger and dismiss as crass pragmatism a teacher's desire for practical tips?

Obviously, teaching strategies and learning activities must work. Suppose someone says to you: "Look here, I have this wonderful, exciting, creative teaching method for you—unfortunately, it doesn't work!" How would you respond? Probably somewhat in the same way as a vegetarian responds to a thick slab of greasy pork roast. The point seems clear: What you do in the classroom is intensely practical. Teaching strategies are intensely practical. Your teaching methods and learning activities must work. Conclusion: You are perfectly justified in looking for the practical stuff at teachers' conventions and in staff development sessions. Right?

A problem

The question "Will this strategy work?" is indeed a key question. But it cannot be the only question, and certainly not the *fundamental* question. I can think of at least four reasons for this claim. First, when you choose a certain strategy or learning activity merely on the basis of its workability, you can easily lose sight of the larger demands of the will of God. The truth is, what works is not always right. If, for example, a student in your class gets to be a serious problem, a workable solution might be to lock him up in a dark and dingy closet. Second, what works today may not necessarily work tomorrow. So what is right today may be wrong tomorrow. The principle of workability, therefore, easily snuggles up to relativism.

Third, to judge teaching methods simply on the basis of whether they work begs a larger question: They work for what? What learning outcome do they achieve? Do the practical activities merely meet the limited objectives stated in the textbook or spelled out in the teacher's manual? Or do they really contribute to our overarching task of guiding, unfolding, and enabling? Some teaching strategies—such as certain games, for example—do an excellent job of promoting a self-serving desire to beat out the competition. They really work if you want to teach your students to be aggressive, ambitious, success-seeking individuals. Yet these same strategies may be totally useless for cultivating a sense of Christian servanthood.

Finally, when the only question you ask about a teaching method or learning activity is "Will it work?" you misunderstand, even distort, the very nature of a teaching strategy. To clarify this claim, we must focus our scope and zoom in.

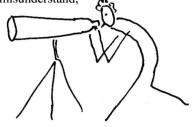

A definition

What is a teaching strategy? A working definition might go as follows: A teaching strategy is a way of intentionally ordering and organizing the classroom and classroom procedures to help students learn. Several key elements in this definition require discussion.

In the first place, a teaching method or teaching strategy is "a way." It is a pathway which you travel through the curricular terrain towards a destination. What destination? "To help students learn," our definition declares. Student learning is the *outcome* of a strategy. Be careful not to gloss over the significance of the term "outcome"! Remember that *outcome* includes not only the various goal areas we examined in an earlier chapter—mastery of content, critical thinking abilities, development of creativity, and so on—but also the ultimate, overarching goal of equipping for knowledgeable and competent discipleship.

But a strategy is more than just a pathway through a curricular terrain. Rather than merely a hit-or-miss let's-see-once-if-it-works bumbling about, a teaching strategy is an *intentional* pathway, a pathway of your own careful design. You construct the pathway through the process of *ordering* and *organizing* the classroom and classroom procedures. What is the difference between "ordering" and "organizing"?

Ordering means to put the pieces, as it were, in an appropriate sequence. Just as you would build a road by first leveling the surface, then scraping it smooth, and finally pouring the concrete, so a teaching strategy begins with philosophical perspectives, considers goals and objectives, and ends with learning outcomes. *Organizing*, on the other hand, means to integrate this ordered sequence with other relevant factors into a coherent whole. To build a road you need to consider not only the roadbed and the cement, but also the equipment needed, the 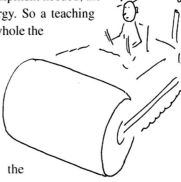 time it will take, and the required energy. So a teaching strategy must organize into a coherent whole the various relevant pieces: the desired classroom environment, the content of the lesson, the number and nature of the students, the resources and equipment needed, and the like. When you take all of these elements into account in your planning, order and organize them, you "structure" the classroom for learning.

As suggested in an earlier chapter, you might regard the process of intentionally ordering and organizing your classroom and classroom procedures as an expression of the *guiding* function of teaching. The metaphor of the "pathway" I used just a moment ago suggests this point. When you construct a "pathway," you thereby acknowledge that you are framing a "road to follow," a direction to pursue. You would not build a road that dead-ends in nowhere. In the very act of structuring the classroom for learning you are guiding—nudging—the students towards the goal of Christian discipleship.

Can we distinguish between teaching strategies and learning activities? I think so. But don't separate them! Teaching should always evoke learning. Classroom teaching and classroom learning go hand in hand. You would not be very far afield if you see teaching activity and learning activity as the two sides of the same pork chop: strictly speaking, you cannot have the one without the other, at least, not on your plate and not in the classroom.

Of course, you can teach in such a way that the students don't learn. Recently I peeked into a classroom where the teacher was showing a video. Roughly 75% of the students—I counted!—were sound asleep. Was there teaching going on? Yes. Learning? No. In the classroom, teaching activities and appropriate learning activities, like air and wind, should be intimately connected.

A picture of a teaching strategy

Are teaching methods "neutral," that is, can they be used by any teacher in the same way? Or do we need to differentiate between Christian and nonchristian teaching methods? Are some teaching methods inherently Christian and others are not?

On more than one occasion I have heard it argued that teaching methods are indeed neutral. Believe it or not, I have been told in no uncertain terms that there is no such thing as a Christian way of teaching. As proof of this assertion it was suggested that both Christian school teachers and public school teachers can use any given method, such as lecturing or cooperative learning, in exactly the same way. The method, presumably, is identical for Christian and nonchristians alike.

But such a view is clearly reductionistic. It looks at a teaching method as merely a technical procedure, implementable regardless of the situation and context. Such an approach is actually quite compatible with the "effective teaching" mentality, a philosophy we have had occasion to criticize before. "Effective teaching" research attempted to identify and describe a number of universal, key "teacher behaviors" guaranteed to produce desired learning outcomes no matter what the situation. Such an approach turns teaching into a set of scientifically proven, universally applicable techniques.

It is a highly technicistic approach. To put it more simply, this approach transforms a repertoire of teaching strategies into a box of recipes.

Actually, as our proposed definition suggests, a teaching method can never be merely a technique or a standard procedure, but is always a part of the larger web of classroom reality. Every teaching strategy is controlled by a religious vision, driven by a philosophical perspective, guided by goals and objectives, brings about learning activities, aims at certain learning outcomes, and is implemented by unbelievably complex entities called teachers. Apart from philosophies, goal priorities, multifaceted classroom situations, and live, infinitely varied people, teaching strategies do not exist.

Teaching methods are somewhat like words. True, you can find words and their definitions described in a dictionary. But they become alive and acquire true significance only in human utterances. In live communication, identical words can take on entirely different meanings. The very same words can be spoken in love or they can be spoken in hatred. The very same words can heal or they can cut. It depends on the speaker, the context, the audience, and the intent. So it is with teaching strategies. While you can, to some extent, objectively describe or define them on paper, in a real classroom they are implemented by living, breathing, feeling, and believing people—each one unique—in different ways in different contexts for different purposes.

How can we describe a teaching strategy in general terms and at the same time maintain its unique distinctness? The key is to remember that teaching is a craft. Every teaching strategy consists of two dimensions: an individual, personal touch, and a universal, standard technique. Those who claim that teaching strategies are essentially neutral see only the universal, technical side, the technical know-how comprising the standard procedures that allow us to describe or define a teaching strategy. They ignore the other, equally important ingredient: the "personal touch" that you bring into your teaching and thereby make the strategy your own personal possession as you seek to meet certain goals. This personal touch refers to individual factors such as your perspective on what you believe to be important in life and education, your unique style, your creativity, the specific setting of your lessons, and the learning outcomes you aim for.

Perhaps a diagram can summarize our discussion thus far:

This diagram maps out the reality that teaching strategies are not objective, neutral methods unaffected by where you come from or where you want to go. It brings out that teaching is not just the technical implementation of a barrel of tricks. On the contrary, the diagram shows that the character of every teaching method or strategy is determined by at least five or six variants.

Let's look at some examples to illustrate the point. Take lecturing, for instance. Is the lecture method simply a neutral teaching strategy, the same for everybody? I do not believe it. For one thing, personal style will play a determining role. And since personal styles differ, lecturing strategies will differ. The truth is, while we certainly can abstractly speak of a general category called "lecturing," there are no two lectures exactly alike.

I come from a church tradition in which the sermon is central in a worship service. Back in the fifties, many immigrant church communities sprang up in Canada. There were not enough preachers to serve them all. So the custom of "sermon reading" became widespread. When no preacher was available, an elder would read a sermon written and published by an ordained clergyman. It was interesting to note how a poor reader could effectively destroy the impact of what could have been an excellent sermon! So it is with lectures.

Lecturing is lecturing is lecturing? Look at it in still another way: Lecturing in an individualistic classroom will function differently than in a collaborative classroom. In an individualistic classroom, lecturing will reinforce the individualism: no student-to-student contact, private notetaking, and "every man for himself." In a collaborative classroom, on the other hand, lecturing will serve as a preparation for further collaboration. In this context the technique of lecturing will slip into an entirely different garb. In all likelihood it will become interactive, with frequent opportunity for student response, or it will include pauses for student reflection or writing.

Or take cooperative learning as a second illustration. Is it a neutral, value-free technique? Of course not. In an individualistic classroom cooperative learning will be used to teach the students the skill of cooperation, a skill they will need as *individuals* when they get out in the big bad world. This approach differs radically from cooperative learning intended to promote a collaborative classroom and to teach discipleship and servanthood skills. What may outwardly appear to be the same strategy actually functions in fundamentally differing ways.

General comments

Teaching strategies come in a wide variety of colors and shapes. Before I move on to consider some ways of categorizing this variety, I remind you of a number of general truths.

- *Teaching strategies should have a pivotal place in every one of your lesson or unit plans.* You should think them through carefully, well before you get into your classroom. You need to plan them thoughtfully, all the while asking yourself: What will best help the students learn? What problems does the strategy create? What unexpected decisions might it call for? You need to pose these questions if you are to engage in productive reflection about your teaching. Such reflection, of course, may never be neglected. Only if we tirelessly analyze and evaluate our work in our classrooms can we grow as *Christian* teachers.

- *There is no single "best strategy."* The educational world is replete with persuasive voices claiming that their classroom approach is the panacea teachers have been seeking for centuries. As soon as you hear someone suggest that a perfect solution is available, assume a most skeptical attitude. The "single best strategy" is always reductionistic: teaching cannot be reduced to a single best strategy. For this reason, claims about phonics, whole language, cooperative learning, and the like must be met with a very critical attitude. I have found that conferences on these topics often assume a religious, even totalitarian character: the educational approach endorsed in such conferences becomes a tyrant—use it or else be excluded from those who *really* know what education is all about. I recall the difficulties I personally experienced when I decided to present a lecture at a national conference on cooperative learning. The fact that I did not use group activity in my session turned out to be an unpardonable sin!

- *Every strategy can be overdone.* Once I heard someone suggest that no teaching strategy should be used more than 60% of the available classroom time. As soon as we use it more than that, we face problems. Intuitively I tend to agree with this judgment. Now we need to take into account that teachers have "comfort zones." Depending on our own learning styles, we naturally gravitate towards certain comfortable ways of teaching, and tend to stick with them. But just as is true for learning styles, we need to cultivate the ability to flex teaching styles, lest we end up using only one or two strategies all of the time. Flexing our teaching styles involves taking risks. Then we need collegial and administrative support. If you can flex your style, assured that failure will not be held against you, the door is open to more effective and creative teaching.

- *Effective teachers employ a wide range of strategies.* Note that this generalization follows from the previous one. Effective teachers avoid getting stuck with only a few tried and trusted methods. They recognize that students learn in many different ways and are motivated in many different ways. In sum, teaching strategies may not be divorced from what we know of child development and about how children learn. How do you do justice to all the diversity the children display? One way you can do it is by enlarging your teaching strategies repertoire. This extra effort and risk taking make your teaching task much more enjoyable, exhilarating, and productive in terms of student learning.

- *Most strategies can be used in all subject areas and at all grade levels.* I became aware of this generalization when I began to hear objections to my proposals for new strategies. For example, I frequently do workshops in cooperative learning. Inevitably some of the responses will be as follows: "But you should see the kids I have to teach! They won't work together. Besides, I have to teach (fill in the subject). Cooperative learning won't work here. . . ." And so on. Such objections merely hide the fear of the new. We are comfortable with what we always do, especially if what we always do works! Nevertheless, if we encourage each other to flex our teaching styles, to reach out to different ways of meeting the diverse needs of our students, we must reject such objections and insist that in fact almost all teaching strategies discussed in a standard textbook on teaching can be used in every kind of classroom with students of every age level.

• *Not all strategies are clearly distinguishable: they can overlap and "blend."* Anyone who observes teaching practice carefully will note how good teachers quickly alternate and integrate a variety of teaching strategies. A good lecturer, for example, will suddenly call on his audience to identify his main points, and before you know it, the class has changed from a passive audience to a lively, participating, brainstorming group. Teaching strategies are not static procedures. They are dynamic and easily adapted in light of student response and a shifting classroom atmosphere. This reality requires especially careful planning. Not only do we design and construct teaching strategies, but we include in our lesson plans a number of alternatives to be used whenever the situation warrants.

The blending and overlapping of teaching strategies confirms the point made earlier: there is no single best strategy. Every so-called "best strategy" is actually a combination of others.

• *In selecting strategies, questions of discipleship must play a primary role.* Guiding and unfolding must be of an enabling character. The ultimate question continually undergirding your classroom decisions is simply this: is the strategy enabling in the full sense of the word? Does the strategy contribute to equipping the saints—yes, the children in my classroom!—for servanthood?

A proposed taxonomy

How can we make sense of the bewildering array of possibilities? Can we categorize a box full of random tips? Can we organize the items scattered out on the yard-sale lawn? Various authors have suggested a variety of interesting and sometimes useful categories.[1] They surely are worth our attention.

To classify teaching methods requires criteria—principles on the basis of which we differentiate between one category and another. What criteria can we use to categorize classroom teaching methods? I suggest we base our distinctions on the interplay between two themes, both of them crucial to our understanding of teaching Christianly: the metaphor of the teacher as a guide, and the vision of a collaborative classroom. The teacher, as officebearer, guides by pointing the way and setting the direction; the students become collaborating fellow-travelers, joining with the teacher as together they journey onwards towards an increasingly competent walk in Christian wisdom.

This picture readily suggests a continuum between teacher-guided direct instruction on the one hand, and, on the other hand, participatory teaching and learning strategies in which the students collaborate in the construction of the classroom teaching/learning situation. In between these two we may postulate an intermediate category of indirect instruction. In this way we can construct a spectrum ranging from direct through indirect to participatory forms of teaching.

Direct teaching, the first of the three categories, represents the sort of classroom activity in which the teacher—as guide—generates, initiates, and controls the content to be learned. Examples are the lecture, teacher explanations and demonstrations, programmed learning, and the use of film and video for certain purposes. In all these cases, it is the teacher who places the subject matter "on the table," as it were.

Indirect teaching, on the other hand, invites a good deal of student participation. In this category we see teachers initiate the content and set the parameters, but students are asked to expand and interpret. Story telling and the use of the parable are good examples. The parable does not present a straightforward message: it needs interpretation, expansion, and application by the audience. Guided inquiry and discovery learning can also be regarded as forms of indirect teaching. The teacher has a pretty clear idea of what it is that needs to be discovered, but invites the students to go through the process of actually doing so.

Finally, we may single out a category called participatory teaching. This is the sort of teaching in which the students become participants in the construction and acquisition of content. Cooperative learning can function this way, if we allow the students a good deal of self-direction and give them responsibility for their learning. Brainstorming is a participatory classroom activity which places all sorts of new thoughts on the table. Shared praxis—a strategy we will consider in a later chapter—usually does not reflect predetermined content, but develops general themes in particular, personal, often unpredictable ways. Drama and simulation, too, can be effective ways of having the students participate in the formulation and construction of content.

In the following chapters I shall consider these three categories in more detail. As I do so, recall that none of them represents a clear-cut category. There is much blending and overlapping. My intent, therefore, is not to play games by assigning various strategies to a specific home. Rather, if we are to construct a useful taxonomy of teaching strategies, we need to look for a few pivotal points towards which and from which the various strategies will inevitably drift.

Let's also be clear that none of these three categories is superior to or more effective than any of the other two. In view of the increasingly fashionable critique of direct instruction, we need to maintain that our preferences for teaching strategies cannot be based on whether or not they belong to one category or the other, but on the question of what combination we judge most likely to encourage knowledgeable and competent discipleship. At the same time, as soon as we begin to gravitate to one of the categories to the exclusion of the others, it is time to rethink our teaching methods.

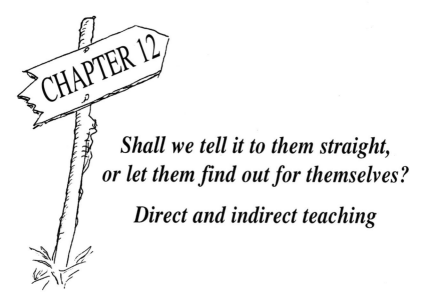

Shall we tell it to them straight, or let them find out for themselves?

Direct and indirect teaching

Alex: You know, Lisa, I tried some of that cooperative stuff you're always talking about. Nothing but trouble, I tell you! Kids off task, a lot of noise, and virtually no learning. I'm going back to my tried and tested method: I tell them what I'm going to tell them, then I tell them, and then I tell them what I just told them. That way they really get to know the stuff cold, and besides, in one fell swoop I've eliminated all the discipline problems. The kids are quiet like mice and work like Belgian horses—colts and fillies, of course!

Lisa: Wow, Alex! Your class must be the quietest and calmest class in this entire school! But do the kids enjoy learning?

The desire to talk

I must confess that I like to lecture. Maybe my desire to talk is what drew me into the teaching profession in the first place. Somehow I tend to be comfortable with the assumption that I have a lot to say that others should hear, whether they want to or not. I suspect many of us teachers are that way.

Even before I considered a teaching career, I thought of becoming a preacher. Preaching seemed like an immensely satisfying pastime. I would talk, a large audience would quietly listen, and my pontifications would carry the authority of the Lord himself!

Over the years I have begun to question this attitude. One reason for my growing skepticism is that, as I get older, I realize that I know much less than I once thought I did. Maybe the pearls of wisdom of the past turn out to be no more than sandstone pebbles—not worth much and easily pulverized.

I have also begun to see that my desire to talk reflects a certain degree of arrogance: I should talk and others—whether a church full of people or a classroom full of kids—should respectfully listen. I pretty well know it all, and I don't need to hear from anybody else. Or so it seemed. Alas, it is not so. I *don't* know it all, and I *do* need to hear from a lot of other folks, not the least among them, my students. Their wisdom can easily exceed my own. And above all, I need to listen very carefully to the instruction of my Lord.

Sometimes, when I observe certain teachers teach, I see some of these same traits: a desire to talk, to control, and to be center stage. And, yes, sometimes I even detect a bit of arrogance—suggested by the teacher's condescending tone, authoritarian attitude, and unwillingness to confess ignorance.

Avoiding a caricature

Lest you conclude that I believe all lecturers are smart-alecky, arrogant egomaniacs, let me describe Mike, a high school teacher. Mike liked to talk. But his talk was not propelled by a power trip. On the contrary, he talked, explained, lectured, even cajoled, because at the deepest level he was moved by compassion, by a keen desire to share, to teach, to enrich the lives of his students. Mike not only talked, he also listened. His talk was spurred by service, not self-service.

Much of direct instruction involves teacher talk. What motivates this talk? Is it simply because we like to talk, or is it because we deeply believe that our talking will be good for our students? If the former is true (even subconsciously), we have cut ourselves off from the possibility to teach Christianly. Such talk is no longer truly serving or enabling. Instead, it disables our students, and, in the long run, disables ourselves as well.

Direct teaching

Direct instruction occurs in your classroom when you present and control the content you want your students to learn.[1] You should interpret this statement rather broadly. It does not mean that direct instruction consists of only teacher talk. Your direct instruction can be assisted by textbook assignments, worksheets, videos, and computer programs. And by "content" I do not mean just a set of facts. It includes a large variety of learning outcomes, ranging from very specific information and skills to critical thinking abilities and artistic appreciation.

In essence, direct instruction relies heavily on the theme of transmission. When you use direct instruction strategies you take, as it were, the material to be learned and transmit it to the learners. It is this transmission process that has given direct instruction a bad name and generated metaphors like "filling empty vessels" or "pouring in the information." But such metaphors are not always justified. After all, a teaching strategy evokes a learning activity. In direct instruction, too, the students are required to respond in some way. Perhaps they do so by listening and reflecting, or by taking notes, or by rethinking or repeating the points made by the teacher, or by practicing their learning on a worksheet. Direct instruction, in short, is always a much more complicated process than first meets the eye. Whenever you use direct instruction, be sure to ask yourself questions about the accompanying student learning activity.

Some review

Direct instruction is undoubtedly the teaching method with which our students are most familiar. It has a long history. In some ways, the Old Testament advocates direct teaching by stressing the importance of *imprinting* on our children's minds the laws and the deeds of our God. These laws are to be told our children so that they will not forget the marvelous doings of the Lord, and be able, in turn, to retell them to their children and their children's children.[2]

As we saw in an earlier chapter, some Christian educators conclude from these Old Testament passages that all modern Christian school teaching must consist of direct instruction. We should avoid, they say, all this new-fangled faddish stuff about discovery and cooperative learning, because, after all, truth is truth, and such truth has to be clearly spelled out to the children so that they can understand it and repeat it. Group work or discovery learning is nothing but an exercise in pooling ignorance and ultimately a mucky bath in relativism.

But arguments of this sort suffer from numerous defects, as we saw. In the first place, they overlook that, in the New Testament, Jesus—the Master Teacher—frequently ignored direct instruction methods in favor of highly ambiguous parables. At times his disciples did not even understand what he was talking about. "He who has an ear let him hear" is one of those phrases Jesus commonly used that left many of his followers baffled and bewildered. In the second place, the "imprinting of truth" philosophy works, I believe, with a static, propositional, Aristotelian notion of truth, quite foreign to the Scriptures. Such a view has difficulty interpreting passages such as "doing the truth," "walking in the truth," and Jesus' claim that he is the truth.[3] This static, unbiblical notion of truth has played a major role in perennialistic educational philosophy, a philosophy that has often been uncritically adopted by Christian educators. It has encouraged academic, cerebral, factual learning while losing sight of our calling to bring up the *whole* child.

We need to remember, too, that the Old Testament is characterized by *direct* teachings not from gurus and wizards, but from the *Lord*, either by his own mouth or through the prophets. Direct instruction in those days was the norm. But in the New Testament dispensation the Spirit has come to dwell with us, a Spirit who leads us—co-laborers one and all—

onward in truth as together we seek to do His will. Making the Kingdom visible in this dark and hurting world has become a participatory, collaborative enterprise.[4]

Types of direct instruction

Think of your own classroom practice: How do you initiate, present, and control what you want your students to learn? Suppose you want them to learn the difference between snakes and lizards. The simplest, most direct way would be to show some graphic pictures of these beautiful creatures and clearly explain the differences. Or you could bring live samples into your classroom and demonstrate some of the differences. You could also assign a relevant section in your textbook and ask the students to outline and summarize. Or a good video would be useful. In all these ways of direct instruction—explaining, describing, defining, illustrating, demonstrating, assigning—you present the basic content to the students without significant input from them. The questions they ask simply elicit more information from you or the text or another authoritative source. You answer the questions by simply providing more content.

No classroom, no matter how collaborative, can do without direct instruction. You need to take time to explain, give guidance, and issue directives. In some ways, every declarative sentence you utter and every command you give represents an instance of direct instruction. Some explicit forms of modeling, too, can count as direct instruction. And not to be overlooked is that the students, too, frequently instruct directly. That is, their responses and suggestions function as just the right kind of information needed at a given point in the learning process.

Normally, however, we think of direct instruction as a teacher presenting to the students material to be learned. Giving a presentation or a lecture is still the clearest example of such instruction. In a lecture the teacher directly transmits the content of the lesson to be learned. Traditionally, such direct instruction requires little response other than the taking of notes, the memorizing of content, possibly some worksheet practice, and the passing of tests.

Madeline Hunter

A widespread model of direct instruction is Madeline Hunter's ITIP (Instructional Theory Into Practice).[5] Some schools used to require—and some still do—that all teachers adhere to and use the Hunter model. The story has it that a volleyball teacher in Texas was fired because she omitted one of the steps in the model. Requiring compliance with one specific teaching strategy is obviously a very unwise thing to do: it fully accedes to the effective-teaching-as-technique approach and destroys the personal side of the craft of teaching.

The basic steps of the Hunter model are the following:

1. Select objective
2. Motivate instruction (anticipatory set)
3. State the objective
4. Teach the main concepts (directly!)
5. Check for understanding
6. Provide guided practice
7. Provide opportunity for independent practice

Note that this model allows very little room for student input. The content to be mastered is entirely determined by the teacher. Student experience, insight, and background are bracketed and remain non-functional. This is not to say that all of the Hunter method is bad. Of course not. In order to teach some basic concepts, the Hunter approach may well be the best available. It is designed to make sure that the students thoroughly learn what the teacher wants them to learn. But as soon as we think that the Hunter method is *the* method to be employed throughout the curriculum and at all grade levels, we cut ourselves off from the possibility of teaching Christianly. We then reduce our task to a mechanical, reductionistic style of teaching and close our eyes to the need for collaboration.

Strengths of direct teaching

As suggested at several points, you should not believe some current voices which claim that direct instruction is to be avoided as vegetarians avoid pork roast. On the contrary, direct instruction plays a meaningful role, even in the collaborative classroom. Perhaps you can understand this claim more clearly when we consider the numerous strong points associated with direct instruction. The following are some of the more important ones:

- Direct instruction is always required, even if only to give directions and explanations of the work to be done collaboratively.
- Direct instruction usually goes hand-in-hand with good organization. Presentations and lectures, for example, can be planned and implemented in minute detail.
- For this reason teachers who are somewhat insecure gravitate toward direct instruction: it allows the teacher to maintain control of the class more easily—at least, so it seems to the teacher.
- Research has shown that direct instruction is effective, especially in teaching basic concepts and skills. For higher level thinking, however, the studies on the use of direct instruction are much less conclusive.[6]
- Direct instruction provides an attractive measure of efficiency. It delivers content to an entire class quickly and concisely.
- It is attractive to first-year teachers, for direct instruction requires much less planning time than, for example, carefully crafted cooperative learning strategies.

Weaknesses of (excessive use of) direct instruction

In spite of the strong points just explained, you should understand the serious concerns about the excessive use of direct teaching. Its weaknesses are quite glaring. It is worrisome, therefore, to observe the trend of relying more and more heavily on direct instruction as one proceeds through the grade levels. A "top-down pedagogy" appears to be operating: high school teachers imitate the teaching style of their college professors who mostly lectured; in fact, at university levels professors are appointed as "lecturers"! Junior high teachers, not to be outdone, in turn follow the high school style of teaching.

This top-down pedagogy reaches down into the earlier grades to an alarming degree. I recall visiting a fourth-grade class in which the teacher lectured for an entire 50-minute class period, while the students diligently—and not so diligently—took notes.

Well, what are the concerns? The following are among the most significant:

- Direct teaching tends to shut down creativity. This consequence follows from our definition of direct instruction: the teacher controls the content. The children need not contribute much to the expansion and interpretation of the content, and so their creative powers are not tapped.

- Direct instruction limits the scope of learning. It tends to remain focused on basic cognitive information.

- At the later stages of schooling, particularly past the grade six level, one wonders about the legitimacy of the "efficiency" argument. It is claimed that much information can be delivered to many students by means of direct instruction. But could this method be considered a *time-waster*? Why spend an hour giving a lecture when it would be much more efficient to write out the lecture and have the students read it as a homework assignment? Centuries ago, when there was a shortage of paper, relying on the lecture indeed made sense. In our time, however, recycled paper and photocopying machines provide teachers with new opportunities. And isn't much of our lecture rephrased information from the students' texts? Sometimes our lecturing excuses students from careful reading.

- A more serious worry is that direct instruction tends to promote individualism. Normally, direct instruction does not require inter- action between and among students. They are individually respon- sible for processing and recording the information presented.

- In a similar vein, excessive direct instruction approves of and fosters what we might describe as "egalitarianism." Students are exposed to a very restricted teaching style, one geared to auditory and sequential learning styles. An egalitarian philosophy assumes that all the students are basically alike in achievement levels and learning styles. All the students are treated alike. Direct instruction supposes that all the students are equally capable of processing what is presented and can therefore be held equally accountable. Such egalitarianism encourages conformity, much as the use of performance objectives does.

- I do believe that excessive reliance on direct instruction techniques fosters laziness and selfishness. The students do very little work other than listen, take notes, memorize, and regurgitate. Excessive teaching of this sort programs the students to expect such limited learning activity. They begin to identify such teaching with good education. They expect the teacher to dish up the goodies on a silver platter, as it were. Yes, there will be assignments and research requirements, but the essence of the curriculum is simply *given* to the students. I have noted this phenomenon in my freshman college classes. Students come fully prepared "to take notes." If a class period is spent in discussion or group activities, and the students do not leave with a set of notes, some feel that they haven't learned anything, and the class was "a waste of time."

- Most worrisome of all is that direct instruction encourages passivity. Students are recipients. But passivity is incompatible with the goal of active discipleship. A disciple of the Lord does not sit by and wait for things to happen, but *actively reaches out* to do the work of the Lord.

- Finally, direct instruction is often accompanied by boredom and routine. True, lectures can be presented in an exciting and engaging way. Some teachers have a gift for doing so. But in my experience, such teachers are few and far between. If you are not a spellbinding, stimulating lecturer, choose alternative teaching methods.

In summary, excessive direct instruction contradicts the very purpose of teaching Christianly in a collaborative classroom in a number of significant ways. It contradicts both the overarching goal of teaching Christianly and the collaborative classroom context in which such teaching is to proceed.

I know I sound like an echo in the Alps, but I do want to say it once more: my critique is not of direct instruction as such, but of its *overuse*. A classroom without direct instruction is not possible, as the open classroom of the progressivists more or less proved several decades ago. The question is not: Do we use direct instruction yes or no? but: *How* can direct instruction facilitate a collaborative classroom? How can we transform direct instruction in such a way that the goals of discipleship are promoted?

The answer to this question consists of a tried and tested technique: Get the kids involved! All good teachers know that the more the students are involved in their learning, the better they will learn. To put it differently, try to make the direct instruction as participatory as possible. I do not mean that the children respond in a canned way, as the Hunter model prescribes. Rather, aim to have the students contribute new insights, develop new ways of thinking, and make use of their creative and imaginative gifts. So, for example, if you must lecture, limit your lecture time to no more than 10 or 15 minutes (in secondary schools too), and stop frequently to ask students to summarize what you have just said. Or, better yet, put them in pairs to recall the main points you have just made. Ask the students how they could say it differently, or what questions should be raised about the topic under consideration. In these and other ways, direct instruction enhances both the participatory style of teaching and the collaborative classroom.

Indirect teaching

In this category I place all those teaching approaches that invite your students to expand, interpret, and contribute to the material you put "on the table," so to speak.[7] Most of the problem-solving assignments are of this sort. Presenting a problem, whether in science, language arts, math or social studies, requires a student's direct involvement in the sense that the student must provide what you did not begin with, namely, a solution. A solution is a student-developed contribution to the topic at hand.[8]

Of course, there are different sorts of solutions. Some may merely reflect a standard procedure that reveals a predetermined right answer. Problem-solving in this sense comes close to direct instruction. Proceeding through predetermined steps to come to a predetermined right answer is not unlike taking lecture notes to be memorized and recalled. Problems of this sort are frequently encountered in science education. The students are told to follow a sequence of steps, and presto! they arrive at the right answer. In these cases "discovery" is not really discovery at all. It resembles much more the programmed instruction as delivered by computers.

True hands-on projects and experimentation, however, do count as instances of indirect instruction. In such projects the student is to come up with something new, perhaps unpredictable, something that reflects the student's personal character and gifts. The teacher provides the guidelines; the students take it from there. It is often useful to have the students collaborate on such projects.

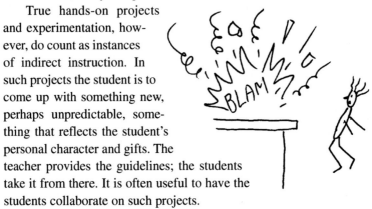

What sorts of problems should you ask your students to solve? I believe we can learn from John Dewey on this point. In his publications he insisted that the problems teachers choose should be both important to the culture in which we live and important and relevant to the students.[9]

The various inquiry and discovery methods described in any standard textbook on teaching strategies offer additional examples of indirect instruction.[10] In such an inquiry approach, the teacher sets the parameters and provides the guidelines. But the student arrives at self-generated—not spoon-fed—conclusions. Suppose in a science class you want your students to learn about the different ways leaves are attached to the stem of a plant. In the direct instruction mode, you would explain to the students that the leaves of a plant are opposite, alternate, or whorled, and show examples of each. In an indirect inquiry approach, you would ask the students to collect plants with different leaf structures (or you could provide examples), and have the students discover the leaf arrangements.

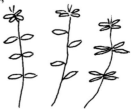

In English class you can get the students to learn about figures of speech in an indirect way. Instead of introducing, explaining, and illustrating them, you provide numerous examples and have the students deduce the various categories. Similar approaches can be taken in almost every subject and at every grade level.

Earlier I mentioned that story telling and parables are good examples of indirect instruction. In this approach the students are asked to reflect, interpret, and make personal applications. These will differ in accordance with the diversity of students.

Inquiry approaches tend to be inductive, that is, you ask the students to draw conclusions and state generalizations on the basis of specific, particular examples. Your students could explore, for example, a variety of totalitarian governments in order to discover the general characteristics that mark all forms of totalitarianism. However, inquiry is certainly not limited in this way. You can also present the students with generalizations

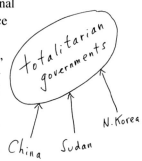

and ask them to generate a number of specific examples to illustrate them. You could explain what totalitarianism is, then have the students find specific instances. The key difference between direct and indirect instruction lies in the extent to which the students are involved in expanding the learning to be attained.

Learning centers and research projects can be understood as fine examples of indirect instruction. In both cases, you set the parameters and guidelines, then let the students do their thing. What they come up with can significantly enhance your understanding of the subjects you teach. I discover this truth anew every time I ask my senior seminar students to write a brief research paper in which they describe a problem they encountered in their student teaching, along with a proposed solution. It is delightful to see the insights these students contribute.

Final remarks

I encourage you to view indirect approaches as opportunities for your students to develop their gifts and insights and to take responsibility for their learning. Indirect instruction allows you to construct lesson plans that more readily meet the various goal areas discussed in chapter 5 than direct instruction is able to do. It can help you focus your curricular content on the larger and more important themes we face in the world today, and stimulate a more integrated approach. Indirect teaching, in short, should find a welcome place in your Christian classroom.

Indirect instruction, especially inquiry approaches, should be closely coordinated with questioning techniques. After all, the very term "inquiry" refers to a questioning attitude. Before we turn our attention to the third category, namely, participatory teaching, let us spend some time exploring the relation between questioning techniques and teaching Christianly.

The Craft of Christian Teaching

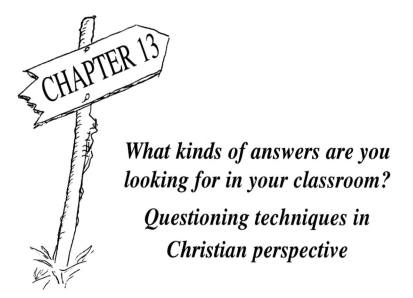

CHAPTER 13

What kinds of answers are you looking for in your classroom?

Questioning techniques in Christian perspective

Jim: Say Lisa, what do you do about those shy students—the kids who never volunteer a single answer in your class? And what do you do about the eager beavers who always have their hands up, even when you're not asking them anything? I use tricks like pulling names out of a hat, checking off a class list, and what have you. The fact remains, some bubbly kids just love to respond, and others just turn into Egyptian mummies every time I ask a question. Any ideas?

Lisa: I find this whole question-and-answer business frustrating too, Jim. I guess I do what you do: try to get everybody to participate, and ask good questions that will make kids think. Sometimes it helps to have the kids talk with each other before they raise—or don't raise—their hands. Sometimes I think I shouldn't ask any questions at all.

No questions in the classroom?

Not so long ago I had a terrifying nightmare. Most nightmares tend to be scary, of course, but this one was particularly bloodcurdling. I dreamt that I had accepted a job in a school where questions were outlawed. The classrooms were to be entirely question-free. Teachers were not permitted to ask a single question at any time. Students risked expulsion from the school if they so much as raised a hand.

I wonder what prompted this nightmare. It could be that I was still smarting over a fruitless debate with someone about teachers teaching and students learning. Teachers, I was told, should make their lessons so clear that few, if any, questions would be needed in the classroom. Or perhaps I was reliving an experience I had while working with education students in Indonesia. Professors at the universities there, I was advised, do not ask questions of students because doing so might suggest that the students are too thickheaded to understand the first time. Conversely, students do not ask questions of the professor, for doing so might suggest that the professor was unclear. In either case, asking questions amounts to an insult.

Questions in the classroom

Actually, asking questions of students is a standard procedure used by virtually all elementary and secondary teachers. Studies show that some elementary teachers can easily ask more than a hundred questions per hour.[1] The number drops off when we get to secondary levels. Why the decline? No doubt this phenomenon has something to do with stages of development. Increasing self-consciousness of the students probably plays a role. Other factors may be that as we move through the grades, the material we teach tends to become more abstract and less obviously connected to life; consequently, genuine interest in questions and answers is on the wane. Few students care to ask questions about things they don't care about. Whatever the cause, it is hard to imagine—except in a nightmare—any kind of contemporary K-12 classroom in which the teacher does not ask questions.

Types of questions

One of my daughters was a member of a high school quiz bowl team for several years. The team traveled to different places to compete with different schools. Sometimes the contest was taped and shown on public television. On occasion I watched the program—just to see my daughter perform, of course. The four team members would be seated on some kind of bench, while a gray-haired gentleman posed the questions. The questions ranged over a variety of topics, not unlike in the popular Jeopardy game.

Quiz bowl and Jeopardy events rely on one-right-answer questions. When was Julius Caesar assassinated? Who wrote *The Sound and the Fury*? What is the capital of Madagascar? None of these questions allow for a range of possible right answers. All such possibilities except one will be wrong. You can't respond to the question "When did Brutus stab Julius Caesar?" with "Well, let's see now, it was in 54 B. C., 44 B. C., as well as at the time of Napoleon." You will no doubt remember from your teacher education program that questions that allow just one correct response are called convergent questions.

Studies show that classroom teachers generally lean heavily towards convergent questions.[2] More than 75% of all questions asked in classrooms are of this type. And no wonder. They are easy to judge as correct or incorrect. For this reason convergent questions frequently appear in test instruments. They allow for so-called "objective testing," the kind of testing that is easy to score. True or false quizzes usually consist of convergent questions.

A second type of question, generally labeled divergent, *does* invite a multiplicity of correct responses. Examples include the following: Why did Napoleon lose the war? What effect does the sun have on planet earth? What uses can you find for an empty pop bottle? Observe that each one of these questions permits a variety of answers.

Sometimes convergent questions can masquerade as divergent questions. Suppose you tell your students: "List three ways in which salamanders differ from lizards." Does this request not allow a multi-plicity of right answers? Not really. In all likelihood the students will select the three ways from a list available to them. Had you asked them to quote the entire list, we would be back in the one-right-answer category. Admittedly, however, the line between convergent and divergent can be thin.

Evaluative questions constitute a third category. They are sometimes classified as a version of divergent questions. An evaluative question reaches farther than many divergent questions do. They require that students not only propose options or alternatives, but that they make judgments about the relative merit of the options and alternatives. For example, I could ask the students not only to identify their favorite TV shows, but to go on to arrange them in order of the value they attach to them, along with reasons for their choices.

Some other characteristics

Convergent questions involve mostly recall. Divergent and evaluative questions, on the other hand, require higher level thinking skills. They force the students to generate, express, and assess thoughts and ideas. Consequently, they address a larger number of goal areas than convergent questions. If you place the development of critical thinking among the objectives for your lessons, you should pay much attention to divergent questions.

If, in addition to critical thinking, you also want to emphasize creative thinking, consider still another category of questions: the "What if?" questions. Such questions are clearly divergent. They are especially serviceable for fostering creative and imaginative thinking skills. Suppose you ask your students, for example, What if the earth had three moons instead of just one? What if everyone in the world could speak ten languages? What if a day were 48 hours long? Questions like these would certainly call for basic knowledge and understanding, yet they are sufficiently open-ended to provoke a good deal of creative thought.

It should be evident that convergent questions are most at home with direct teaching. Much of direct teaching deals with basic information. Divergent and evaluative questions, on the other hand, are more attuned to indirect and participatory modes of teaching. They require the students to not merely recall and repeat (teacher-supplied) information, but to generate new thoughts that contribute to the topics under study. These statements are general-izations, of course. Nevertheless, we do well to reflect. It is important that you and I check our teaching and assess the extent to which we use different sorts of questions. A tape recorder or a video camera is very helpful in making such an assessment.

An important question

The important question is this: Is there a distinctively Christian approach to your classroom questioning practice? Or are questions simply questions—a neutral, mechanical procedure used by all good teachers, whether Christian or not? As long as teachers use convergent, divergent, evaluative and what-if? questions generously, does it really make a difference whether or not they are Christians? You will recall that in an earlier chapter I raised a similar issue in connection with teaching methods. Strategies, too, are sometimes regarded as merely technical components of teaching, skills free of religious values. But if Christ is Lord of all, He is Lord of all aspects of our teaching, including our questioning strategies.

To get at this significant issue, let's begin with an exploration of the reasons why teachers ask questions in the classroom. This is an intriguing issue. After all, we normally ask questions when we need an answer to something we don't know. Teachers are the only folks who ask questions about things they already know.

Why ask questions in the classroom?

Why do teachers pose questions in their classrooms? This is itself a good example of a divergent question, since it allows an unlimited number of responses. Here are some that show how important questions are in a classroom:

- A well-formulated question can be the right trigger to start a lesson or a lively class discussion.
- Questions function as an effective formative check, to see whether or not the children have sufficiently grasped the concepts you are teaching.
- Questions can help students study or review difficult material.
- Questions form good transitional points between lessons.
- They can function as "sponges," sopping up transitional time between classes or topics, time that might otherwise be wasted or allow for behavioral problems.
- They provide a useful mechanism to close a lesson.
- Careful questioning is an excellent strategy to develop thinking and communication skills.
- Questioning students in a positive way helps build their self-confidence.

Many teachers include the formulation of questions in their lesson planning. I strongly recommend this practice. Carefully designed questions can be enormously helpful in starting off, continuing, or concluding a lesson, or in making a transition from one topic to another. Don't count on being able to come up with the appropriate question at the appropriate time. Planning in advance assures you're asking the right sort of questions.

The list of reasons we generated illustrates that asking questions is a purposeful activity. They are not simply time fillers or occasions for empty chit-chat. Questions are *directional* in nature: they aim at something, they seek to achieve a goal. As soon as I mention "goal," I think, of course, of the largest, overarching goal, the goal of knowledgeable and competent discipleship. Let me pursue the point a little further.

Suppose you are a hard-core, drill-them-in-the-basics teacher. Your aim is to fill heads with facts. What sort of questions are you likely to ask? Most likely the emphasis will fall on convergent, factual questions. Suppose, on the other hand, you are a progressivist: more than likely your interest would be to ask divergent, problem-solving types of questions. Clearly your philosophy of education has much to do with your questioning techniques.

Further, suppose you are an intellectualist. To you the cultivation of the mind is the essential focus of schooling. Again, what sort of questions would you most likely ask? Certainly the scope of your questions would be limited to intellectual and cerebral concerns. Questions dealing with personal feelings and social hurts would probably be raised in only the most marginal fashion. On the other hand, if you espouse a we-must-save-the-world reconstructionist philosophy, your questions would have much to do with the evils that pervade our society. You would seek to get your students upset and ready for action. Thus not only the types, but also the scope and range of your questions are influenced by your philosophy. My point is that your educational perspective exerts a strong influence on both (1) the types and (2) the scope of questions you ask in your classroom.

The context for questions

Questions are not raised in a vacuum. They occur in the context of, first, your specific units and lessons, and, second, the larger classroom environment you cultivate and maintain.

Lessons

Your lessons involve subject matter, and most of the questions you pose in your classroom are likely to be associated with the subject matter you are busily unfolding. But, as we saw, subject matter is to be placed in a Christian perspective. The great biblical themes of creation, fall, and redemption must encompass and direct the material you teach. This perspective must be reflected in the sort of questions you raise. If our teaching degenerates into, say, a focus-on-the-facts approach, then the biblical perspective will be eliminated, and our questions will change in character.

Of course, the environment should reflect the collaborative classroom, as I have argued in an earlier chapter. Such an environment will make a critical difference to your question and answer procedures. Take, for example, an authoritarian, fear-filled classroom. How does questioning proceed? Children will be afraid to respond, for fear of getting it wrong and invoking the wrath of the teacher. Or consider a classroom in which the teacher is perceived largely as an arbitrary judge. In such a classroom, too, the students will be hesitant to speak. Or take an individualistic and competitive classroom: the students will compete with each other for the attention and approval of the teacher. Individual students will secretly hope that their classmates will respond incorrectly, or worse, they may hope that others will make fools of themselves. It is clear, then, that the classroom environment has everything to do with questioning.

In contrast, in a collaborative classroom the children will be invited to respond in freedom from fear. They will be encouraged to speak and to take risks. They will be encouraged to ask questions themselves, of the teacher and of one another. Since there is mutual support and acceptance, students do not put each other down when the questions they ask or the responses they give supposedly aren't what they should be. Students will encourage each other to try again and to succeed.

Suggestions

I conclude this brief introduction to questioning by listing a series of suggestions, designed to help you ask questions Christianly.

- At the beginning of the term, when introducing and discussing classroom procedures, make your expectations clear. Students need to know that you will be asking plenty of questions, and that they will do much responding. Explain to the children that they are to respond in a positive Christian manner to the teacher and to each other. Give them some examples of what you mean, ask them to come up with additional examples, and allow them to practice good responding skills.

> Be nice!
> Be good!
> Smile!
> Pay attention!

- One of the most important classroom expectations will be: No put-downs or sarcasm of any kind! Assiduously avoid even a hint of disrespect or sarcasm in your own responses to the students, not even in jest, and immediately stop the proceedings when such put-downs occur among the students. Do not allow them to go unnoticed. Do not ignore them.

- Be sure to listen carefully to student responses. Model good listening skills. Look at the student when he or she responds, and give some indication that you have heard and understood the response accurately. Be generous with remarks such as "Let's see once if I understand what you said." Follow up with further questions, to show that you are taking the student's response seriously.

- Refrain from making hasty judgments about correctness or incorrectness of a response. Often students have difficulty articulating a response clearly and are cut short by teachers who demand instant accuracy. Students are often well on the way to offering excellent insights, if only given plenty of encouragement and opportunity to express themselves. Be quick to encourage the students to rephrase questions and responses. Ask other students to do so as well.

- When a student gives an obviously incorrect answer, be sure to avoid setting him up against another child. For example, avoid disastrous remarks such as "That's quite wrong, Kyle! Raveena, please give us the right answer." Perhaps more subtle—sounding less harsh—but equally problematic is a response like this: "Raveena, can you help Kyle out?" Such pronouncements fracture relationships and make it doubly difficult to maintain a collaborative classroom atmosphere. Instead, ask a clarifying question or ask students to rephrase.

- Encourage students to be creative and imaginative in their answers.

Give them the freedom to speculate and to conjecture. I realize you run the risk of setting up your class for frivolous responses. I believe it is a risk worth taking. Frivolity will even out with serious, responsible questioning and responding activity. Expect the best from them. And besides, humor is always in style.

- Seek to involve all the students. Studies show that teachers believe that they are in fact involving all the students, when in actuality some students receive much more opportunity to respond than others. This reality is especially a problem on elementary levels. In the later grades, an opposite situation may develop: whereas in elementary grades all the students will raise their hands when asked a question, in secondary schools getting the students to respond is at times exasperatingly difficult. As I suggested, this phenomenon may be due to an increasing irrelevance of subject matter and to a teacher's habit of asking obvious or meaningless questions. Carefully crafted questions associated with carefully crafted lessons can go a long way in solving the nobody-volunteers problem. In any case, be sure to involve all the students. Not doing so conflicts with the meaning of a collaborative classroom. If you are not sure how equally you are distributing your questions, give a student a class list and have her keep track of who responds.

- Encourage the children to ask each other questions. Too often questions are only teacher's questions, and dialogue is only between the teacher and an individual student.[3] Instead of acknowledging a student's response and going on to the next question, stop to ask other students what they think of the response. Specifically design situations in which the students have to ask each other questions, and learn to respond to each other, not just to the teacher. Seating arrangements play a major role. Arranging the students in a circle obviously promotes interaction and reciprocal questioning.

- Avoid repeating student responses. Doing so promotes individualism. The students then learn to depend on the teacher as an "answering machine," rather than to develop the listening skills required for meaningful collaborative interaction. Repeating student responses word for word teaches them to listen only to the teacher, not to each other. The practice hampers inter-student discussions.

- Ask a variety of questions. Be sure you do not limit yourself to simple, convergent questions. Press for divergent, evaluative, and what-if? questions, and follow up on student responses.
- Enlarge the scope of your questions. Do not limit yourself to purely academic, intellectual, or content-specific questions. Ask the students how they feel about the topic at hand, what they believe about it, what values they attach to it, and how it relates to their sense of priorities. Remember, we are teaching the whole child, not just a mind in a body.
- Don't be too quick to dismiss questions and responses that have to do with the students' experiences and seem to be off task. True, little kids especially can quickly get side-tracked in discussions about their grandmother and the puppies at home. Nevertheless, remember the principle of "connectedness." Ask questions about student experiences, about how they might relate to what they are learning, and about ways in which they think what they are learning will make a difference in their lives. The experience and insights of each one of your students are important. Invite them and receive them with thanksgiving.
- Remember that there really is such a thing as "wait time." Research has convincingly shown that the more time we allow for the students to respond, the better the quality of the responses.[4] From a Christian perspective we want to add here that, first, students are unique in their gifts and learning styles, so some require more time to process a response than others, and, second, patience is an important virtue to model and cultivate.
- Avoid always directing questions to individual students. Consider the "letterhead" approach: place the students in groups of, let's say, four, and assign a letter to each group member, A, B, C, D. Then, when asking a question, ask the students to stick their heads together and frame a response. Announce that you will call on a B, or a C, or whatever. This approach encourages collaboration and diminishes individualistic competition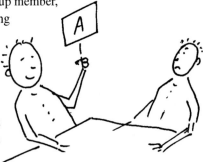

between students. It also fosters a sense of self-confidence and fear-lessness: after all, the responses are team responses. Should there be an error, no individual student will bear the brunt of scorn. Obviously you can't use this method for every single question you ask. Plan what situations you will create in your lessons and what questions you will reserve for the letterhead approach.

Questioning techniques can indeed bear a Christian stamp. The difference will show when we begin to pay close attention to what otherwise might appear to be simply a standard procedure. I suggest you get together with your colleagues to discuss this matter, compare the formulations of your questions, and encourage each other to hone your skills. It would be especially useful if your board and principal could free up time for you to get into each other's classrooms, to observe closely one another's questioning strategies, then spend time reviewing, evaluating, and supporting each other's practice.

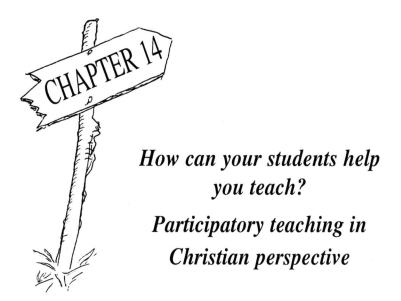

How can your students help you teach?
Participatory teaching in Christian perspective

Alex: Wow, Lisa! You must be doing something right in your class-room! Aren't you doing a unit on birds? Well, I overheard Travis and Ashley in the hallway this afternoon, discussing blackbirds! I thought Travis was interested only in spaceships, and I don't think I've ever heard Ashley talk about anything but movies and the mall! How did you manage to keep these kids talking about what you're teaching them?

Lisa: Well, for one thing, I've had the class do a lot of discussion lately. Today we carried on quite a conversation about the zillions of blackbirds that congregate in town every fall and decorate it so liberally. Nice to hear that the kids actually continued the discussion after class.

Alex: I'm impressed! I'm lucky if my kids are still thinking about the lesson topic when the bell rings.

An initial description and distinction

If your students are like the ones Alex describes in the scenario above, you might consider doing more participatory teaching in your classroom. Of course, doing so is no guarantee that your students will suddenly perceive the closing bell as an unwelcome intrusion and practically force you to keep your lesson going. In classroom teaching, there simply are no guarantees—despite what the salespeople at teachers' conventions try to tell you. The classroom is just too complex a place to allow simple solutions and easy recipes.

Nevertheless, there are ways of getting the students more involved in their learning than they might be if you lean too heavily on direct modes of instruction. Participatory teaching situations can help pull kids like Travis and Ashley from their obsessions with spaceships and movies and actually motivate them to look at what you want them to learn.

What are participatory approaches? Participatory teaching is the sort of teaching that invites the students to collaborate in the construction of the classroom teaching/learning situation. It cultivates opportunities to teach each other and to learn from one another. It encourages student initiative to a much greater extent than do either direct or indirect instruction.

But how, you might ask, does participatory teaching differ from indirect teaching? Don't both of them require student involvement? The question is somewhat similar to asking: What is the difference between cumulus clouds and nimbus clouds? Aren't they all clouds? Yes, sometimes they are hard to tell apart, at other times they look quite distinct. The one may even turn into the other. So it is with teaching strategies. Recall a point I made earlier: teaching strategies are not always clearly distinguishable; they overlap, and good teachers frequently intermix, even blend, a variety of approaches and learning activities.

To me, the difference between indirect and participatory teaching is but a matter of degree. The key lies in a shift of focus from more to less teacher control. Indirect teaching situations still require students to work within parameters set and controlled by the teacher. Participatory approaches, on the other hand, deliberately encourage the students to play an active role in generating the content to be learned and in structuring and controlling classroom procedures.

To be truthful, I do not see a clear distinction between indirect and participatory teaching; that is, I know of no specific criteria that permit us to differentiate clearly and sharply between them. I see participatory teaching as a general area on a continuous spectrum, rather than as a distinctly defined, sharply delineated category. It represents the sort of teaching that invites the students to contribute, as much as possible, to what is going on in the classroom.

Why make the distinction when there is no clear distinction? My sense is that if we do not explicitly recognize the category of participatory teaching, we will tend to remain wrapped up in largely teacher-controlled classroom activity. Ask yourself some hard questions about your own teaching style and comfort zone: To what extent do you need to be "in charge" in order to be able to teach effectively? Do you believe that your students must be "controlled"? Do you feel most comfortable when the students do exactly what you tell them to do? How open are you to spot and make use of the teachable moment and to adjust your lesson plan accordingly? Or is your motto "My objectives must be met, come heat or high water"? How willing are you, really now, to flex your style and allow the students to help shape what you are teaching, to encourage them to teach each other, and thereby to equip them to act responsibly?

Three quick reminders

Participatory approaches do not rule out diligent study of what is traditionally described as subject matter and skills. Of course not. After all, one key assumption of this entire book is that Christian education is for competent and knowledgeable discipleship. Without a deep understanding and a wide range of skills, the potential for effective discipleship in our world is seriously compromised.

Nor does participatory teaching eliminate the need for direct instruction. Recall the "rule": no method should be used for more than 60% of the available class time. Besides, as we saw, even the most collaborative of classes needs direct instruction.

Finally, participatory teaching, too, always presupposes that teachers are officebearers and guides. They retain the ultimate authority in the classroom, and they retain responsibility for setting the direction of student learning. I summarily reject—and I invite you to do the same— any notion of "open classroom" or "Deweyan democracy"; these educational approaches are incompatible with the character of teaching Christianly.

An example of a participatory teaching method

A simple example of participatory teaching is the practice of brainstorming. Most teachers use this technique in order to quickly generate a multitude of ideas to be considered in class. Brainstorming clearly requires a divergent or evaluative

leading question. A convergent, one-right-answer question cannot initiate a brainstorming session. Now the critical point is this: What does the teacher do with the results of a brainstorming session? Are they simply incorporated into a predetermined plan or outcome, designed by the teacher? Surely there is place for such a strategy. In a more imaginative, participatory brainstorming session, however, the suggestions made and the conclusions drawn play a significant part in the procedure of the lesson. They make an authentic contribution to the teaching/ learning situation. They may even change the intended outcomes of a lesson.

A simple illustration: One third-grade teacher conducted a brainstorming session as part of a lesson on classification procedures. Her intent was to get the class to construct a complete list of all the characteristics that separate horses from cows. One little boy suggested the adjective "mean." "Why do you think horses are mean?" the teacher asked. "Because," the boy responded, "a horse kicked my uncle in the head and killed him!" He added with a sob: "He was my favorite uncle." A teachable moment! The theme of classification was transformed—or, at least, extended—into a discussion about the relationship between "mean" and "dangerous," about practicing safety around horses, and about comforting the hurting. Rather than glibly dismissing the boy's contribution, the teacher incorporated it and worked with it in her lesson.

In the remainder of this chapter I shall consider two participatory approaches: "participatory discussion" and "shared praxis." These should serve as models for other forms. An examination of cooperative learning as a participatory approach is reserved for the next chapter.

Participatory discussion

The term may puzzle you. Isn't all discussion participatory? Does it not always require "discussion partners"? Well, yes and no. True, unless you are talking about soliloquies or singing in the shower, discussion normally refers to a conversation among multiple participants. In a classroom, however, it makes sense to distinguish between participatory and nonparticipatory discussion. Teachers sometimes report that they have a lot of "discussion" going on in their classrooms, when in fact they are really talking about something else. They may be talking about a non-participatory discussion. So what is a *nonparticipatory discussion*? Here are some features that identify it:

- Not all those who ought to participate in the discussion do in fact participate. Often what goes for a "class discussion" is in fact no more than a dialogue between a few vociferous vocalists. The "discussion" is actually more of a spectator sport than anything really participatory.

- The "discussion" is essentially a question-and-answer dialogue between the teacher and selected students. The teacher does 80% of the talking.[1] In essence, there is only one real participant: the teacher. This form of "discussion" could better be called a "recitation." There is no more genuine discussion going on here than in the quiz bowl event in which my daughter "participated."

The Craft of Christian Teaching

- The students, along with the teacher, state their opinions without listening to each other, responding to each other, or seeking to understand each other. Their "discussion" easily ends up in a shouting match, not unlike the political roundtables—such as *Crossfire*—that masquerade as discussions. Every "participant" is out to prove that all the others are wrong.
- The teacher rules certain contributions out of order on the grounds that "they do not advance the discussion" or as simply "wrong." In other words, some kind of subtle—or not so subtle—censorship controls the conversation. Contributors need to ask themselves first whether or not their opinions meet certain acceptability criteria arbitrarily assumed by the teacher.

I am toying with the idea of designating what I call "participatory discussion" as an "authentic discussion." What makes a class discussion "authentically participatory"? At least three characteristics come to mind:

- An authentically participatory discussion is a conversation among participants in which information, insights, and ideas are solicited, shared, and heard. As in brainstorming, no ideas are summarily dismissed because they might be "wrong" or clash with the teacher's opinions. Of course, the formulation of ideas and the tone in which they are expressed may be inappropriate. I'll return to this point in a moment.
- The purpose of an authentically participatory discussion is not just to check student understanding—as in recitation—but to create the conditions in which all participants, including the teacher, will grow in knowledge and wisdom. There is not only teacher-student exchange, but also much student-student interaction. A participatory discussion should be enabling, rather than disabling. While recitations have their place, they should not be confused with participatory discussions. Participatory discussions do not require predetermined answers but aim to bring out the experiences and understandings of every one of the partners.
- In a participatory discussion there is commitment to hear one another out. It assumes basic rules of communication. There is civility and mutual encouragement. There is willingness, even eagerness, to listen to each other.

Conducting a participatory discussion

Getting an authentically participatory discussion going in your classroom is no simple task. It won't do to gather your kids together and declare "Let's talk!" What are some of the key steps you must take?

First, make sure the discussion topic is of some significance. To get a meaningful discussion going on the question whether or not banana cream pie tastes better than apple strudel is as difficult as preparing a pork chop from bacon strips. You need more meat.

The topic should engage not only the intellectual prowess of the students, but also their sense of values, their priorities, their feelings, and their belief systems. Sometimes it is best to focus an anticipated discussion on a problem that begs for a solution. Examples of meaningful topics in different areas might be the following: What happens to the rightness or wrongness of mathematics when it is used to make bombs? In view of changing hypotheses, is there such a thing as an "objective body of scientific knowledge"? What should be done with the blackbirds decorating our town? Do video games contribute to violence in our schools? What makes a good friend? How is a community built?

I am not suggesting that in every case the topic be something so profound even philosophers can't handle it. I do believe, however, that participatory discussions require the kind of "higher-order" sophistication that we often avoid or dismiss as impractical or as bringing the students too far away from the content we want to teach. They require the potential for unpacking a diversity of ideas. Questions or problems with easy answers or ready solutions do not lend themselves to a classroom discussion where the sharing of insight leads to a deepening of wisdom. So I encourage you to look over the content of your lessons and your units and ask yourself: Where and when do I have an opportunity for a good participatory discussion? Do not think, by the way, that participatory discussions have a place only in middle schools and high schools.

Younger children, too, can share their thoughts. Whenever students are able to speak, a participatory discussion becomes possible.

Once you have decided on a topic, you need to appropriately prepare. Normally, participatory discussions do not suddenly emerge. They can, of course. And sometimes they do. We should receive such unplanned opportunities as gifts from God and celebrate them as occasions for gratitude. More often than not, however, participatory discussions require some preparation on the part of both you and the students. Students should know something about the topic—including the topics they themselves suggest. They should have opportunity to reflect and relate it to their previous experience, their current situation, and their future life.

Assuming you have the preparations in place, how do you proceed? Here are some suggestions:

- Break up the class into smaller groups, especially if your class has little experience with authentic class discussion. In a smaller group the chance that all will function as partners will be greater. Should such groups be homogeneous or heterogeneous? This is a judgment call. Heterogeneous groups invite greater diversity of viewpoints, while homogeneous groups foster more cohesiveness. You need to experiment.

- Arrange the small groups in circles. Participatory discussions do best when the partners are face-to-face.

- Appoint a facilitator. I would avoid a "discussion leader" since leaders tend to produce followers. You want partners, not leaders and followers.

- Spend a good deal of time establishing or reviewing expectations. Kids do not by nature know how to partake in a participatory discussion. They need to be taught. Here the discipleship skills we have referred to earlier play a role once again. Specific expectations might be the following: One person speaks at a time; no put-downs or sarcasm; listen carefully and attentively—ask for clarification to make sure there is understanding; aim to come to consensus; be willing to be convinced; encourage all partners to participate; avoid dominating the discussion; be patient and gentle with each other; always look for the best in what the other person is saying. It helps to demonstrate and illustrate these discipleship skills.

- Make sure the partners see the process as authentically participatory: The discussion aims to expand everyone's knowledge (including that of the teacher). The goal is to teach one another, in all wisdom, and to learn from one another. The activity should enable all of us to grow in our ability to function as knowledgeable and competent disciples of the Lord.

Remember that in participatory discussions, too, you remain the guide. Monitor the discussion and offer encouragement. Also be willing to admonish when the formulations of ideas or insights are not appropriate. Bad language, badmouthing, insulting or suggestive talk, or a mean-spirited tone should not be tolerated.

I have spent considerable time with the practice of authentic discussion. Doing so is necessary before proceeding to the next participatory teaching approach: shared praxis. Shared praxis assumes familiarity with well-conducted participatory discussion models.

Shared praxis

Jennifer is a sixth-grade teacher. Parents, the principal, and her peers regard her as exceptionally creative. One of her strengths is her desire to gain new insights to improve her teaching effectiveness.

Recently Jennifer attended a two-day workshop on shared praxis. Her principal was supportive, even though he was not always so sure about "new-fangled stuff." Jennifer herself did not know exactly what the topic was about, but—always eager to try participatory approaches in her classroom—she decided to go, to see what she could learn. Well, what did she learn?

She learned that "shared praxis" is a teaching approach first described by Paulo Freire, the late Brazilian Catholic educator who became widely known for his work in adult literacy. Influenced by neo-marxism, Freire used the term "shared praxis" to designate the teaching methods he developed.[2] Literally "praxis" refers to the intertwinement of theory and practice. Rather than seeing theory as distinct and to be applied to practice, the two form one indistinguishable, seamless interactive process.

Jennifer also learned that Freire had been extremely critical of direct instruction. Freire called such teaching "banking," that is, the depositing of stuff into an empty vault. Freire opposed such teaching and urged the use of methods that begin with the experience of the students. Intuitively Jennifer felt herself in agreement with this approach. She had always objected to a view of students as empty containers. So she liked the definition of shared praxis she was offered: In its strictest sense, shared praxis describes teacher and students sharing their insights and experience through structured dialogue, thereby building up each other's knowledge and experience, and so coming to the desired learning. "Amen!" said Jennifer. "I think I've been doing this sort of thing all along. But some more specifics might be helpful."

And Jennifer did learn more. She learned that Freire's approach has been extended by others including Thomas Groome.[3] Groome had actually applied this method largely in the context of church education. Yet, as a classroom teacher, Jennifer felt she could use Groome's procedure. Groome suggested that our lessons consist of five "movements," beginning with a conversation about the students' experience with the topic to ways of integrating what they learn about it into their future lives. At the workshop, Jennifer received a handout summarizing these five "movements":

1. The students (along with the teacher) are invited to describe some personal view or experience directly related to the topic to be addressed.
2. They are invited to reflect on what they believe about the topic, and what the likely or intended consequences of their views or experiences might be.
3. The teacher presents whatever basic information concerning the topic the group needs.
4. The students are invited to appropriate this information into their lives in a dialectic cross-examination with their own experiences.
5. There is opportunity to choose a personal response for the future.

On the second day of the workshop, Jennifer was paired with another teacher and instructed to create a unit plan based on this handout. Since the schools in which they were teaching were not all that far from the California coast, they decided that a unit on the ocean as a distinct biotope would provide an opportunity to practice shared praxis Groome-style. Using Groome's five steps, they constructed the following general lesson plans:

1. Ask students to share their experiences of the beaches and in the ocean.
2. Have the students discuss how their experience of the California coast has affected (or might continue to affect) their lives.
3. Present basic information about the ocean (use a textbook along with several videos available from various educational agencies).
4. Create some discussion sessions in which this new information enlarges, diminishes, supports, or contradicts what they articulated in step 2.
5. Ask the students to write a journal entry in which they indicate what they will now do about the beach and the ocean as a result of what they learned in this unit (for example, protect the whales, clean up the beaches, support bird sanctuaries, and so on).

Specific steps—a proposed model:

Groome's "movements" lay a solid basis for a classroom shared praxis approach. In working with teachers and experimenting with this strategy, I have come to believe that we should adapt and expand Groome's proposal as a *six-step* shared praxis model, as follows:[4]

1. First, invite the students to articulate their experiences with the topic at hand. Ask them to place these experiences "on the table," so to speak. Open the discussion by posing carefully crafted questions. Ask them to freewrite in response. This first step ensures that your lesson will be rooted in the experience of the students. Shared praxis ceases to be shared praxis if you toss curriculum at the kids without first inviting them to articulate their experiences with the topic of the lesson.
2. Encourage your students to question one another. The intent is to

probe their understanding, and in so doing enlarge the concepts they are working with. This sort of activity can easily be combined with cooperative learning strategies. It is best to seat the students in small groups, in circles, and have them systematically share their experiences and knowledge. This step provides opportunity for mutual, shared dialogue, for authentically participatory discussion.

3. Only at this point is it appropriate to provide additional input. You can deliver such input via a lecture, a video, reading assignments, or research projects. Take care that the additional input is directly linked to the experiences presented and discussed in steps one and two. Note that this step eliminates the criticism that a shared praxis lesson degenerates to nothing but an exercise in "pooling ignorance."

4. Now you must ask your students to demonstrate (or practice) the new understanding of the concepts they learned. They could do so by explaining, describing, comparing, paraphrasing, redefining, and the like.

5. To make sure that you retain collaboration and build community, step five consists of "mutual checking." The students check each other, question each other, teach or reteach each other, and encourage each other as they probe each other's new understanding. The objective is to make sure that everyone in the group has understood the new concepts or has learned the new skill. Shared praxis is clearly an enemy of individualism.

6. Finally, and probably most importantly, direct your students to consider how the newly-learned material can be channeled back into their lives. What difference in their lives will the new learning make? How will the new learning equip them to carry out their task more effectively and Christianly? What specific redemptive action steps can they design? Are they willing to commit themselves to implementing, in a healing way, as agents of reconciliation,[5] the material they have learned?

Some examples

To make these steps more concrete, I offer two illustrations. The first is an example applicable to middle or high school. Suppose I want to teach a unit on the nature and task of government. The first step, that of articulating some relevant experience, could begin with questions such as the following: What is our government? When do you see it in action? What have you experienced as a direct result of government? Have you, for example, ever received a speeding ticket, or seen immigrants going through admission procedures, or observed your parents at income tax time, or witnessed some military exercises? Perhaps your local government has established zoning laws or issued curfew laws? Or you may have opinions about parking meters, "no loitering" signs, political TV commercials, and local school bond issues. What do you think is good or bad about our government?

The second step encourages reflection and discussion about these personal views and experiences: Why do you think this or that is good or bad about the government? What was your response to what you experienced as a result of government action? How did you feel about the speeding ticket you received?

In step three I would present basic information about the government and confront the present feelings, views, and experiences of the students. I could, for example, give a brief presentation outlining the tasks and duties and limitations of our system of government, provide some biblical givens and background, show a film, bring in a guest speaker such as a city council member, or assign a chapter in a textbook.

The fourth step asks the students to compare this new information with their own experiences and to express their reactions to it. Would they now view their experiences described earlier in a different light? What do they now see that they had not noticed before? This step should naturally lead to the next one: the students ask each other questions about what they have just presented. The goal should be to teach the students to take responsibility for each other's learning: they should make every effort to make sure that the new learning is clear and appropriated by all the participants.

The sixth and final step urges the students to evaluate their own lives and futures in view of what has transpired in the first five steps. What will their stance be towards the government? How do they intend to participate in citizenship in this town or in this country? What can they do to promote a healthy patriotism? What contributions can they make to the political climate in their town and county? And so on.

A second, rather down-home example shows how the shared praxis approach might work in an early elementary mathematics lesson, in a school in a rural farming community such as we find in Iowa. Suppose the topic is simple addition and subtraction. The steps might go somewhat as follows:

1. Invite the students to share their experience with counting: Are there cows on your farm? How many are in the corral? Can you count them one by one? Does your dad count them every day?

2. Encourage reflection about personal experience: What happens to your counting when a cow has a calf? Or when some cows die? Or when your dad buys or sells some cows?

3. Provide input by presenting the basic addition or subtraction algorithms to be learned.

4. Students now practice the algorithms by relating them directly to the cows on the farm. For example, 3 cows + 7 cows = 10 cows. How many cows will your dad have when he sells three of them? The children would do a number of counting exercises to ensure mastery.

5. The students ask each other to demonstrate their counting abilities. They might make up some review sheet questions. Some cooperative jigsaw strategies (to be considered in the next chapter) might work well here.

6. Students transfer the algorithms from their immediate experience with cows and link them to other areas of life, and finally come to master more abstract computation applicable to their future lives.

Is shared praxis practical?

Shared praxis at first glance looks cumbersome and might even remind you of the old and by now stale "relevance movement." Indeed, the approach would become insufferably cumbersome if I were to suggest that every single lesson would need to be cast into an iron grid of six steps. But this work is not necessary. Once you understand the six steps you can use them in a simplified form. The summary structure of shared praxis, in fact, is simple. It does what all good teachers know they should do: tie the lesson material to the students' experience, both at the beginning and end of the lesson. In some ways programs such as math-their-way and the whole language approach seek to do just that. Not only do we need to tie our lessons to the students' experience, we need to *keep* them tied to the students' experience, and encourage the students to integrate the material into their lives. Thus shared praxis makes use of some of the latest learning theories, especially those promoted by constructivism. Shared praxis assumes that students learn best if they graft the new learning into their previous understandings and experiences, and are encouraged to work out the implications of the learning for their own lives.[6]

Clearly, shared praxis lessons require time. For this reason they may be difficult to implement in a school that prizes efficiency and on-task behavior. In such situations I advise teachers to select only some of the most important components of the prescribed curriculum and transform them into shared praxis lessons.

Shared praxis: its Christian character

The shared praxis approach is eminently suitable to the Christian collaborative classroom. Like the first step, it takes the lives and experience of the students seriously and invites thorough participation. It allows the students to express and share their knowledge, feelings, beliefs, and commitments. The dynamic interaction between teacher, students, and the material to be learned inevitably involves an equally dynamic relationship between student and student. In shared praxis sessions there is a subtle transition from "*my* experience" to "*our* experience," from "*my* past and *my* future" to "*our* past and *our* future."

The lives of the students and teacher become closely intertwined. Shared praxis is just that: theory and practice inseparably connected and *shared* with one another.

Shared praxis is not yet a commonly used teaching strategy. General class discussion sessions come closest. Shared praxis goes beyond discussion to achieve full student participation.

Shared praxis goes hand-in-glove with cooperative learning strategies. To see this connection more clearly, we turn our attention in the next chapter to a much discussed phenomenon: the spectacular rise of interest in cooperative learning.

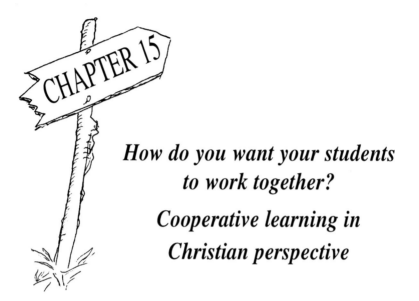

CHAPTER 15

*How do you want your students
to work together?*

*Cooperative learning in
Christian perspective*

Jim: I can't believe it! And I thought this was a Christian school with Christian parents! I just don't believe it!

Lisa: Wow—are you upset! What happened, Jim?

Jim: I sent a letter home with the kids yesterday, announcing that we were going to do some cooperative learning in my class. I explained that the kids would work in groups and that they'd help each other learn. Well, this morning Tim handed me a note from his mother. She made it quite clear that she strongly objects to "this cooperative learning fad." Her Timmy, she says, is in school to learn so he can make it in the world! "I don't want my son," she wrote, "wasting his valuable time helping other kids!"

Lisa: I don't believe it.

Jim's decision

Jim is convinced that fostering a collaborative classroom is the Christian way to go. Of course, as a middle school teacher, he knows that this conviction, like an ambitious New Year's resolution, is more easily put into words than into practice. Cooperative learning, he believes, can help him do so. Jim has heard about it and read about it, even attended—with the principal's blessing—several workshops. He has come to see that what he used to do—simply telling the kids to pair up or "get into groups"—will not do. Such instructions merely create an illusion of collaboration; in reality they permit some of the students to get by with doing nothing, or, conversely, encourage some to take over the show and turn the group work into a spectator sport for the others. Jim has decided to avoid such ineffectiveness and try a more structured approach.

What is cooperative learning?

Let's follow Jim into his classroom to observe how he implements the seven essential principles of authentic cooperative learning. Jim knows that each one of them is critically important to the success of cooperative learning. Ignoring even one principle may well have him end up saying: "Cooperative learning? A great idea, but it doesn't work for me!"[1]

Let's find a seat in the back corner of Jim's seventh-grade language arts class and watch the proceedings. Jim is particularly interested in cultivating both critical thinking and creativity in this classroom. So he wants to assign an essay in which his seventh graders argue for or against an issue current in his school: Should the students be required to wear uniforms? Jim wants to use a cooperative learning strategy to achieve his goals. How does he go about it?

1. Setting the tone

Before actually implementing the cooperative learning lesson, Jim takes considerable class time to discuss with his students the expectations for group behavior. "What can we do," he asks, "to make sure that we will work well together?" Jim and his students brainstorm, list, and describe several specific discipleship skills such as encouraging, listening, deferring to others when appropriate, and the like.

> encouraging
> listening   helping
> respect   be gentle

Jim asks the students how such skills might be expressed in the classroom. He suggests they create some scenarios. Brianna, Gerrit, and Jessica propose a way to encourage each other. They suggest a skit in which they express specific, encouraging remarks, such as "I like this metaphor you used here!"

While some of this activity may at first appear artificial and has some students looking askance, Jim is undaunted and persists. He inquires about their previous experience with cooperative learning. "Tell me," he asks, "what sorts of group activities have you done in your classes so far?" The students volunteer a variety of answers. Brianna says: "In sixth grade we did a lot of group work, but I hated it because I always ended up having to do all the work!" After some discussion Jim senses that their experience with cooperative learning is rather limited, so he decides to spend even more time working on the expectations.[2]

What do you think? Is Jim wasting a lot of time that should be spent on covering the curriculum? Perish the suggestion! Don't underestimate the importance of what Jim is doing here! Jim is working on establishing a collaborative classroom. Too often teachers assume that by nature students know how to work together. Not so. Jim has done the right thing by not plunging into cooperative learning activities on the first day of the term. On the contrary, he deliberately waited several weeks until he had enough time to lay out the expectations and to get to know the students well enough to group them effectively. Indeed, by doing this preliminary work, he set the tone of the class for the entire year.

2. Forming groups

Let's watch what Jim does after all the tone-setting activity. He quickly and efficiently arranges his students into preassigned groups. As much as possible, each group is composed of a mixture of male and female students and low and high achievers. Jim tells the students that once in groups, they will remain in their groups for quite some time, to allow them to become tuned in to each other and learn to work together.

But wait a minute. Why preassigned? In a truly collaborative classroom shouldn't the students have a say in how the groups are formed? Yes, you are right. And eventually Jim will no doubt encourage the students to choose. He recalls, however, that in the early stages of cooperative learning activity the preferable route is to assign students to groups rather than permit them to select their own. Allowing the students to choose, at the outset, their own partners may actually interfere with the establishment of a collaborative classroom.[3]

Jim makes sure that his groups are arranged properly. He insists that the students face each other, in a cross arrangement, like so:

He does not allow students to slouch or to tune out. Note how he has located the groups: he can walk a complete circle around each one. He has kept groups away from walls (to discourage leaning back and tuning out). He is quietly thankful for the tables the school board purchased for his classroom. Jim successfully persuaded the board members that the old rickety desks with downward-sloping tops he used to have in his classroom could better be donated to the local Heritage Village schoolhouse.

Jim gives each group a Roman numeral (I, II, etc.) and assigns a letter (A, B, C, D) to each group member. He encourages each group to select a team name.

3. Assigning roles

What roles should Jim assign to the group members? Well, that depends on the group task to be performed. In this first cooperative learning session Jim wants his students to help establish the criteria for a good persuasive essay. Clearly this task will require a recorder and a reporter. A group manager will also be useful—someone who will have the special duty of making sure that every group member contributes to the group task.

Jim wisely picks students who will be able to model the roles. For recorders, he selects students who write clearly; he chooses reporters who speak clearly. The managers will be kids who have demonstrated a measure of confidence. After this initial session, Jim plans to rotate assignments within groups, so that eventually each student has an opportunity to learn each role.

Jim has already devoted considerable thought to other roles he may wish to assign over the following weeks. He plans to avoid appointing a "leader." That move, he knows, would encourage a one-man show. Roles he *is* considering are observer, encourager, morale sergeant, noise monitor, prober, summarizer, checker, researcher, runner, praiser, proofreader, and materials handler. Whatever task Jim may assign, he will take time to explain clearly how the roles are to be performed.

4. Explaining the task and structuring interdependence

Now that he has his groups in place, Jim explains the assignment. "Listen carefully," he says. "I will explain your task only once. If you have questions, check first with your group." We recognize at once the reasons for these instructions: he wants to help the students to develop their listening skills and to learn to depend on each other rather than just on their teacher.

Cooperative learning requires what the literature calls "positive interdependence." Every member of the group must contribute. No single group member should be able to do the work alone while the others idly sit by. Let's observe how Jim puts this important principle into practice in his creative writing class.

First he asks every group member to quietly, independently list some of the criteria for evaluating a good persuasive essay. What aspects of writing should we remember as we write an argument for or against mandatory school uniforms? Jim expects some of the following issues to emerge: giving a clear opinion, having good reasons, distinguishing between right and wrong, and using paragraphs with topic sentences.

Next, the group recorder tabulates the results, first as a rough draft, then on a transparency. Brianna suggests that we will need very good reasons for requiring uniforms. Kimberly urges her peers to include topic sentences. Jim quietly reminds the managers to make sure that each group member contributes to this final list. To ensure individual accountability, Jim requests that every group member submits his or her individual list to him at the end of the hour.

5. Closely monitoring the group work

Jim resists the temptation to sit at his desk to correct papers or to head for the staff room to grab a cup of coffee. Instead, he moves around the groups, occasionally reminding students of their role assignments. With a clipboard to keep notes, he observes the students carefully and keeps track of individual students' participation. He encourages them to solve their own problems. He does not intervene too quickly. If there is a disagreement, he first asks the group members how they intend to solve it.

6. Closure

Jim brings the activity to closure by inviting the reporters to come to the overhead projector and share the group results with the whole class. He asks the groups to make sure to add to their own lists any new idea they see. This activity leads to a class consensus about the essential criteria to be used for evaluation of the persuasive essays the students will write. Jim has now set the stage for subsequent writing of paragraphs and essays and for group peer checking. For these activities, to be conducted over the next few days, Jim plans to assign roles of "author," "friendly critic," "reviewer," and "prober."

7. Processing

We might expect Jim to end the lesson at this point, or move on to the next stage of writing an individual essay. Instead, watch what he does now. "Okay, class," he says, "let's stop for a moment and ask ourselves:

How well did we work together?" He distributes a brief questionnaire. The students respond to two questions: (1) What discipleship skills did our group practice? (2) Which ones should we work on next time? This debriefing, reflecting activity—referred to in the literature as "processing"—neatly ties the students' work into the expectations set earlier. Since this is the first cooperative learning session in his class, Jim has the students simply fill out an individual processing sheet. He wants his students to become familiar and comfortable with the processing phase. Eventually he expects his students to be able to discuss their group work freely and without inhibitions. Processing, he knows, is a skill that needs to be learned. Its effectiveness increases as group members begin to establish trust relationships.

Cooperative learning: its Christian character

Class is over, and we walk back with Jim to the staff room. "We enjoyed watching you teach, Jim! But tell us," we ask, "what really is so Christian about this cooperative learning stuff? Aren't you simply using a secular teaching technique? What's so Christian about forming heterogeneous groups, making role assignments, and attempting positive interdependence?"

While Jim may not always be able to articulate a response clearly, his basic approach is unmistakable. Cooperative learning strategies, he thinks, reflect some of the Lord's intentions for educational practice. Cooperative learning, even when secularly distorted, is an example of educators encountering God's will.[4] Don't the Scriptures make it unmistakably clear that human beings are to constitute a community of image bearers, engaged in service of the Lord, of each other, and of the entirety of God's wonderful garden? Aren't selfishness and disregard for one another and for God's will the primary results of the fall into sin? Cooperation, then, is clearly akin to redemptive, healing, and peace-making activity. Cooperative learning, when carefully crafted in a collaborative classroom context, can help shape your class as an expression of the Body of Christ. It provides your class with opportunities for training in specific servanthood skills (such as respect, listening, sharing, encouraging, exercising patience—in general, the fruit of the Spirit). It creates an environment favorable to the practice of knowledgeable and competent discipleship.

A few other examples

One Bible teacher I know wants his students to memorize the seven last sayings of Jesus when he hung on the cross. To accomplish this task the cooperative learning way, he gives one of the four group members the relevant text from Matthew, another from Mark, a third from Luke, and the fourth from John. Together they have to construct a list of the seven sayings.

A math teacher frequently assigns a set of calculations to each one of the group members, then has them total up their scores to come to a specific number. Kindergarten or first-grade teachers structure activities in which every group member plays a role: one has the scissors, another the crayons, another the construction paper, and together they create a collage.

Cooperative learning, indeed, is appropriate across the curriculum at any grade level.

Group "tests" and mutual checking

From time to time you want to hold your students individually accountable for mastery of material. I am thinking, for example, of work in math (multiplication tables, solving basic equations, measuring and estimating); language arts (spelling, reading and writing skills); foreign languages; social studies (basic facts, reasons for events, learning of capitals); science (basic physical/biological taxonomies). Perhaps you have them practice with worksheets and you assess their mastery by administering a test of some sort.

Before you succumb to assigning individual seat work, work-sheets, or tests, consider the opportunities built into cooperative learning strategies. Rather than individual review leading to individual testing, try a group test. Allow the students to work together. Encourage them to help each other. You may have to explain that a "group test" does not mean cheating. In any case, such an activity usually reveals that some students know the material you want them to learn, and some don't: a splendid opportunity for the students to help each other achieve mastery. Encourage them to take responsibility for each other's learning. Once every group is satisfied that all members have mastery, you may wish to go to an individual check or test.

Objections

The parent's position in the opening scenario above is not a fabrication. Some time ago one of the B. J. Haan Education conferences, held annually at Dordt College, dealt with the topic of cooperative learning. At one of the public evening sessions a big crowd of parents and teachers attended an open forum on the pros and cons of cooperative learning as a teaching strategy in Christian school classrooms. I must say, the vast majority of the audience that evening appeared supportive of our claim that cooperative learning is eminently compatible with teaching Christianly. One woman, however, stood up and declared with impressive finality that she would not allow her Timmy to "waste time helping others."

I must confess that I was slightly flabbergasted, if not discombobbled, by the remark. How can someone who claims to be a Christian object to helping others? I suspect that the lady believed in the old saying that God helps those who help themselves. Or perhaps she envisioned Timmy as the future president of the United States, so he should be trained early in the harsh realities of political, self-enhancing competition.

An extreme exception, you say? Not so. In Christian circles objections to cooperative learning are frequently voiced. I have personally heard the following reasons asserted as sufficient grounds for banishing cooperative learning from Christian schools forever. Presumably, cooperative learning is

- just another secular, progressivist fad, destined for the educational trash heap.
- nothing but a pooling of ignorance and therefore a gross waste of time.
- inspired by New Age thinking and other weird Eastern philosophies.
- a form of crass, manipulative behaviorism.
- a practice that will inevitably lead our children down the slippery slope of relativism—kids sitting around the table deciding for themselves what is true and what is false.

What shall we say about these charges? No doubt a number of them can be dismissed without much debate. Calling cooperative learning a New Age philosophy, for example, looks like a guilt-by-association maneuver, commonly used by those who seek to oppose or block a new idea. Linking cooperative learning with New Age thinking pretty well eliminates, right there and then, any possibility of a fruitful discussion.

Two of the objections raised, however, deserve attention: cooperative learning is merely a fad, and it promotes relativism.

A fad

If cooperative learning were to turn out to be a fad, it would probably be due not to the nature of cooperative learning as such, but to an unexamined, often unhealthy "we've-always-done-it-this-way" traditionalism that continues to control too much of Christian education. Fads, moreover, are closely associated with unrealistic expectations. As soon as we hear the cry "Here is the solution to all your classroom problems," we can be sure we are encountering a fad. Whenever I hear fans tout cooperative learning as a panacea, I envision a quick demise of this otherwise promising teaching approach.[5]

Even if cooperative learning were to be a fad, that would not necessarily make it a bad strategy. I suspect that many valuable practices—such as education for women, educational psychology, and integrated curriculum—were considered fads when they were first introduced.

One key problem with calling cooperative learning a fad is that it offers an excuse for educators not to try it. If cooperative learning is here today and gone tomorrow, why should anyone want to invest time and energy working with it? As a result, some teachers—especially those whose comfort zone falls entirely within the range of direct instruction—decide that it isn't worth the effort. Those who have tried it, but ran into difficulties, are also served by the handy "fad" excuse. They say, "Well, I gave it the old college try! I did some cooperative learning in my class, and wouldn't you know? It bombed. It just doesn't work for me. Oh well, it's just a fad anyway, so I won't try to figure out what went wrong. I'll just go back to what I know works for me." In short, the cooperative learning=fad argument shuts down the expansion of a teacher's repertoire of strategies.

Relativism

Does cooperative learning promote relativism? Does it encourage students to set aside right and wrong, and to generate their own opinions and their own conclusions? Does it foster a let's-reach-consensus-at-all-costs mentality at the expense of truth?

Some time ago I was asked to debate this very question with the staff of a Christian school in Canada. There was a sticky problem in this school: about half of the staff held to the opinion that cooperative learning was but a version of a pernicious relativism, while the other half voiced support of the method. The principal waffled. While I was unable to resolve the dispute, one thing became clear: those who equate cooperative learning with relativism are working with a caricature. They generalize that all cooperative learning is a close cousin of values clarification or some other type of humanistic approach, in which every student could well end up with nothing but a personal opinion. Add to this the fact that we live in a postmodern culture where anyone's viewpoint is as valid as that of anyone else, and you can see there is reason for concern.

True, cooperative learning can indeed foster unbridled relativism. But before you now decide that cooperative learning is out, think again. The potential of an unwanted result does not by itself disqualify a given practice. Does the possibility of a head-on collision stop you from driving your car? It is said that most people die in bed: so now you'll do all your sleeping in a chair? Besides, remember that not only cooperative learning can lead to relativism. Virtually all teaching strategies can bring about similar results. Even an exclusive reliance on direct teaching cannot prevent students from getting the wrong message.

In a genuinely Christian classroom, cooperative learning does not lead to relativism. For one thing, as we saw, the teacher remains the guide. Though the journey through the curricular terrain may skirt relativism, it never ends up there. The road is always to Christian discipleship.

Other cooperative learning strategies

The Jigsaw Strategy (for "higher-level thinking")

Some years ago, I worked a semester with Doyle Smiens, formerly an English teacher at Unity Christian High School in Orange City, Iowa. We experimented with a variety of cooperative learning strategies. One of these was the jigsaw, a very powerful strategy that allows the students to become deeply involved in considering and understanding complicated issues.

Take a look at how we worked a simple jigsaw pattern in Doyle's 11th-grade American literature class. One poet we wanted the students to study was Emily Dickinson. Among the objectives we had listed the following: the students will understand and be able to articulate clearly Emily Dickinson's concept of God. A jigsaw strategy helped us meet this objective.

First, we considered the poems that address the issue: Who is God? Dickinson gives clues. We selected four different poems, and identified them as A, B, C, and D. We arranged our students in "home groups" of four. Then we distributed the poems in each home group: student A received the A poem, student B the B poem, and so on. Each home group had four different poems to work on.

Then we rearranged our students as "expert groups": all the A's got together to work on the A poem, the B's on the B poem, and so on. In the expert group the task was to determine what the particular poem says about God. Each "expert" had to return to the home group, ready to share the result of the expert group's discussion, and ready to work on integrating the result with the conclusions the other experts would bring to the home group.

After the expert groups had sufficient time to work on their assigned poems, we reconstituted the home groups. Each home group now had four "experts." We suggested a procedure for the reconstituted groups: Student A reads the A poem and explains what it says about God. Then student B, and so on. In their home groups the students as a group tabulated a list of characteristics of God as portrayed in the four poems.

The recorders wrote the conclusions on a transparency. Reporters shared the transparency with the whole class.

You can see the power of this procedure: students work through their assigned poems twice. The jigsaw strategy produces deep levels of understanding not readily achievable through direct teaching or individual research. Once you try it, you will quickly discover that the group results will invariably be superior in quality to what any single student could achieve.

The jigsaw is particularly useful for reviewing material: Divide the material into four parts, assign each part to "experts," have the experts formulate review questions and ask them to check their teammates' knowledge. Using the jigsaw in this way reveals its participatory character.

Conflict resolution strategies

The New Testament stresses the unity of the Body of Christ. It calls us to be "of the same mind" and instructs us to live harmoniously with one another.[6] Does this injunction mean that there cannot be disagreement among us? Of course not. Given the uniqueness of each one of us, it hardly seems possible that we could blend into an identical, uniform mass of humanity.

There is a difference, however, between disagreement and conflict. Conflict describes situations where two or more people not only disagree, but where such disagreement leads to hostility and anger. To avoid such anger and hostility, we need to teach one another to disagree appropriately, in such a way that the unity of the Body of Christ is not impaired. How can Christians learn to disagree agreeably, each seeking the welfare of the other and building up the entire Body?

This question is what conflict resolution is all about. Conflict resolution has been a neglected topic among us. As a result, we see conflict everywhere. Recently I wrote a report of observations and recommendations for several Christian school systems I visited in Australia. I prefaced my remarks by sharing a deep pain: wherever I go in the world of Christian education (whether in Australia, the United States, Canada, Europe, or wherever), I find unresolved conflict. I see boards pitted against principals, parents against teachers, teachers against each other, and, worst of all, much conflict among children. We spend a good deal of time telling the kids to get along together; we rarely—or only superficially—provide them with the tools to do so.

I believe we do well to correct this traditional neglect. At least two questions need to be addressed: First, how can we introduce conflict resolution as a meaningful component in a K-12 curriculum? While we teach mathematics and language arts from K-12, we seldom address conflict resolution skills in a sustained way. But isn't conflict resolution an even more important skill than solving equations or figuring out square roots? Secondly, conflict resolution must become an integral dimension of our teaching practice. We must develop teaching strategies that promote the ability of the students to resolve conflicts. Reliance on direct instruction can hardly do such a task. Participatory modes of teaching and learning are much more productive. I have come to believe that certain types of cooperative learning strategies can do much to enable our children to resolve conflicts.

To teach conflict resolution skills requires

- the context of a collaborative, rather than a competitive classroom: competition tends to lead to conflict.
- discussion skills: authentically participatory discussion does much to help kids learn to resolve conflict.
- expectations: once again, it is critically important that we review and practice discipleship skills. Simply talking (or preaching) about them is not enough, any more than you can teach a child to speak a foreign language without giving him opportunity to practice it.

It is with some regret that I cannot point to effective conflict resolution models developed within the Christian educational community. Rather, we must look to the larger educational arena. In response to the growing threat of violence and an apparently accelerating moral decline in the Western world, much interest has developed in peace education and character education. David and Roger Johnson have devoted much time and energy developing conflict resolution models to be used in schools.[7] One of these goes as follows:

1. Select a controversial topic to be debated.
2. Arrange students in groups of four.
3. Divide each group into two pairs.
4. Each pair prepares a set of arguments to support one side.
5. The groups debate.
6. The pairs reverse positions, each pair now arguing for the position it just finished attacking.
7. The group comes to consensus.

Much work on this important topic awaits the Christian educational community.[8]

Some concluding cautions

As we saw, there is a risk that cooperative learning turns into a fad. This risk is enhanced by claims that cooperative learning is the solution to all our classroom problems. So we need to take a realistic attitude towards implementing this potentially rich strategy. Some warnings:

- Avoid the "panacea (i.e., this is the final solution!) mentality."
- Start small.
- Plan carefully (in detail).
- Do not use cooperative learning strategies for more than 60% of total class time.
- Communicate with principal and parents (some parents have very strange—and sometimes silly—notions about cooperative learning!)
- Seek a support group among your fellow teachers.
- And, as always, seek to establish a larger context of the collaborative classroom. Cooperative learning does not work when it is introduced as a half-hour diversion in an individualistic or competitive classroom![9]

Is cooperative learning a method for you? Of course it is! Go to it!

CHAPTER 16

How can I teach all my students when they are so different?

Celebrating individual gifts and meeting individual needs

Randy: You know, Lisa, I don't think I've ever met a teacher who believes that there are kids who have no gifts whatsoever. Have you?

Lisa: No, I don't think so. I *do* know some teachers who treat some kids that way—as if they're zombies or dunderheads, or whatever word you want to use.

Randy: To be honest, Lisa, for a while I almost thought that Bryan—you know, the new kid—had no gifts: he can't draw a decent picture, can't carry a tune, has trouble with the academic stuff, and often—I hate to put it this way—doesn't seem to be "all there." But now, thank God, I have discovered his gift!

Lisa: You have? Tell me about it!

Randy: Well, somehow the conversation turned to horses. All of a sudden, Bryan came alive! Horses? This kid knows everything there is to know about horses: how many kinds there are, how to tell them apart, how to raise them, how to train them, you name it, he knows it! I was aware that he came from a farm, but I didn't realize his dad was in the horse-breeding business. The kids were surprised, too. Now that they know about Bryan's expertise, they all look differently—more admiringly?—at him. Just wish I had known about this sooner.

Lisa: I guess looking for hidden talents is never a waste of time!

Can we overstress community?

In one of my workshops on the collaborative classroom, a teacher raised an interesting and important point. He put it somewhat like this: "While I appreciate all the stress you're putting on cultivating a collaborative community, sir, your talk also troubles me. You see, my problem is not so much how to establish community. It's just the reverse. My problem is every single individual kid. I just don't see how all this talk about community is going to help me meet the specific needs of every student in my classroom. In fact, sir—and let me put it to you gently—I think that your emphasis will make it even more difficult for us teachers to meet these needs. In the kind of classroom you advocate, isn't every unique kid simply going to blend into a communal whole? How come I haven't heard you say much about individualizing instruction, of working with one kid at a time, of making sure that no single child falls through the cracks?"

The question triggered some sober reflection. Yes, I concluded, my heavy emphasis on collaboration and community could easily cloud the role and significance of the individual student. So I asked myself: Have I said too little about the nature and meaning of individualized instruction and personalized learning?[1] Have I unwittingly fostered an imbalance— perhaps even a tension—between community and the individual person? Indeed, have my missiles aimed at individualism bombed out individuality as well?

If I have left this impression, I stand to be corrected. Let me put it plainly: Individualized instruction and personalized learning are absolutely indispensable in my classroom and in yours. After all, as Christian teachers we are to express deep concern and uninterrupted care for each one of our students. Since each one of our students is unique and differently gifted, it is our Christian obligation to provide classroom conditions in which each child can flourish as an individual.

So we face a problem: Since individualized instruction encourages students to work in relative independence and stresses a measure of "self-sufficiency," how can such instruction and personalized learning fit into a collaborative, service-oriented classroom? How can we construct a classroom environment in which communal and individual concerns are not in tension with each other? Let's explore this question.

Complications: "the kids in the middle" and egalitarianism

Tension between community and individuality is aggravated by several factors. In the first place, we teachers tend to see our classes as composed of three groups: the high achievers, the low achievers, and the "kids in the middle."[2] As you know, the individuality of both the high achievers and the low achievers is commonly recognized. High and low achieving students are recipients of special, often individualized attention. High achievers frequently have opportunity to participate in accelerated or enrichment programs. Similarly, low achievers benefit from remedial programs, special education teachers, and classroom aides.

The kids in the middle are regularly regarded as a homogeneous group of "average students." Of course, teachers really know that this perception is not true; yet, in practice the kids in the middle represent a group of students whose special gifts are not always celebrated and whose special needs are not always met. They move from grade to grade without much special attention. They don't stand out. Only when they either rise above this medial group or fall significantly below it do they become special, individual cases (or special problems!).

What happens to these "kids in the middle"? Here a second factor comes into play, namely, the spirit of egalitarianism. Egalitarianism encourages teachers to see students, especially the "kids in the middle," as basically alike with respect to ability, potential for achievement, and learning style. Again, teachers know in their hearts that this assumption is not so. Even though in their hearts teachers know the falsehood of egalitarianism, 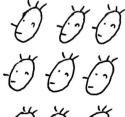 circumstances and classroom situations often force teachers to adopt an egalitarian stance. Egalitarianism, furthermore, leads teachers to assess students on the same basis. As a result, the kids in the middle are likely to range between B- and D+ on the grading scale. They will come out "average." The term "average" is fundamental to egalitarian philosophy.

You might think that egalitarianism contributes to community. After all, in some ways you can argue that in community we are all the same. However, there is a sharp difference between community and conformity. In contrast to community, conformity suggests compliance and agreement with a standard stereotype, regardless of individual variation. Conformity requires the abandonment of uniqueness and diversity, and ultimately acquires a totalitarian character. Conformity homogenizes differences and blurs uniqueness. Egalitarianism leads to this kind of conformity and uniformity, not to true community in which various diverse parts harmoniously function as a whole.

You can observe egalitarianism at work in the ways in which teachers frequently speak to the students. For example, teachers often address the students as "Class!" But "class" is a collective term which does not allow for individuality. When individual students are homogenized into a "class," they lose their distinctiveness and blend into an undifferentiated whole. "Class" does not really suggest community either, for true community always acknowledges the value of the individual. Addressing the students as, for example, "third-graders" is an improvement, for at least it recognizes that each student is a distinct member of the group. Even better is to have the children choose their own class name to create communal identity. In a school in Australia, I once worked with a teacher named Janet Berry. The class she taught called themselves the "wild berries," every one a "wild berry" indeed!

Egalitarianism is powerfully reinforced by the overuse of mass (or whole-class) instruction. While obviously there is a place for whole-class instruction, a heavy dependency on this method prevents teachers from meeting the needs of many of their individual students. When more than 60% of class time is devoted to whole-class (often direct) instruction, the process that marginalizes students inevitably sets in.

Summary

Let's summarize: The Scriptures call us to be one body made of many different parts.[3] There is no reason to believe that the Body of Christ refers to church congregations only. Our classrooms, too, should be communities in which the individual students are recognized and honored. Distortions, however, are created by two paradoxical forces:

On the one hand individualism destroys genuine community, and on the other hand egalitarianism destroys individuality. The following diagram depicts this situation. Note that the straight lines suggest proper relationships, while the wavy lines symbolize destructive attacks:

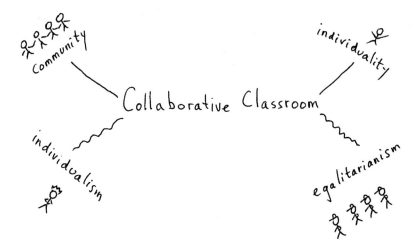

What can you do to counteract the destructive effects of individualism and egalitarianism? How can you do justice to both community and meeting the needs of every one of your students? I suggest you consider structuring a "multifunctional classroom" as one avenue towards a solution.[4]

Implementing the multifunctional classroom

A multifunctional classroom is *not* something different from the Christian collaborative classroom described in earlier chapters. Perhaps you can best understand a multifunctional classroom as an *elaboration* of a collaborative classroom. It is a collaborative classroom that aims to specifically address both communal and individual concerns. As the term suggests, a multifunctional classroom is a place where many things are going on simultaneously, as the teacher seeks to establish community without doing injustice to the individuality of the students.

What key characteristics are integral to a multifunctional classroom? Here are the features needing attention:

- the recognition of the individual needs of all students (not just of low achievers, those with learning disabilities, or those with behavior disorders) in your class.
- the recognition of the gifts of all students (not just of the high achievers) in your class.
- the recognition of individual learning styles. Learning styles should be seen as gifts. Thus you could subsume this point under the previous point. I do single out this category because learning styles are currently widely discussed in educational literature, and because learning styles are directly and immediately related to and affected by classroom teaching styles.
- a diversity of concurrent tasks. Implementing this principle will be helpful in breaking the grip of egalitarianism. And in any case, recognition of the uniqueness of every student should make continuous whole-class teaching a highly problematic practice.
- a diversity of opportunity to learn by creating classroom conditions that allow every student, given his or her gifts and needs, to succeed in becoming the kind of knowledgeable and competent disciple he or she was meant to be.
- student ownership of their learning. A multifunctional classroom will be a highly participatory classroom, and encourage students to take responsibility for and ownership of their diverse learning.
- pursuit of the overarching goal of enabling for discipleship. Though listed last, this characteristic is, of course, the first and ultimate purpose of all Christian educational effort.

A multifunctional classroom, then, contrasts not only with traditional whole-class instructional settings in which learning is largely controlled by the teacher, but also differs from classrooms heavily skewed towards cooperative learning and grouping techniques.

Underlying philosophy

I make it a practice to invite teachers to work with me, to help me test the practicality of my proposals. Some time ago I arranged with a teacher in a certain Christian school to try out various steps in the multifunctional classroom. The teacher in question was enthusiastic and eager to get started. As always, we needed the approval and support of the principal. Here we ran into an unexpected snag: the principal declared that while the multifunctional classroom idea may be a fine theory, it is not grounded in biblical principles.

This surprising turn of events prompts me to affirm that we can never take a grasp of biblical principles for granted, especially not in education. Let's assume that at this point you are asking the same question: What makes the multifunctional classroom a biblical pursuit?

Probably the most fundamental principle at stake is a *biblical view* of the child. Each child is a unique image bearer of God, endowed with unique gifts and personality characteristics, as well as unique learning needs. Surely our classrooms should be places where each one of God's children can flourish. The goals and objectives listed in the lesson plans of a multifunctional classroom teacher will consider the growth of each individual student, not just of "the class."

Further, the multifunctional classroom recognizes and addresses the *reality* of sin visible in the personal and social distortions children bring with them into the classroom. Particularly in its efforts to identify and meet the needs of each one of the students, the multifunctional classroom aims to encourage, build up, heal, restore, and make peace.[5]

Remember that the multifunctional classroom is still a collaborative classroom. It must be a caring community, an expression of the Body of Christ exercising the fruit of the Spirit. It is a classroom which promotes relationships in which teachers and students take responsibility for each other's learning and lives. There will be much love and prayer for one another.[6] Practicing the fruit of the Spirit will have high priority on the list of objectives in the teacher's lesson plan. And so a multifunctional classroom views learning as learning for *redemptive service* rather than for success.[7] In this kind of classroom "success" is measured, first of all, by the ability to function as a knowledgeable and competent disciple, not by high grades, honor rolls, and whether or not the student is on the way toward college and a lucrative career.

To put it in still different terms: in a multifunctional classroom no student is permitted to "fall between the cracks" or to become marginalized. Note, of course, that becoming a leader or heading for college is not at all to be despised. But if these "successes" are not expressions of a commitment to servanthood and love, they mean nothing.[8]

Getting there

How can you begin to establish a multifunctional classroom? How can you design an environment in which the children can individually learn within a context of community? Let's explore some possibilities.[9] I suggest we examine at least five areas. In what follows I briefly discuss each one of them in some detail. It should be clear that these five areas are by no means the only ones to be considered. Be aware as well that I intend to do no more than provide a general framework, not a step-by-step program of implementation.

Extensive inventory work

In chapter 10, I encouraged you to try the "first-step" approach. The first step of the first step, you will recall, consists of inventory work. To review:

From the very beginning of the term you must make every effort to understand the experiences, personality, gifts, and needs of every student in the class. Everything I advocated in that chapter I could repeat at this point. But rather than risk smothering you in tedium, I will focus specifically on the issue of gifts and needs.

In sessions with teachers I frequently ask the following three questions: (1) What categories of student needs do you experience in your classroom? (2) What different kinds of gifts or giftedness do students display in your classroom? (3) In what ways do you identify and assess student needs and gifts? Responses to these questions suggest that teachers sometimes reach diverse, even contradictory conclusions. For some teachers certain kinds of needs or gifts overshadow others. An additional problem is the vagueness of the terms "gifts" and "needs." Actually, how one understands gifts and needs is determined by what one takes to be the purpose of life and the purpose of schooling. If, for example, we see the school as primarily an institution that extols academic excellence, we will believe academic gifts to be much more important than, say, musical or athletic gifts.

If we see the purpose of Christian teaching as enabling for discipleship, then we may define gifts and needs as follows: gifts are all those abilities, talents, and interests that help students to enhance and advance their service to God and neighbor. Some of these gifts are academic in nature (for example, highly developed intellectual abilities), or artistic gifts, or practical gifts, and the like. We might think of Howard Gardner's eight "intelligences" and recognize giftedness in each one of them.[10] I shall return to the catalog of gifts in a moment.

What are needs and what kinds of needs are we talking about? Again in a broad sense we may define needs as all the factors that prevent students from serving God and neighbor as effectively and meaningfully as they could or should. Such needs come in a variety of categories: learning disabilities, undeveloped artistic skills, faith needs, physical impairments, emotional difficulties, and the like. To these needs, too, I shall return in a moment.

In short, I suggest we view gifts and needs as enhancing or limiting knowledgeable and competent discipleship. Now it is important that gifts and needs not be seen as static, unchanging constituents of human beings. Needs can be met and gifts can be cultivated. To see them as permanently fixed leads to pigeon-holing and labeling. Rather, we should see gifts and needs as dynamic enhancers and detractors within ongoing developmental processes. For this reason we must insist that the identification of gifts and needs not be done in a scientifically abstract, detached way (as is often the case with, e.g., certain instruments to identify learning styles), but must flow from personal interaction with the children and an understanding of the background and context from which they come.

Since human life is complex, no simple taxonomy of gifts and needs is possible. Maslow proposed a "hierarchy of needs," ranging from biological needs to the need for self-actualization.[11] More recently Glasser's control theory has proposed the five fundamental needs for survival, love and belonging, power, freedom, and fun.[12] For our purposes, however, the following large, roughly delineated categories may be helpful:

- The road to discipleship: What is the relationship between the student and his Lord? Often this category is referred to as the "spiritual dimension." Some students will be farther advanced (and, therefore more "gifted") than others, while some will show lack of development (and thus exhibit a "need") in this area.

- Social relationships: How does the student relate to her parents, siblings, and peers? What social problems (occasioned by family situations such as divorce, substance abuse, poverty, racial or religious tension, and so on) does he carry along into the classroom?

- Physical/physiological strengths and weaknesses: impairment of sight, hearing, and speech must obviously be recognized. Similarly, some students possess outstanding physical abilities.

- Emotional status: What self-concept does the student have? What fears and hopes govern the student's life?

- Learning styles: What kind of learner is the student? Learning style theories abound. They sometimes contradict each other. Unhappily, I don't know of a coherent, Christian approach to understanding learning styles. We are dependent on theorists like David Kolb, Bernice McCarthy, and Anthony Gregorc.[13] Happily, their work is often insightful and can be helpful. We do well to become familiar with their models. The research by Rita and Kenneth Dunn, too, is important.[14] They identify environmental factors and how they affect a child's learning. What areas of strength and weakness in learning does the student display? Take time to explore the implications of the "multiple intelligence" model proposed by Howard Gardner.[15]

- Sometimes I hear Christian educators say that learning styles theories are not important, as long as we vary our teaching approaches. I'm not so sure. While in all likelihood learning style assessment instruments are not necessary, it is at the same time probably not sufficient to count on varying our teaching strategies to meet the learning style needs of all our students. As we know from personal experience, even in classrooms where we find much variety in teaching approaches, the learning needs of numerous students are still not met.

- Academic/learning skills: I have in mind here such competencies as reading, writing, thinking, computing, and communication, and the variety of hindrances at work in these areas, frequently leaving students learning disabled.

How we might determine gifts and needs we have already explored in Chapter 10. You might consider reviewing that chapter at this point.

Classroom arrangement

The way we arrange our classrooms says much about our educational philosophy. Perennialists will probably insist on straight rows and little student activity other than taking notes and filling in worksheets. Progressivists may want to do away with the furniture. Social reconstructionists prefer to eliminate the classroom altogether and take the students into the heart of urban city life. To implement a multifunctional classroom, we will need flexibility and variety. This means that at some time straight rows are in order, while at other times changes should be made in order to meet needs and celebrate gifts. Here are some suggestions:

- Use learning centers. Even though we see them mostly in elementary schools, they are appropriate at the high school level as well (high school libraries sometimes function as large learning centers). Too often learning centers are limited in scope, allowing only narrow skill development. I suggest you aim for multifaceted centers which combine cooperative learning with individualized instruction, permit meaningful and responsible choice, encourage self-evaluation, and work with an integrated curriculum.
- Arrange for special student areas:
  - areas where students can study quietly and independently
  - discussion areas, where students in small groups can discuss a topic, assignment, or project

- areas for pairs of students
- an area where you can work with small groups of students who need special help

Designing this kind of a classroom would require close examination of the results of the teacher's inventory work. Learning style preferences must also be taken into account: some students learn best in dim light and cool environment, for example. Be sure to invite student input into the arrangements.

Curriculum

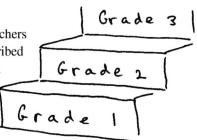

A major problem most teachers face is the requirement of a prescribed curriculum. At the end of grade 1 all students should presumably be at a certain level, at the end of grade 2 they should be at another level, and so on. Such curricular prescription often rides roughshod over everything this chapter has been talking about: needs, gifts, diversity, and uniqueness. Our schools too often ignore what all parents know: not all six-year-olds are ready for first grade, not all seven-year-olds should be in the second grade, and so on. Yet the old industrial model of herding groups of kids, who happen to be at the same age, through an assembly line sequence continues to control much of our schooling practice.

Obviously, attempting to redo an entire school's curriculum is unrealistic. Nevertheless, in a multifunctional classroom, in which diversity of tasks and diversity of opportunity to learn are stressed, some redesign of the curriculum will be necessary. One should distinguish between *core material* and *parallel learning activities*. Core material is part of the school's overall macro-curriculum. All students in a given grade level need to master this material. But right along with the core curriculum there should be parallel learning activities, opportunities that allow the students to indeed master the core material at their own pace and in their own style and that take account of student needs and gifts. So the teacher would plan special projects, design options among various ways of learning, provide supplementary activities, and the like.

Harro Van Brummelen has suggested something similar. In fact, Van Brummelen points to a multifunctional classroom when he says:

> If you want learning to be personalized, discuss and reinforce basic concepts or present information using methods that best suit the whole group, altering your teaching on the basis of student response. Then take individuals or small groups apart to meet particular needs. You may want to give individual students or small groups several options to further reinforce concepts, to examine some specific part of the topic under consideration, or to expand what has already been learned. In this way, you see your pupils as having special gifts which they use in the context of a community of learners. This type of personalized learning calls for a variety of classroom groupings that suit particular needs.[16]

Teaching strategies

As we have seen earlier in this book, there is no one best way to teach anyone anything. Teaching strategies need to alternate between cooperative learning, whole-group instruction, and personalized instruction. Particularly important will be to plan the teaching strategies and activities carefully. No doubt, mass teaching from the textbook or giving all the students identical worksheets is much easier. But doing so without regard for needs and gifts and individual uniqueness lands us in egalitarianism again. Lesson goals and objectives would have to be diversified as well: what may be a learning goal for Bryan may not be an appropriate goal for Tiana. What Bryan already knows about horses Tiana may have to learn from scratch. And finally, evaluation procedures would also have to be reconsidered. The issues of goals, planning, and evaluation in a multifunctional classroom will require thorough investigation, and probably innovative revision.

One way to help you vary your teaching methods is to review the assignments you make. Ask yourself: How can I assign diverse tasks to diverse students and yet achieve my overall goals? Some time ago I collaborated with a high school teacher designing a differentiated ninth-grade unit on the industrial revolution. We asked the students: What would be a good way for you to learn about the industrial revolution? How should we teach? Lectures and note-taking? Do a research project? Read some novels reflecting those times? Create a play or video depicting the tensions between parents and their exploited children at the time of the industrial revolution? Or what? As we asked these questions, we kept our unit objectives in mind. The thing to avoid is a multiplicity of learning activities all leading to a diversity of unrelated learning outcomes.[17]

Expanded use of contract systems, personal goal-setting, and self-evaluation

Ideally, there should be a contractual arrangement between the teacher and every one of her students. Together the teacher and the student should discuss what learning outcomes are to be achieved, how obstacles ("needs") are to be overcome, how gifts are to be encouraged, and how we will know whether or not the terms of the contract have been met (self-evaluation). We might consider contracts between the teacher and groups of students as well.

Conclusion

Obviously the discussion of the multifunctional classroom thus far has been general and sketchy. My emphasis has been on context and a few key components. Consequently, numerous questions remain. Consider the following:

- What conditions must be in place if a multifunctional classroom is to have a chance at all? How does it fit into a traditional school structure with all its pressures of time, staff, and resources? Can a classroom change without concomitant school change?
- Does meeting the needs and celebrating the gifts of every student in a class require a multifunctional classroom, or can this be done by means of appropriate adjustments in traditional classrooms?
- Is it likely that many school principals and teachers believe that all the goals suggested in this chapter are already being met?
- What kinds of assessment procedures would be needed to test

whether or not a multifunctional classroom is more effective than a traditional classroom?

- Is there not a risk that teachers, insufficiently prepared, might jump on a multifunctional bandwagon and actually make things worse, rather than better?

- What kind of expertise do teachers need if they are to engage, e.g., in the kinds of inventory work we discussed earlier? Could such inventory actually harm the child? Where does the professional social worker or psychologist come in? And won't teachers, by investigating the family background of their students, be tempted to blame the home situation for their students' difficulties?

- Is a multifunctional classroom, as described in this chapter, merely a general, sweeping and idealistic vision, or will it be possible to design a step-by-step program for implementation, easy for teachers to follow? Or can this type of classroom become a reality only through long-term, incremental changes under the guidance of a consultant or adviser?

These and other questions readily come to mind. I encourage you not to see them as deterrents. Resist allowing good old Western pragmatism to take over. Such pragmatism whispers: it's too complicated, it won't work, and it can't be done! Well, can it be done? We won't know until we try it.

CHAPTER 17

How do you get Kristi to behave?
Managing the collaborative classroom

Alex: I'm having some trouble managing my class, Lisa. I've got some pretty bad eggs in there. Take Kristi, for one. She's a sullen kid and obviously dislikes me. I hate the way she disrupts the class. She doesn't come off as a bully or a loudmouth, but in a subtle way she undermines the class atmosphere. She annoys me to no end!

Lisa: I think I know the type. I suppose she's unmotivated as well?

Alex: Unmotivated? She couldn't care less! Funny thing is, somehow she manages to get good grades. She's a smart kid all right. But I can't stand her bad attitude. She's got these sneaky, clever tricks that foul up my classroom discipline. I know she calls me names under her breath, just loud enough for kids around her to hear and snicker.

Lisa: How have you responded to Kristi?

Alex: The usual, so far. I've talked with her, put her name on the board, vowed I'd send her to the office, moved her off in a corner, gave her detentions and time-outs, even tried to bribe her with rewards. Nothing helps.

Lisa: Have you any idea why she might be like that?

Alex: No clue! And I really don't care either. She's obviously a natural brat! I've just got to sit on her more; I'm still too lenient, I think. I wish this school allowed corporal punishment. She's not too old for a proper spanking, if you ask me!

233

The fundamental issue

When our student teachers return from their first stint at full-time teaching and gather in my senior seminar, I invite them to list and rank the problems they encountered. Two issues invariably reach the top of the list: classroom management, and dealing with the unmotivated student.

Student teaching - Problems:
1. Classroom management
2. Unmotivated students
3. grouchy coop. teacher
4.

I ask them to share their stories, to solicit suggestions from one another, and to demonstrate their experiences by means of skits. Classroom management creates hours of animated discussion.

The literature on classroom management is vast and expanding.[1] It is also controversial and confusing. A cacophony of voices claims the last word. Different authors promote conflicting classroom management models.

Some basic distinctions are much debated. To illustrate the vigor of the conversation, consider the following frequently discussed contrasts:

- *The contrast between proactive and reactive classroom management.* Proactive management aims to prevent management problems. Reactive management aims to solve the problems after they arise. During the past 20 or 30 years or so, there has been a remarkable shift away from reactive towards proactive management. It finally dawned on educators, I suppose, that a gram of prevention is indeed worth a kilo of cure!

- *The contrast between classroom management and discipline.* Often the difference is said to be as follows: Classroom management deals with the entire picture of creating and maintaining a classroom environment conducive to teaching and learning, while discipline refers to the procedures and consequences for dealing with infractions of classroom rules. However, this point is contested. Some authors find this distinction unacceptable.[2]

- *The contrast between preventative and corrective discipline.* Preventative discipline is akin to proactive classroom management. Corrective discipline refers to measures taken to punish or correct unacceptable behavior.[3]
- *The contrast between imposed discipline and self-discipline.*[4] Imposed discipline generally reflects a coercive approach; self-discipline aims to get the students to take personal responsibility for their behavior.

Meanwhile, recent discussions pose questions about the term "classroom management" itself. Alfie Kohn, for example, reminds us that "'management' is a term borrowed from business . . . with overtones of directing and controlling employees."[5] Frankly, I am quite sympathetic to Kohn's concern. While teachers as guides are surely responsible for setting direction, must they also control? To this question I return in a moment. In spite of the troubling questions, I suspect that the term "classroom management" is so firmly entrenched that, for the sake of communication, we may as well work with it. What content to pour into this term, however, is for us to decide.

I do not intend to add more verbiage to the continuing debate. Rather, I propose to focus this chapter on a single question: What implications for classroom management flow from our definition of teaching Christianly? What do guiding, unfolding, and enabling for discipleship in the context of a collaborative classroom have to do with the way you conduct your classroom?

The scenario

Let's return to the problem Alex is experiencing with Kristi. The picture looks pretty grim. Kristi is being more than a kingly ache. She is making life miserable for Alex. The facts seem clear: While Kristi does not have a learning disability, she does not like to learn what Alex is asking her to learn. She expresses her dislike of learning by doing her level best to prevent it from happening. To make matters worse, Kristi doesn't like Alex either and she makes sure that he knows it. So what does Alex do?

The first in the list of actions he reports is "talk with her." Apparently this effort has met with no success. It might be interesting to listen to a tape recording of his conversation with her. For one thing, did Alex really talk *with* her? Or merely talk *to* her? Did he ask her any questions? Or did he recite a litany of threats and punishments?

That the latter is likely the case we may safely infer from his next moves: He put her name on the board (a threat), vowed to send her to the office (another threat), moved her off to the side (somewhat of a punishment), and gave her detentions and time outs (clearly punishments).

But wait a minute! Alex tried one other tactic: bribe her with rewards. Apparently he reasoned as follows: If the stick doesn't work, try the carrot! Instead of warning "If you don't behave, some bad things are going to happen to you" he suggested "If you do behave, something nice is going to happen to you." Sadly, as it turned out, neither approach worked. Now what? In his frustration Alex concluded that the reason why his methods failed is simply a matter of bulk: the weight of punishment hasn't been heavy enough—and by extrapolation, the rewards probably weren't big enough either. What do you think? To me the entire scenario looks like a classic case of a teacher who won't learn: he knows he's doing something that doesn't work, yet believes that simply doing more of what won't work will work!

The scenario raises another point. Somewhat in passing Lisa asked Alex if Kristi was unmotivated. That seems like a silly question, doesn't it? When did you ever see a highly motivated on-task student dislike both the teacher and what he's trying to teach? As we know from experience, lack of motivation to learn is commonly related to behavior problems. Note, by the way, that it is not the case that Kristi isn't motivated. She surely is! She is motivated to let Alex know that she doesn't like him and that she doesn't like what is going on in the classroom. Now here is a puzzle for you: Is Kristi's misbehavior the result of her being unmotivated, or is she unmotivated because she is a behavior problem in the first place?

Lingering behaviorism

Alex's methods of getting kids to behave are all too familiar to many teachers, including Christian teachers. Essentially, these methods reduce to programs of threats and punishment, along with rewards. They are rooted in behaviorist assumptions about negative and positive reinforcement. They assume that the teacher must be able to control—even manipulate—the students in order to teach. They assume that a major part of being a student is to comply with what the teacher requires. They assume, in short, strict obedience.

The classic example of this type of behaviorist classroom management is Lee Canter's program of "assertive discipline," an enormously influential and successful commercial enterprise. Assertive discipline aims to provide a bag of tricks to ensure that students will be compliant and obedient. It teaches teachers to get kids to do what teachers want them to do. It reduces kids to animals to be tamed and trained. It translates the guiding function into a control function.

Assertive discipline and similar management programs that advocate show-them-who's-boss philosophies are, in my view, incompatible with teaching Christianly. Here are some of my reasons:

- Such programs prevent students from learning to be responsible for their actions. Since children are told what to do and how to behave, they have no opportunity to reflect on what is and what is not morally acceptable action. Do what the teacher says, no questions asked and no discussion or reflection needed. But learning to be a disciple of the Lord requires much discussion and reflection.

- Behaviorist programs of management give students no choice over the affairs that involve them deeply: being part of a classroom teaching/learning situation. They silence the students' voices. Students' experience, insight, and input are ignored. Children are no longer seen as responsive and responsible image bearers of God. The only choice they have is "Do as I say or suffer the consequences."

- Behaviorist strategies address only the outward behavior of the students, not who they are as persons. Rewards do not necessarily promote goodness and responsibility. Rather, they teach kids to do something not because it is good and right, but because they get a reward. Similarly, punishment does not necessarily bring about a sense of "I guess I did wrong—I must better myself." It is just as likely to prompt the question: How can I get away with misbehavior the next time? It is not surprising, then, that more and more studies show that systems of punishment and reward do very little to turn people into responsible, caring and compassionate persons.[6]
- Perhaps most important of all, these behaviorist management programs confuse punishment with discipline. I want to expand on this point.

Discipline vs. punishment

Punishment normally follows a wrongful act. Presumably such punishment pays for the sin and teaches the perpetrator a lesson. But now I ask you: What do we mean when we say that Jesus Christ paid for all of our sins once and for all? Do we mean *all* of our sins? Including the sins of the kids in our classrooms? Do we really have to punish again, as if the work of Jesus was not adequate?

I know that there is a huge debate about the relationship between repentance and forgiveness. My view is this: If I read the Scriptures correctly, I see that forgiveness is to be our fundamental attitude, just as it was for Jesus himself. Jesus talks about the extra mile, the other cheek;[7] he even forgave those who crucified him. We should do no less. When our kids do wrong, we do not first ask, How can we punish them? but How we can forgive them and set them on the right road?

This point brings us to the question of discipline. It may be that you think I'm advocating a see-no-wrong-just-forgive-and-forget-and-every-thing-will-be-hunky-dory attitude. Of course not. Does not the Lord himself "chasten those whom he loves"? Such "chastening," however, is not to be understood as punishment, but as discipline. What is discipline? It is essentially guiding our kids to stay on the right road. To do this, punishment is not necessary. In a forgiving attitude we should ask: How can I help this child understand that what she did is wrong or unacceptable? How can I get her back on the right road? How can I guide her?

Discipline, in distinction from punishment, must always be restorative and corrective, rather than punitive. Punishment by itself does not restore and correct. It often leads to more anger and frustration. Punishment always carries with it connotations of getting even, taking revenge, or hurting someone to pay for hurt done. Punishing may well be equivalent to exasperating our children, which Paul warns against.[8] Discipline, on the other hand, is always corrective action in the context of love and forgiveness, of bearing with one another, of both admonishing and encouraging one another.

Behaviorism, or assertive discipline, or any other strategy of reward and punishment has no eye for this biblical picture of discipline. It merely cajoles and coerces and manipulates, in an attempt to "modify behavior," without asking, Who and what is this person we are trying to coerce and manipulate?

The scenario revisited

Let's return one more time to Alex and Kristi. What should Alex have done? I trust you understand that when it comes to discipline, there are no recipes. Sometimes teachers ask me: What would you do if so and so does this or so and so does that? It would be nice to be able to provide a foolproof remedy. Alas, there is none. Every so-called discipline case is unique, since every human being and each situation is unique. No two cases, though outwardly similar, can elicit identical responses. However, there are general guidelines—guidelines that I think Alex should have considered in dealing with a tough case like Kristi. The guidelines I suggest assume everything I have said earlier in this book about a collaborative classroom. The guidelines can best be stated in the form of questions.

Let's begin with the question Lisa asked: Why do you suppose Kristi is so negative? Alex thinks it's just a case of bad character. The fact is, there are usually reasons for misbehavior. I remember an elementary class I was teaching in Australia. One kid was as sullen and negative as Kristi. Then we discovered that his parents were going through a messy divorce. The kid felt abandoned and lost. Once we recognized the cause, we had an opportunity to work with him.

But there may be other reasons for Kristi's misbehavior that Alex should inquire about. Apparently Kristi is not motivated. Why not? Could it be that the curriculum Alex is trying to teach is uninteresting and irrelevant? One of the quickest ways to turn students off and to create both motivation and discipline problems is to teach kids boring stuff in boring classrooms. Sometimes we are told that we should ignore students' complaints about a boring classroom. "All kids think that everything is boring!" is what I hear said as sufficient grounds to ignore the complaint. But such advice, in my opinion, is dead wrong. When students complain that lessons and teachers are boring, they might be right. Some hard questions about the what and how of teaching should be asked.

I remind you of the important principle of connectedness: what you teach should relate to the previous experience of the children, to their current situation, and to what they intend to do with their lives. If you cannot answer the question "Why do I have to learn this stuff?" you are setting yourself up for serious classroom management problems.

Another question Alex needs to ask is, How can I establish a positive, trusting relationship with Kristi? Am I treating her as merely an object to be cajoled and manipulated? Why do I dislike her? What can I do to establish a good relationship with her? One way to do this is to talk *with* her, instead of *to* her. Alex needs to set up a situation in which he is willing to listen to Kristi, not just preach at her.

Alex also needs to review his expectations of Kristi. Apparently he expects nothing good from her, since she is an "incorrigible brat" anyway. But such an attitude is a self-fulfilling prophecy. If you think your kids are brats, they will not disappoint you!

Another question: How much voice in classroom decisions has he allowed Kristi to have? Apparently Kristi has no interest in Alex's classroom. One reason may be that she has experienced no ownership. She merely walks into Alex's class and is told what to do, what to learn, and how to behave.

Collaborative classroom management

As a model alternative to punishment-and-reward behaviorism, I suggest that you consider a genuinely collaborative management approach. I admit, such an approach is very difficult for us to adopt. We are so deeply steeped in a tradition in which the teachers call the shots and the students comply and obey without question. We are afraid that if we give students voices and responsibility to manage themselves, we will lose control and bring about chaos in our classrooms. It seems safer to tell the kids what to do and to control them. Yet let's ask once again: How can we expect our children to learn to be responsible disciples if we don't give them responsibility, right from the start, at appropriate levels?

To introduce and cultivate collaborative management, consider the following steps as guidelines (not as a foolproof recipe!):

- Decide firmly against assertive discipline methods. Decide that your management style will not be patterned after reward and punishment programs. Decide you will guide, yes, and discipline, yes, but you will not manipulate your kids into compliance by treats and threats.

- Recall that the children you are teaching are image bearers of God. Children are experienced, gifted, responsible creatures, precious in God's sight. They are not objects whose behavior needs to be modified or animals to be trained.

- Decide that you will structure your classroom for grace, not for sin. That means that you will approach the students with high expectations and trust, rather than always expecting them to be their worst.

- Adopt a discipline stance rather than a punishment stance. Cultivate a forgiving and forbearing attitude. Instead of saying, What punishment must I mete out? ask, How can I help the child to return to and stay on the right road, as we journey together?

- Recall our conversation about the first-step approach. Invite the children to participate in structuring the classroom. Be sure to give them a genuine voice, not just a voice that echoes what the teacher wants. Be ready to ask for input, listen to the input, and work with it.

- When you ask the students to collaborate with you on classroom rules, remember that such rules should govern not simply individual behavior, but the entire classroom. Ask not simply How do you and I behave? but What should this classroom be like? How can we help each other make this classroom a safe, secure, and exciting place?

Ask students to suggest ways of helping children who misbehave to stay on the right road.

- Remember what we said about goal areas in chapter 5. Recall a critically important goal area: the development of discipleship skills. Encourage the children to help each other identify and practice discipleship skills, such as showing respect, listening, encouraging, seeking to resolve conflict, and above all, giving love.

- When students do misbehave—like Kristi—try to figure out why. Look first at what you as a teacher might be doing to elicit negative behavior. Is your teaching dull? Is your curriculum irrelevant and pointless? Are the tasks you assign nothing but drudgery? Or is she struggling with situations outside the classroom?

- Rather than merely impose punishment or consequences, do your level best to help the misbehaving child understand why the behavior was unacceptable. Remember, we need to work together at helping the child to become a better person, not merely to adjust some behavior. Consider misbehavior not as a punishable event, but as an opportunity to teach.[9]

- Consider establishing contracts. Have the kids agree to help maintain an appropriate atmosphere by putting suggestions down in writing. You might have the students write their views down, then place them in an envelope, and return the envelopes periodically to check to see how well the whole class is doing.

- Encourage your colleagues and your principal to study alternative classroom management models currently entering the educational world.[10]

Given these guidelines, what might a collaborative management procedure look like? I suggest this basic version:

- Begin the program with an upfront discussion about discipleship. Explain that discipleship consists of hearing and doing the will of the Lord. Ask what such discipleship might mean in the classroom. Use strategies such as authentic discussion, brainstorming, cooperative learning, and shared praxis to get at these issues.

- Invite the students to set rules for the class. Ask what a "discipling" class would look like. Be sure to *listen* to the students and to take their suggestions seriously.

- Invite your students to determine consequences. What should we do, as a class, when problems and conflicts occur? Again, *listen* to what the students think and say.
- Consider assigning roles. I am not suggesting you appoint "police officers." But do think of the possibility of selecting students to observe, monitor, and admonish when necessary. Try to share your task of managing, encouraging, and correcting the students in your class.
- Try to "redirect," rather than squelch or threaten "trouble spots." Aim to turn negative into positive behavior.
- "Process" frequently. At regular times invite the students to respond to the question: How are we doing as a class? What is going well? Where do we need work? How can we achieve the type of classroom atmosphere discussed in step 1 above? Continuous self-reflection will be an indispensable component of a collaboratively managed classroom.

Is collaborative management possible?

Is collaborative management possible? No, not if you believe that children are not only totally depraved, but also untouched by the grace of God and unaffected by the redemption of Christ. No, not if you believe that your classroom is boot camp and you are the drill sergeant. No, not if you allow your classroom to be turned into a competitive, let's-see-who-can-be-the-best war zone. No, not if you believe that the biblical concept of the Body of Christ has nothing whatsoever to do with your classroom.

But you want to teach Christianly. And you want to manage Christianly. It will not do to give lip service to community and love and all that if a system of punishment and rewards controls your classroom. A collaborative approach, reflecting authentic community, is surely a better way.

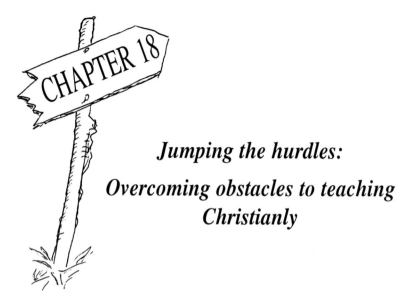

Jumping the hurdles:
Overcoming obstacles to teaching Christianly

Jennifer: You know, Lisa, I really enjoyed this year's education conference at Dordt College. Good presentations on evaluations and assessment, and plenty of opportunity to stick our heads together and work on some specific action steps to take back to our schools. You should have been a member of our team, Lisa!

Lisa: I would have loved to go. What sort of report and what kind of action steps will you present at our staff meeting next week?

Jennifer: I'll explain some neat ideas about parent-teacher conferences. I recommend we look at student-led conferences. I'm not sure how this idea will fly. Worse, I'm not sure I'll be able to find the time to work up a good proposal. Taking the time off for the conference has really set me back. I'm way behind on correcting papers and lesson planning. No time to reflect at all!

Lisa: Time! Sometimes I think it's more of an enemy than a friend.

Lest we are discouraged . . .

It is, of course, one thing to say that we should seek to teach Christianly in our classrooms; it is an entirely different matter to actually do so. Or to be able to do so. All sorts of factors militate against our best efforts to teach Christianly. In fact, when you consider all the obstacles we face, we might be tempted to chuck the whole thing and go fishing! It is no wonder that "teaching Christianly" is easily neglected or written off as an idealistic buzzword.

Discouraging, you say? Well, yes, but there is another side. Let's begin by making some firm decisions. First, let's decide that what it means to teach Christianly must remain a central question if Christian education is to flourish. We can have beautiful buildings, well-disciplined children, even high performance test scores, but if we teachers do not really teach Christianly, is it worth the effort and, for many, the financial sacrifice? Secondly, though the temptation to chuck it all and go fishing may seem irresistible, let's decide right now not to capitulate. Instead, let's boldly address the problems. A first step is to identify and describe the obstacles. Then we can look at ways to counteract them. Let's aim to turn these nasty stumbling blocks into exciting challenges to meet.

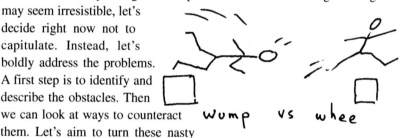

Wump   vs   whee

Three common interconnected obstacles

Time

A shortage of time is invariably the first stumbling block the typical classroom teacher will identify. Repeatedly I hear teachers bewail their lack of time: "I'd love to sit down, reflect on what I'm doing, and work on improving my skills, but I just don't have the time. I have too many kids to teach, too many school duties, too much paperwork, too much to plan. In addition, there are church activities, and what about my own needs? And, of course, I must spend some time with my family!"

What are the standard responses to this growing and widespread problem? You know them as well as I do. Here are some of them: Get organized! Learn the tricks of good time management! Learn to say no! Plan a schedule! Make a list of things to do, and be sure to prioritize them! Do the most unpleasant tasks first thing in the morning! Don't procrastinate! And on and on.[1]

Now I don't mean to pooh-pooh these suggestions. They are indeed excellent, and many of them will help you offset the time problem. I have also come to believe, however, that there is no single time management model that will work for each one of us. We are all different people. Some of us are highly organized, while others of us can work effectively in a mess. So I suggest that we add to all the good, standard ideas one more: Look for your own personal, tailor-made solution to the time problem rather than simply adopt a prescribed model. How do you do this? Consider working on the problem with others. The time problem is not just your personal problem. It's a communal problem. We need to confront it as a community. Within the school community you may be able to find a colleague whose personality and working style are similar to yours.

I should not have to remind you that time—in spite of Lisa's musings—should be our friend, not our enemy. Time is one of the great gifts we all receive from the hand of the Creator himself. We need to use it wisely. But there is no one standard way of using time wisely. The workaholic will have a different conception of the use of time than a person who prefers a lackadaisical, it-will-all-come-out-in-the-wash approach. You need to make some prayerful decisions about what "using time wisely" means to you. I suggest that at the very least a wise use of time should include opportunity to reflect on your teaching practice.

Important, too, is the need to avoid reductionism, that is, the tendency to spend too much time on one thing and neglect others. You know of musicians and athletes who think and live nothing but music or sports. Teachers are particularly prone to this malady. I know of teachers who think of their classroom all the time. When on vacation, for example, they spend all their time looking for things to take back to be used in their lessons. They think and live curriculum.

It is easy to be overwhelmed by time pressures. I encourage you to face the problem head-on and design a personal, relatively balanced approach you are comfortable with. As I already suggested, included should be time set aside for personal reflection on and evaluation of your teaching strategies. But also press your colleagues and principal to make time for communal discussion of pedagogy: What teaching methods do your colleagues use? Why? What sort of classroom atmosphere do we seek to maintain? What do we mean by teaching Christianly? Questions like these have no easy answers. They require time. Spend some time encouraging your fellow teachers to take the time.

Stress

A second obstacle is the reality of stress. Teaching is a physically and emotionally draining task. It can be a terribly stressful task. Part of the stress is due to the many decisions a teacher must make while in the classroom. Only air traffic controllers make more decisions on any given day than teachers do. Some teachers, like some air traffic controllers, habitually take a nap as soon as they return from duty.

Frequently we teachers compound the stress by worrying about what others think or expect: Will the students like me? Am I really a good teacher? What will the next grade level teacher think of my work? How do parents *really* see me? Questions like these quickly turn to self-doubt and translate into added stress.[2]

Add to this stress the "BDB phenomenon": the Bad-Day Blues. One inescapable characteristic of teaching is that good days are invariably followed by bad days. One day we experience the joy and satisfaction of teaching, the next day we wish we had decided on a different career. In my younger years I spent some time as a logger in British Columbia. Over the 30-plus years of my teaching career I have heard myself say on more than one occasion: I should have stuck with logging!

To the problems of stress we also find a set of standard answers. These, too, you know: Be sure to take good care of yourself—eat well, get sleep and plenty of exercise; look at immediate problems in a larger perspective (by asking yourself, Will I remember this problem a year from now?);

cultivate hobbies; take regular time off from work; keep your Sundays free. And so on.

Again, these are helpful suggestions. Most important of all, be in steady conversation with the Lord. A prayer early in the morning is not sufficient. Too often we pray while we are still at home. We pray for strength and patience—especially when a low-pressure weather system is predicted and we know the kids will likely be climbing the walls—or we pray that Ashley may be absent today so that she will not make our life miserable. After such prayers have been uttered, we get ready for the day and enter our classrooms—alone. Don't! Be sure to invite the Lord with you into your classroom. Cultivate a "we-attitude" for teaching. Say not "*I'm* going to teach today" but "*we're* going to teach today." (A cynic remarked that this way you can always blame God when the day goes wrong! I recommend you ignore the cynic.) Keep in step with the Spirit, as the Apostle Paul reminds us in Galatians 5.

Frustrations

A third, related obstacle consists of the many frustrations that continually plague the life of the teacher. From the survey to which I referred earlier, I learned that effects of TV and videos in the lives of children can loom large as an enemy of the classroom. Leaving aside the many ways in which excessive television and video watching negatively affect the learning of children, I mention only two of the key problems introduced into the classroom. First, teachers sometimes feel compelled to compete with TV and videos. However, usually such competition is altogether too unmatched: teachers have virtually no chance to keep their students as interested in classroom work as in watching TV or videos. A second key problem mentioned by the teachers is the distorting influence of TV and videos. They effectively counteract and break down the values and priorities the teachers seek to instill in the youngsters.

When it comes to our efforts to teach a Christian perspective on life, it is evident that not only TV and videos, but family life style as a whole can easily contradict and nullify what we seek to accomplish in the classroom. It is hard to teach the virtue of conservation and simple, altruistic living, for example, when parents own mansions for homes, are accustomed to annual vacations overseas, and spend loads of money on things they do not need. It is hard to address the evils of materialism when at home the children are engulfed in materialistic spirits.

Similarly, it is difficult to inculcate discipleship skills when the students come from broken homes or dysfunctional families, from backgrounds where love and care are at a premium, or from situations where might-makes-right is the prevailing philosophy. A frustrating sense of helplessness can easily overpower the serious Christian teacher.

Frustrations like these sometimes drive teachers to quit and look for other workplaces. For those of us who stay, the frustrations can seriously undermine our understanding of what it means to teach Christianly. Like combating stress, meeting and overcoming these frustrations require much reliance on the Lord. We must maintain a deep conviction that teaching Christianly is a high calling—even when our efforts can't seem to get off the ground or when the results may not seem spectacular. We must hold to a living faith in the coming Kingdom of God. No matter what, our work for the Lord will be blessed. You remember the saying: The Lord does not ask us to be successful, only to be faithful. Dr. Stuart Fowler says, "Be faithful and prophetic."[3] Call a spade a spade. Boldly seek to counteract the materialism, selfishness, and brokenness that ⟵ = a spade surround us everywhere.

Happily, teaching Christianly has many rewards that help offset the frustrations: seeing children learn, affecting lives for the better, and remembering that one's work as a teacher, though not the most lucrative, is nevertheless among the most significant of occupations. These rewards ultimately overcome the frustrations. Every frustration can evoke from the creative teacher a positive response, from using television programs as a tool for developing critical skills to designing experiences that encourage children to reset their priorities.

Additional obstacles

The three stumbling blocks described above are of the ready, easy-to-spot sort. But teaching Christianly is further hampered by more subtle factors—by powerful, subversive spirits that are not of the Lord. These spirits, often expressed in philosophical terms, have firmly established themselves in the course of history. It is important to note that we are not now talking about quaint ideas suggested by dizzy philosophers and enshrined in treatises that nobody reads. On the contrary, we are dealing with powerful forces that take hold of human hearts and capture entire populations. Specifically important for our consideration of Christian teaching practice in our Western culture are the following philosophical perspectives:

Intellectualism

Intellectualism is a spirit that arose in ancient, pagan Greece. Intellectualism regards the intellect as the central determining component of human beings. The ancient Greeks believed that by training the mind we train the person. They thought of the "mind" as a faculty designed to engage in abstract theory. In the Middle Ages this type of intellectualism encouraged notions such as the "rational soul" and the "natural light of reason." In modern times this perspective led to centuries of rationalism and scientism. Only recently, thanks in part to the rise of Postmodernism, has the philosophical world begun to break away from assigning a privileged status to abstract, scientific theory.

Christian education has not escaped this powerful spirit frequently exhibited in an undue stress on "academic excellence." It has created classrooms which cater to the intellectually gifted, often leaving those with other talents to fend for themselves. It has blinded teachers to the emotional and social needs of our children. Academic rigor and inflexible evaluation procedures control intellectualistic schools.

Positivism

This spirit can be understood as a stepchild of intellectualism. It held sway for a considerable period of time in the Western world by emphasizing analytic methods leading to objective, indisputable facts.

The positivist believes that true knowledge is factual, observable, and scientifically verifiable. This approach, too, has powerfully affected Christian education. Many teachers have contented themselves with teaching facts. Students are asked to take notes, put them to memory, and recall them. Most of us have experienced this kind of learning and know that such learning is quickly forgotten. Of special concern is that such positivism reinforces the dualism I described earlier: factual learning is placed alongside devotional classroom activities. Facts are facts, objectively true, while devotions are devotions, religious and personal in character. The two do not meet.

Perennialism

Meet another stepchild of the intellectualistic tradition! Perennialism likes to believe that the core school curriculum should consist of the abiding truths articulated throughout the ages, particularly as found in Western classical literature. More often than not, these "truths" tend to be of a rationalistic character, mentally grasped "great ideas." Like positivism, perennialism leads to a stress on facts and promotes a "subject-centered" approach to education. Students tend to be regarded as empty containers to be filled with teacher-transmitted knowledge.

A Christian critique of perennialism must avoid the suggestion that nothing can be learned from the wisdom of the past, as if every generation must fashion its own wisdom anew to suit its own purposes. There is always a perennial wisdom, an ongoing story as it were, that needs to be incorporated into our curriculum and pedagogy. We need to identify, affirm, celebrate, and learn from such wisdom.

Two issues emerge at this juncture: (1) What exactly is wisdom? What, in the classical authors, can be celebrated as genuine wisdom and what is mere foolishness? (2) What role does this wisdom play in our educational efforts? How does it meet the various goal areas we have considered earlier? When the "wisdom of the ages" is uncritically accepted as good and true and becomes the kingpin of our teaching practice, a perennialist philosophy takes control.

Pragmatism

Aha! you say: I've heard about this one before. I read about it in chapter 1. Right! But let's take another look. Pragmatism is a home-grown American philosophy. Its basic premise is that truth is to be determined by practice. Thus if a proposed course of action works, it is true, good, and just. If it does not work, it is to be discarded. We need to be careful as we consider such pragmatism. It is important to distinguish between pragmatism and being appropriately pragmatic. An -ism attached to a word more often than not suggests an exaggeration and distortion of the root word. Think of rationalism, intellectualism, and humanism, for example. These positions clearly attach too much importance to rationality, the intellect, and the place of human beings. Ultimately such -isms represent forms of idolatry.

In combating pragmatism we must not close our eyes to the need to plan strategy or to check if a given course of action works. We need to be wise as serpents, as the Bible puts it.[4] We *should* consider the question— Will it work? But when this question becomes the fundamental, primary question, we need to be concerned. For such a question cannot be the first, rock-bottom question. The first question to ask is this: Will a proposed course of action serve God's Kingdom? Only when we are clear on what the Lord requires will it be legitimate to ask what might be the most work-able approach to solving a specific problem.

Teachers tend to become pragmatists when they become fixated on recipes, teaching tips, and easy answers. Teachers become pragmatists when they seek only the answers to questions of what will or will not work in the immediacies of the classroom, all the while having lost the larger vision, purpose, and context of Christian education. Pragmatism, then, can be a powerful obstacle to teaching Christianly. For, after all, though teaching Christianly should be practical, it is rooted in commitments and assumptions that cannot be measured by any kind of pragmatistic yardstick.

Progressivism

Progressivism no doubt supports many of the suggestions made in this book. Consequently, a progressivist philosophy may inadvertently slip into our classrooms. We could then confuse a Christian collaborative classroom with a secular, Deweyan democratic classroom. To avoid this trap, we must reject a number of fundamental tenets espoused by progressivism. One of these is that children will naturally flourish in an appropriate environment. Progressivism, in other words, is blind to the reality of sin. Second, progressivism downplays the significance of structured curricular content. To a true progressivist, all that counts is the ability to confront the present world and deal with it by means of problem-solving techniques. Consequently, progressivism bypasses the need to teach our children to be discerning, able to distinguish between antinormative and normative responses to the problems they are asked to solve. Finally, a progressivistic democratic classroom consists of presumed autonomous individuals, each one endowed with equal authority. Progressivists do not see the importance of office and office consciousness. While not as prevalent in Christian classrooms as perennialism, progressivism remains nevertheless a powerful influence. It can quickly turn a Christian collaborative classroom into an unstructured do-what-is-right-in-our-own-eyes situation.

Constructivism

Constructivism is rapidly becoming both a bandwagon and a panacea. In the larger educational world it is uncritically touted as *the* indispensable ingredient of all good classroom practice. So what *is* constructivism? Why the enormous appeal?

Constructivism, in brief, is an approach to education based on the conviction that knowledge is constructed. We do not simply "receive" neatly packaged information from outside sources. Instead, we *make sense* of our experience as we interact with our environment. What we believe and know about the world, in other words, consists of what we make of it. Our knowledge is the product of an active process.

As I pointed out in my discussion of shared praxis, constructivism proposes, in my view, a helpful learning theory. It affirms that students need to be actively involved in their learning and cannot simply function as receptacles. It helps teachers see that they must teach for understanding, not merely memorization and recall.

In spite of these positives, the widespread (and mostly uncritical) acclaim of constructivism makes it easy to lose sight of the dangers implicit in this perspective. From a Christian point of view, the largest of these dangers is the assumption that there is no meaning other than what autonomous individual persons construct. Constructivism has no vision of a God-created and structured reality. While indeed we construct knowledge—we build on our experience, for example—we never do so outside a normed creation to which our constructions respond.

A resulting problem is that constructivism fails to recognize degrees of truth and falsity, or, eventually, of right and wrong. Consequently, constructivism can promote an intolerable tolerance. While as Christians we surely need to be tolerant of other views and to recognize our own limitations and muddleheadedness, we also must maintain that not all views and opinions are equal. The difference between right and wrong, normative and antinormative responses to God's intentions for our lives must remain a cornerstone in all of our teaching. Let's not succumb to the constructivist lure that tempts us to refrain from taking a stand. Teaching Christianly always assumes a stance: Christian teachers seek to teach children to know and to do what is right and true instead of what is wrong and false, and to be able to tell the difference. Knowledgeable and competent discipleship is never merely a matter of personal, subjective opinion.

Individualism

Again a point we examined in connection with our discussions about the collaborative classroom. Individualism is another powerful spirit dating back to the ancient Greek world. It blossomed luxuriously during the Hellenistic Age, went underground during the Middle Ages, and reemerged with strength and vigor in modern times. An important boost for individualism was the period of the Renaissance, when it joined forces with notions of freedom and autonomy.

Individualism proclaims the significance of the individual to the exclusion of community. Human beings are essentially separate islands, disconnected from one another. Communities, such as marriages or social organizations or classrooms, are merely aggregates of individuals, merely social constructs. Only the individual is real and, consequently, only the individual is important. No wonder, then, that individualism lies at the basis of greed, selfishness, competition, and callous disregard for the needs of others. Its power makes a collaborative classroom difficult to achieve.

Egalitarianism

Egalitarianism stresses conformity and sameness. It ignores uniqueness and differences. An egalitarian teaching approach will set aside diversity of gifts, needs, and learning styles, and treat the students as if they were basically cut from the same burlap bag. Egalitarian teachers will treat and evaluate all the students on the same basis, ostensibly under the cloak of fairness and equality. Egalitarianism encourages school boards and principals to approve and support standard curricula, standardized tests, and even a sameness in teaching approaches.

Elitism

This spirit also harks back to the ancient world. The Greek intellectuals declared that philosophers and mathematicians, those who work with their heads rather than their hands, were vastly superior to the general rabble. Closely allied to intellectualism, elitism believed that mental work—especially of the theoretical sort—is superior to manual work. This idea, fortified by a medieval stress on the superiority of the clergy, firmly established itself in the Western world. It fosters the tendency to convert Christian schools into private schools where we have only "nice kids" and potential leaders—followers are of no consequence. Elitism exhibits itself, then, in the tendency to allow "dunderheads" to fall through the cracks. It exhibits itself in the inevitable bias teachers feel towards certain kinds of students, to the detriment of others.

Elitism inevitably leads to exclusivism. Some time ago while in Australia, I worked in a Christian school that accepted kids who, for various reasons, both academic and behavioral, had been dismissed from other schools. The principal, Bill Oates, is part aborigine. He came from a background familiar with minorities and marginalization. One time Bill said to me, "You know, John, when the Lord comes back I doubt whether his first question to us will be about curriculum and evaluations. He probably won't even ask us whether we are really teaching

Christianly. Rather, I suspect he will ask, 'What have you done with my little ones, especially with those who are poor and orphaned, the marginalized and rejected, those who have been expelled from other schools because of behavioral and learning problems?'"

Bill Oates' vision was to offer truly inclusive Christian education. The Christian school is to be a lighthouse, he said, a place where the needs of all the children are met, not just of those who can afford it or who have the required academic gifts.

Let's ask ourselves: Isn't it true that most Christian schools today serve only a middle-to upper-class Christian society? In fact, aren't most Christian schools still set up primarily for those who are not disabled in any serious way? The kids with disabilities are "too expensive" to accommodate in our mainline Christian schools. Students with vocational or industrial talents are often not welcome either.

Secularism

Finally, there is one more -ism to be added to the long litany of spiritual obstacles to teaching Christianly: secularism. Secularism may well be the greatest bugaboo of all, probably because it may be the subtlest of all. You see, secularism comes in at least three different versions. In its most blatant form, it needs no disguise at all. When we hear the claim that God is dead or that religion is but archaic superstition, we know for sure that the dragon of secularism has reared its head. In this, its crassest manifestation, secularism simply sets aside God and his will. The Lord is simply ignored.

But there are two other forms of secularism not so easily recognized. They come disguised under a Christian cloak. In an earlier chapter I spoke of the first of these two disguises called dualism—a philosophy that divides life into a sacred and secular domain. In the classroom this approach can come to expression as a combination of devotional activity plus the standard curriculum and teaching methods. From this point of view the secular domain does not look so dangerous any more. After all, as long as they are contextualized by sincere, explicit

Christian devotions and a model Christian teacher, the presumably neutral areas of mathematics, history, foreign language, and other disciplines can't be all that suspect. In this case, a secular perspective is made acceptable and legitimate.

The second of the two disguises is the one we especially need to worry about. In this disguise secularism creeps into our teaching even though we vociferously deny dualism and claim that we are subjecting our curriculum and teaching methods to the will of the Lord. Some examples: in teaching mathematics we may proclaim the majesty of God as the great Mathematician who created the marvelously ordered world of mathematics, yet teach mathematics from a thoroughly secular formalist perspective that assumes that mathematics is a self-contained and self-validating set of rules. Or we teach history by reminding the students that history is "His story" without giving them any sense whatsoever—except perhaps in a most superficial way—of how the unfolding of historical processes reflects or denies God's ordinances.

This sort of subtle secularism continues to take hold of the hearts of all of us. It prompts us to rationalize or to set the key issues aside uncritically. It encourages us to live comfortable lives and to keep real sacrifice to a minimum. This is also the sort of sneaky secularism that we cannot fight alone. We need to talk about its power and effects more openly with less defensiveness. Teaching Christianly will require nothing less than the unmasking of this sort of secularism.

Concluding remarks

These and other forces violently militate against efforts to bring the rule of Christ and the presence of the Holy Spirit into the classroom. Indeed, we could easily write another book to catalog all that makes "teaching Christianly" a far-off, idealistic dream of no consequence in the real world of schooling today. I say "an idealistic dream." But is it really? No. Christ, through us, is making all things new, including our teaching practice. Undaunted, let us put our hands to the plow.

You have, in fact, already done so! Reading this book says that you are taking your calling seriously. My fervent hope is that you will be prompted to rededicate yourself to your task as a Christian teacher. Your work with children is so incredibly significant to furthering the

Kingdom of God! Remember to see the different topics we have discussed in this book—classroom organization, pedagogical choices, class management, and others—as service to God.

And now, my friend, as we conclude our conversations, I wish you blessings on your efforts. May the grace of God, and the love of Jesus, and the fellowship of the Holy Spirit abide with you and your children every day you set foot in your classroom.

A teacher's prayer

Lord, you know that I am frail and weak. I am often scared. Often I don't believe you when you tell me that indeed you are making all things new—including what I do in my classroom. Often I am stubborn, when I say, "But I've always done it this way, please don't bother me!" In callous arrogance I tend to dismiss what my fellow believers say or think, and I make no attempt to be the agent of reconciliation and renewal you want me to be.

Lord, I commend my work to you. Thank you for giving me such a scary yet marvelous task—the task of helping your precious children grow as knowledgeable and competent disciples, eager and willing to seek to do your will everywhere in their lives. Help me never to ride roughshod over the kids in my classroom. Help me to see Jesus in every one of them, even in kids like Keith or Kristi who seem so bent on going the wrong way. Forgive me when I wish they'd go away.

Help me, Lord, to work together with the students, the staff, the principal, the board, and the parents. May I seek to build community and to practice genuine love.

Lord, help us to teach Christianly. Without you, it's a pipe dream. But when we link our arms with yours, we can do it. Yes, Lord, we can do it!

Amen!

NOTES

Chapter 1

1. Nicholas Wolterstorff, *Curriculum: By What Standard?* (Grand Rapids, MI: National Union of Christian Schools, 1966); Paul Kienel, editor, *Philosophy of Christian School Education* (Colorado Springs, CO: Association of Christian Schools International, 1995); John Van Dyk, *The Beginning of Wisdom: The Nature and Task of the Christian School* (Grand Rapids, MI: Christian Schools International, 1985); Richard Edlin, *The Cause of Christian Education* (Northport, AL: Vision Press, 1997); Harro Van Brummelen, *Steppingstones to Curriculum: A Biblical Path* (Seattle, WA: Alta Vista Press, 1994). See also Nicholas Henry Beversluis, *Christian Philosophy of Education* (Grand Rapids, MI: National Union of Christian Schools, 1971).

2. For a good description of "the shock of the familiar," see Kevin Ryan and James Cooper, *Those Who Can, Teach* (Boston, MA: Houghton Mifflin, 1998), pp. 467-470.

3. The Dordt College Center for Educational Services is a component of the college designed to assist Christian schools and Christian teachers to enhance their effectiveness. Every spring the Center hosts representatives from Christian elementary and secondary schools at the B. J. Haan Education Conference, offering a program for school improvement.

4. In the Reformed tradition we do find examples of concern about pedagogy. The Dutch theologian Herman Bavinck already addressed pedagogical issues nearly 100 years ago. See J. Brederveld, *Christian Education: A Summary and Critical Discussion of Bavinck's Pedagogical Principles* (Grand Rapids, MI: Smitter Book Co., 1928). Later the Dutch psychologist Jan Waterink was much concerned with pedagogy. See Jan Waterink, *Basic Concepts in Christian Pedagogy* (Grand Rapids, MI: Eerdmans, 1954).

5. Cornelius Jaarsma, *Human Development, Learning and Teaching* (Grand Rapids, MI: Eerdmans, 1959).

6. For an initial description of this lengthy and complicated debate, see Larry Reynolds, "Describing Instruction: Basic Assumptions" in *Pro*

Rege, Vol. XII, No. 3, 1984, pp. 12-24.

7. See, for example, David W. Anderson, "Creative Teaching: Education as Science and Art" in *Holistic Education Review*, Vol. 4, No. 1, Spring, 1991, pp. 16-21; Ron Brandt, "On Research on Teaching: A Conversation with Lee Shulman" in *Educational Leadership*, Vol. 49, No. 7, April, 1992, pp. 14-19; and Jere Brophy, "Probing the Subtleties of Subject-Matter Teaching" in *Educational Leadership*, Vol. 49, No. 7, April, 1992, pp. 4-8.

8. For a discussion of the Greek view of knowing and doing, see my articles "The Relationship Between Faith and Action: An Introduction" in *Pro Rege*, Vol. X, No. 4, 1982, pp. 2-7, and "Christian Philosophy and Classroom Practice: Is the Gap Widening?" in *Pro Rege*, Vol. XXIII, No. 1, 1994, pp. 1-7.

9. N. L. Gage, "Theories of Teaching" in *Theories of Learning and Instruction*, National Society for the Study of Education (Chicago: The University of Chicago Press, 1964), pp. 268-285.

Chapter 2

1. I Corinthians 1:10.
2. Matthew 28:18; Revelation 19:16.

Chapter 3

1. Colossians 1:19-20.
2. Galatians 5:25.
3. Ephesians 4:11-13.
4. James 3:1.

Chapter 4

1. Ephesians 4:12.
2. Joshua 4.
3. Galatians 5:25.

Chapter 5

1. Ralph W. Tyler, *Basic Principles of Curriculum and Instruction* (Chicago: University of Chicago Press, 1949).
2. Tyler, pp. 5-33.

3. See, e.g., H. Jerome Freiberg and Amy Driscoll, *Universal Teaching Strategies* (Needham Heights: Allyn & Bacon, 1996) pp. 61-79.

4. Elliot W. Eisner, "Instructional and Expressive Objectives: Their Formulation and Use in Curriculum" in *Instructional Objectives: An Analysis of Emerging Issues*. James Popham, ed. (Chicago: Rand McNally & Co., 1969), pp. 13-18.

5. Benjamin S. Bloom, ed., *Taxonomy of Educational Objectives, Handbook I: Cognitive Domain* (New York: McKay, 1956); David R. Kratwohl, and others, *Taxonomy of Educational Objectives, Handbook II: Affective Domain* (New York: Longman, 1964); Anita J. Harrow, *Taxonomy of the Psychomotor Domain: A Guide for Developing Behavior Objectives* (New York: McKay, 1972).

6. Howard Gardner, *Frames of Mind: The Theory of Multiple Intelligences* (New York: Basic Books, 1982). For a sample of how Gardner's theory is implemented, see the Vol. 55, No. 1, September, 1997 issue of *Educational Leadership*. The theme of this issue is "Teaching for Multiple Intelligences."

7. Nicholas Henry Beversluis, *Christian Philosophy of Education* (Grand Rapids, MI: National Union of Christian Schools, 1971). See especially chapters 3 and 4. In this book Beversluis speaks of "moral growth" rather than specifically a "decisional domain."

8. Donald Oppewal, *Biblical Knowing and Teaching* (Grand Rapids, MI: Calvin College Monographs, 1985), p. 18.

9. Nicholas Wolterstorff, *Educating for Responsible Action* (Grand Rapids, MI: Eerdmans, 1980), pp. 14-15. Of special interest is the appendix "Reflections on Taxonomy."

10. Harro Van Brummelen, *Walking with God in the Classroom* (Seattle: Alta Vista Press, 1992 and 1988), pp. 117-119.

11. Van Brummelen, *Walking with God in the Classroom*, p. 118.

12. Ephesians 5:15-17; James 3:13-18.

13. James 1:22.

14. For further discussion, see my essays "The Relationship Between Faith and Action: An Introduction" in *Pro Rege*, Vol. X, No. 4, 1982, pp. 2-7, and "Christian Philosophy and Classroom Practice: Is the Gap Widening?" in *Pro Rege*, Vol. XXIII, No. 1, 1994, pp. 1-7.

15. Galatians 5:13-14.

16. Daniel Goleman, *Emotional Intelligence* (New York: Bantam Books, 1995).

17. An earlier version of this chapter appeared as my essay "Goals and

Objectives: Pathways to Educational Myopia?" in *Pro Rege*, Vol. XXIV, No. 3, 1995, pp. 19-24.

Chapter 6

1. Ephesians 6:10-17.
2. The literature describing the research on teaching is vast and expanding. For some representative samples see David Ryans, *Characteristics of Teachers* (Washington, DC: American Council on Education, 1960); N. L. Gage, ed., *Handbook of Research on Teaching* (Chicago: Rand McNally, 1963); M. Wittrock, ed., *Handbook of Research on Teaching*, third ed. (New York: Macmillan, 1986); Jere E. Brophy, "Trends in Research in Teaching" in *Mid-Western Educational Researcher*, Winter, 1994, pp. 29-39.
3. See, e.g., Jere E. Brophy, "Proving the Subtleties of Subject-Matter Teaching" and Ron Brandt, "On Research on Teaching: A Conversation with Lee Shulman" in *Educational Leadership*, Vol. 49, No. 7, April, 1992, pp. 4-8, 14-19.
4. An interesting book detailing these movements is Ron Miller's *What Are Schools For?* (Brandon, VT: Holistic Education Press, 1992). This book provides an overview of various person-centered and progressive educational movements.
5. Paulo Freire, *Pedagogy of the Oppressed* (New York: Seabury Press, 1970).
6. Henri J. Nouwen, *Creative Ministry* (Garden City, NY: Image Books, 1978), pp. 3-20.
7. Parker J. Palmer, *To Know as We Are Known: A Spirituality of Education* (San Francisco: Harper and Row, 1983), pp. 69-105.
8. Alfonso Montuori, "The Art of Transformation: Jazz as a Metaphor for Education" in *Holistic Education Review*, Vol. IX, No. 6, 1996, pp. 57-62.
9. Kieran Egan, *Teaching As Story Telling* (London, Ont.: Althouse, 1986).
10. Alan Tom, *Teaching As a Moral Craft* (New York: Longman, 1984).
11. Harro Van Brummelen, *Walking with God in the Classroom* (Seattle: Alta Vista Press, 1992), pp. 21-22. In the 1999 revision of this book, Van Brummelen describes the priestly function of teaching as a metaphor. See pp. 35-36.
12. Parker J. Palmer, *The Courage to Teach: Exploring the Inner Landscape of a Teacher's Life* (San Francisco: Jossey-Bass Publishers, 1998), p. 148.

13. A phrase popularized by Lee Shulman, as acknowledged in the Ron Brandt article mentioned in note 3, above.

14. Harro Van Brummelen uses the metaphor of "journey" to conclude his chapter on the "vocation of teaching," the final chapter in *Walking with God in the Classroom*, pp. 180-182.

Chapter 7

1. Attributed to George Bernard Shaw.

2. See note 2, Chapter 6.

3. There is a variety of current perennialist perspectives. A growing phenomenon is "classical Christian education." For a survey, presented from a classical point of view, see G. E. Veith, Jr. and Andrew Kern, *Classical Education: Towards the Revival of American Schooling* (Washington, DC: Capital Research Center, 1997).

4. Christians differ on the scope of Christ's redemption. The Reformed perspective endorsed in this book sees *all* of creation affected by sin, and *all* of creation in principle redeemed. See Colossians 1:19-20.

5. My description of these dimensions is loosely inspired by the modality theory proposed by the Dutch philosopher Herman Dooyeweerd.

6. Proverbs 4:23.

7. Is teaching an art or a science? The debate goes back at least half a century. A pivotal, early work was Gilbert Highet's *The Art of Teaching* (New York: Random House, 1950).

8. Calvin Seerveld, long-time aesthetician at the Institute of Christian Studies in Toronto, has an interesting and valuable chapter "The Fundamental Importance of Imaginativity Within Schooling" in *Rainbows for the Fallen World* (Toronto: Tuppence Press, 1980), pp. 138-155.

9. *To Know As We Are Known* (San Francisco: Harper and Row, 1982), pp. 79-83.

10. Arnold De Graaff, formerly with the Institute for Christian Studies in Toronto, devoted considerable attention to the role of "the formative" as a key component of teaching activity. See his book, *The Educational Ministry of the Church: A Perspective* (n. l. The Craig Press, 1968), especially pp. 110-111, 129-133.

11. I Corinthians 3:6-7.

Chapter 8

1. In a valuable discussion of the effectiveness of modeling, Nicholas Wolterstorff refers to the earlier studies of Albert Bandura. See Nicholas Wolterstorff, *Educating for Responsible Action* (Grand Rapids, MI: CSI and Eerdmans, 1980), pp. 51-62. For Bandura's later work, see his *Social Foundations of Thought and Action* (Englewood Cliffs, NJ: Prentice-Hall, 1986). See also B. J. Zimmerman and C. F. Kleefeld, "Toward a Theory of Teaching: A Social Learning View" in *Contemporary Educational Psychology*, Vol. 2, 1977, pp. 158-171.

2. Harro Van Brummelen has singled out "structuring" as a fourth component of teaching, in addition to guiding, unfolding, and enabling. See *Walking with God in the Classroom* (Seattle: Alta Vista Press, 1992), pp. 28-33. However, I continue to think of structuring as an important guiding function. When I structure the classroom for learning, I am actually setting the stage for my students to head into a certain direction and nudging them along.

3. The term "enabling" is becoming somewhat problematic. It is used in social work and other fields, often with negative connotations. For example, "enabling" may refer to the factors that continue to keep a person in bondage to addiction.

Chapter 9

1. E.g., Hebrews 3:13, 10:25, and numerous places in the letters of Paul.

2. Bernice McCarthy, *The 4MAT System: Teaching to Learning Styles with Right/Left Mode Technique* (Barrington, IL: Excel, 1980); Anthony Gregorc, "Learning/Teaching Styles: Their Nature and Effects," in *Student Learning Styles: Diagnosing & Prescribing Programs* (NASSP, 1979), pp. 19-26.

3. Harro Van Brummelen, *Walking with God in the Classroom* (Seattle: Alta Vista Press, 1992), pp. 46-61.

4. Kenneth Dunn & Rita Dunn, "Dispelling Outmoded Beliefs About Student Learning" in *Educational Leadership*, Vol. 44, No. 6, 1987, pp. 55-62.

5. Howard Gardner, *Frames of Mind: The Theory of Multiple Intelligences* (New York: Basic Books, 1982). Gardner added the eighth intelligence a few years ago.

6. The distinctions between individualistic, competitive, and cooperative classrooms are frequently described in the cooperative learning literature. E.g., David W. Johnson, Roger T. Johnson and Edythe Johnson Holubec, *Circles of Learning: Cooperation in the Classroom* (Edina,

MN: Interaction Book Co., 1986), pp. 3-4.

7. The concept "Body of Christ" is frequently used by the Apostle Paul. Some key passages are Romans 12, I Corinthians 12, and Ephesians 4.

8. For a further description of these historical developments, see my essays "From Deformation to Reformation" in *Will All the King's Men . . .* (Toronto: Wedge Pub. Co., 1972), pp. 63-91; and "Church and World in Early Christianity" in *Pro Rege*, Vol. 8, No. 1, September 1979, pp. 2-8.

9. E.g., I Corinthians 7:14.

10. II Corinthians 1:7, 2:3; Galatians 6:2.

11. For an insightful exploration of fear in the classroom, see chapter 2 "A Culture of Fear" in Parker Palmer's *The Courage to Teach: Exploring the Inner Landscape of a Teacher's Life* (San Francisco: Jossey-Bass Publishers, 1998), pp. 35-60.

12. See Robert E. Yager, "Wanted: More Questions, Fewer Answers" in *Science and Children*, September 1987, p. 22.

Chapter 10

1. This statement is a generalization, of course. During the last twenty years there has been increasing interest in creating classrooms marked by cooperation rather than by individualistic competition. For discussions and further bibliography, see the following issues of *Educational Leadership*: Vol. 54, No. 1, September 1996 ("Creating a Climate for Learning"); Vol. 54, No. 5, February 1997 ("Education for Democratic Life"); Vol. 55, No. 2, October 1997 ("Schools as Safe Havens"); Vol. 56, No. 1, September 1998 ("Realizing a Positive School Climate"), and Vol. 57, No. 1, September 1999 ("Personalized Learning").

2. For an illustration and further bibliography, see Evelyn Schneider, "Giving Students a Voice in the Classroom" in *Educational Leadership*, Vol. 54, No. 1, September 1996, pp. 22-26. Schneider's program for teaching educational responsibility is grounded in the work of William Glasser—especially his *Control Theory in the Classroom* (New York: Harper & Row, 1984), and *The Quality School: Managing Students Without Coercion* (New York: Harper & Row, 1990); David W. and Roger T. Johnson, *Teaching Students to be Peacemakers* (Edina, MN: Interaction Book Co., 1991); and R. S. Charney, *Teaching Children to Care: Management in the Responsive Classroom* (Greenfield, MA: Northeast Foundation for Children, 1991). See also Alfie Kohn, "Choices for Children: Why and How to Let Students Decide" in

Kappan, 1993, Vol. 75, No. 1, pp. 8-20.

3. I heard Alfie Kohn draw this comparison in a public debate conducted at the convention of the Association for Supervision and Curriculum Development, San Francisco, 1995.

Chapter 11

1. A classic text on teaching methods is the book *Models of Teaching* by Bruce Joyce and Marsha Weil (Needham Heights, MA: Allyn & Bacon, 1972). Since its appearance in the early seventies it has gone through five editions, the latest published in 1996. Since this book continues to be popular, I'll review its contents (references refer to the fifth edition, 1996).
Joyce and Weil group their "models of teaching" into four families:

(1) The social family: The models in this family emphasize "our social nature, how we learn social behavior, and how social inter-action can enhance academic learning" (p. 63). Included are several forms of cooperative learning, group investigation, and role playing.

(2) The information processing family: The emphasis in this family falls on acquiring and organizing data, concept formation, and problem solving. Some strategies discussed in this section are inductive thinking, concept attainment, mnemonics, and synectics.

(3) The personal family: The purpose of the models in this family is to "lead the student toward greater mental and emotional health by developing self-confidence and a realistic sense of self. . . and to develop specific kinds of qualitative thinking, such as creativity and personal expression" (p. 293). Included are nondirective teaching approaches (Carl Rogers) and methods for enhancing self-esteem (Maslow).

(4) The behavioral systems family: In this section the authors focus on models inspired by behaviorism. They take pains to explain the background and principles of behavior theory (pp. 321-328), then consider, as examples, mastery learning and programmed instruction, and include—interestingly—direct instruction and simulation. To understand this inclusion, the reader needs to take careful note of how the authors define direct instruction and simulation.

While this book provides us with many interesting and helpful insights, a major problem remains the lack of clarity about the criteria used to distinguish between the families. It looks as if some of the strategies are classified according to their inner nature (e.g., information processing), while others appear to be determined by what the strategies are to accomplish (e.g., the personal family). Consequently, the problem of overlap looms large. Wittrock observed that "models of instruction derive largely from the behaviorist, cognitive, and humanistic psychological perspectives" (M. C. Wittrock, "Models of Heuristic Teaching" in M. J. Dunkin, ed., *The International Encyclopedia of Teacher and Teacher Education*, Oxford: Pergamon, 1987, p. 69). This suggestion applies quite accurately to the "families" proposed by Joyce and Weil, if we assume that both the social and personal families are oriented to the humanistic school.

A somewhat similar book is *Instruction: A Models Approach* by M. A. Gunter, T. H. Estes, and J. Schwab (Needham Heights, MA: Allyn & Bacon, 1990 and 1995). The authors define an instructional model as "a step-by-step procedure that leads to specific learning outcomes" (p. 73). Unlike Joyce and Weil, the authors of this book do not attempt to classify models into families. They simply describe a series of disconnected instructional strategies: direct instruction, concept attainment, concept development, synectics, the Suchman inquiry model, classroom discussion, vocabulary acquisition, cooperative learning strategies, models for memory, and conflict resolution models. What distinguishes the models from each other are the differences in intended learning outcomes.

Even more random is the list of teaching strategies discussed by Donald R. Cruickshank, D. L. Bainer, and K. K. Metcalf in their book *The Act of Teaching* (New York: McGraw-Hill, 1995 and 1999). An "instructional alternative" is loosely defined as "any teaching maneuver used to facilitate student learning and satisfaction" (p. 163). The authors present their list of instructional alternatives in alphabetical order (pp. 190-192).

On occasion we do find discussions of teaching strategies that reflect some thought about taxonomies. For example, H. Jerome Freiberg and Amy Driscoll in their book *Universal Teaching Strategies* (Needham Heights, MA: Allyn & Bacon, 1992 and 1996) use the continuum ranging from passive to active learning as basis for their survey of teaching strategies. They begin with lecture and end up with chapters on "students as shareholders" and "making learning real."

By and large, however, descriptions of methods appear to support my contention that the world of teaching strategies remains, in general, a fairly incoherent jumble-bumble jungle. Christian thinking about these matters is only in a stage of infancy.

Chapter 12

1. The literature on direct instruction is quite extensive. A recurring problem is the diversity of views as to what should count as direct instruction. A variety of types and models have been proposed. See, e.g., B. Rosenshine and C. Meister, "Direct Instruction," in L. Anderson, ed., *International Encyclopedia of Teaching and Teacher Education*, second edition (Oxford: Elsevier Science Ltd., 1995), pp. 143-148; J. Murphy, M. Weil, and T. McGreal, "The Basic Practice Model of Instruction," *The Elementary School Journal*, Vol. 87, 1986, pp. 83-95.

2. Deuteronomy 6:6-9, 20-23, 11:18-21; Psalm 78:3-7.

3. For some divergent discussions and further bibliography, consult H. Evan Runner, *The Relation of the Bible to Learning* (Toronto: Wedge Publishing Foundation, 1970), especially pp. 35-40, 87-132; John C. Vander Stelt, *Philosophy & Scripture: A Study in Old Princeton and Westminster Theology,* (Marlton, NJ: Mack Publishing Co., 1978), especially pp. 303-322; John Cooper, "The Changing Face of Truth" in *Orthodoxy and Orthopraxis*, John Bolt, ed. (Jordan Station, Ontario, Canada: Paideia Press, 1986), pp. 33-58. To help you understand how the relativism of postmodernism addresses the question of truth, study J. Richard Middleton & Brian J. Walsh, *Truth Is Stranger Than It Used to Be* (Downers Grove, IL: InterVarsity Press, 1995).

4. Mark 16:20; I Corinthians 3:9; II Corinthians 6:1.

5. Madeline Hunter, *Improving Instruction* (El Segundo, CA: TIP Publications, 1976).

6. The diversity of views on the definition of direct instruction complicates the research results. Consult the following sources: N. L. Gage, ed. *The Psychology of Teaching Methods* (Chicago, IL: Chicago University Press, 1976); N. L. Gage & D. C. Berliner, *Educational Psychology*, 5th edition (Boston, MA: Houghton Mifflin, 1991); Donald C. Orlich and others, *Teaching Strategies: A Guide to Better Instruction* (Lexington, MA: Heath, 1990); B. Rosenshine, "Synthesis of Research on Explicit Teaching" in *Educational Leadership*, Vol. 43, No. 7, 1986, pp. 60-69; B. Rosenshine, "Direct Instruction," in M. J. Dunkin, ed., *The International Encyclopedia of Teaching and Teacher Education* (Oxford: Pergamon, 1987), pp. 257-263; P. Peterson, "Direct Instruction: Effective for What and for Whom?" in *Educational Leadership*, Vol. 37, 1979, pp. 46-48; P. Peterson, "Direct Instruction

Reconsidered" in P. Peterson & H. Walberg, eds., *Research on Teaching: Concepts, Findings, and Implications* (Berkeley, CA: McCutchan, 1979); P. Peterson, "Issue: Should Teachers Be Expected to Learn and Use Direct Instruction?" *ASCD Update*, Vol. 24, No. 5, 1982.

7. Like direct instruction, indirect teaching is a wide concept covering diverse definitions. It is variously described as discovery learning, problem solving, inquiry, and inductive methods of instruction. Gary Borich puts the components together as follows: "Indirect instruction is an approach to teaching and learning in which the process of learning is *inquiry*, the result is *discovery*, and the learning context is a *problem*." Gary D. Borich, *Effective Teaching Methods* (Columbus, OH: Merrill Publishing Co., 1988), p. 163. Indirect instruction is as old as Socrates. It was advocated by John Dewey and popularized by Jerome Bruner. See John Dewey, *Democracy and Education* (New York: Macmillan, 1916), *Experience and Education* (New York: Macmillan, 1938), and Jerome Bruner, *The Process of Education* (Cambridge: Harvard University Press, 1960), and *Toward a Theory of Instruction* (Cambridge, MA: Harvard University Press, 1966).

8. Problem solving as a teaching method includes a variety of types. Currently in vogue is PBL (problem-based learning), an approach that presents "ill-structured problems" to students to be solved. The formulations of such problems intentionally omit specific procedures to be followed and encourage the students to design action steps leading to solutions. For a discussion, see Al Bandstra, *The Effectiveness of Problem-based Learning in Middle School Science* (M. Ed. thesis, Dordt College, 1998). Doug Blomberg suggests that problem-solving should be at the heart of the Christian school curriculum and teaching approaches. He advocates a "problem-posing pedagogy" which is the "exploration of a normed problem-space" (*Perspective*, Institute for Christian Studies, Toronto, Vol. 33, Issue 1, March, 1999, p. 7). See his article "A Problem-posing Pedagogy: 'Paths of Pleasantness and Peace'" in *Journal of Education & Christian Belief*, Vol. 3, No. 2, Autumn, 1999, pp. 97-113. For further discussion, see Gloria Goris Stronks and Doug Blomberg, eds. *A Vision with a Task: Christian Schooling for Responsive Discipleship* (Grand Rapids, MI: Baker Books, 1993), pp. 172-175, 192-213.

9. As reported by Donald C. Orlich and others, *Teaching Strategies: A Guide to Better Instruction* (Lexington, MA: Heath, 1994, 4th ed.), p. 296.

10. Examples are Donald C. Orlich and others, *Teaching Strategies: A Guide to Better Instruction* (Lexington, MA: Heath, 1994, 4th ed.), pp. 268-320; Gary D. Borich, *Effective Teaching Methods* (Columbus, OH: Merrill Publishing Co., 1988), pp. 163-191; Donald R. Cruikshank, D. L. Bainer, K. K. Metcalf, *The Act of Teaching* (New York: McGraw-Hill, 1999), pp. 215-223; H. Jerome Freiberg & Amy Driscoll, *Universal Teaching Strategies* (Boston, MA: Allyn & Bacon, 1996), pp. 306-316.

Chapter 13

1. Meredith D. Gall, "The Use of Questions in Teaching" in *Review of Educational Research,* Vol. 40, 1970, pp. 707-721; William W. Wilen, *Questioning Skills for Teachers* (Washington, DC: National Education Association, 1991).

2. There are many studies. For some samples, see Marylou Dantonio and Louis V. Paradise, "Teaching Question-Answer Strategy and the Cognitive Correspondence Between Teacher Questions and Learner Responses" in *Journal of Research and Development in Education,* Vol. 21, Spring, 1988, pp. 71-75; Nathan C. Swift, Thomas Gooding, and Patricia R. Swift, "Questions and Wait Time," in *Questioning and Discussion: A Multidisciplinary Study*, J. T. Dillon, ed. (Norwood, NJ: Ablex Publishing, 1988); Karen D. Wood and Denise K. Muth, "The Case for Improved Instruction in the Middle School" in *Journal of Reading*, Vol. 35, No. 2, 1991, pp. 84-90.

3. Many studies show that in most classes—at all grade levels—teacher talk predominates. Students ask very few questions. See, e.g., the work of J. T. Dillon, *Questioning and Teaching: A Manual of Practice* (London: Croom Helm, 1987).

4. M. B. Rowe, "Wait Time and Rewards as Instructional Variables, Their Influence in Language, Logic, and Fate Control: Part I—Wait Time" in *Journal of Research in Science Teaching*, Vol. 11, No. 2, 1974, pp. 81-94; K. G. Tobin, "The Effect of an Extended Teacher Wait Time on Science Achievement" in *Journal of Research in Science Teaching*, Vol. 17, 1980, pp. 469-475; "Effects of Teacher Wait Time on Discourse Characteristics in Mathematics and Language Arts Classes" in *American Educational Research Journal*, Vol. 23, No. 2, 1986, pp. 191-201; "The Role of Wait Time in Higher Cognitive Level Learning" in *Review of Educational Research*, Vol. 57, Spring, 1987, pp. 69-95.

Chapter 14

1. See J. T. Dillon, "Using Questions to Foil Discussion" in *Teaching and Teacher Education*, Vol. 1, No. 2, 1985, pp. 109-121.

2. Paulo Freire, *Pedagogy of the Oppressed* (New York: Seabury Press, 1970), *Education for Critical Consciousness* (New York: Seabury Press, 1973), *Pedagogy in Process* (New York: Seabury Press, 1978). Also, Clarence Joldersma, "Shared Praxis: Interchange of Words" in *Christian Educators Journal*, April/May 1980.

3. Daniel Schipani, *Conscientization and Creativity* (Lanham, MD: University Press of America, 1984). Thomas Groome, *Christian Religious Education* (New York: Harper & Row, 1980). Groome's book can rightly be called a landmark in the development of the shared praxis method.

4. I have experimented (and continue to experiment) with the proposed shared praxis model at several grade levels. For a description of one of these experiments, see Trent De Jong, David Loewen, and John Van Dyk, "Shared Praxis: Where Content and Process Meet in the Classroom" in *Christian Educators Journal*, Vol. 37, No. 4, April 1998, pp. 12-15. This article reports a successful experiment at the 7th-grade level in two Christian schools in Abbotsford, BC, Canada.

5. E.g., II Corinthians 5:18.

6. The shared praxis approach surely shows kinship with constructivism. Constructivism suggests that learning takes place when knowledge is built on previous experience and reshaped and reformulated—constructed—as students grow and develop. Constructivism strikes me as proposing a helpful learning theory. Unfortunately, much of constructivism becomes problematic when it also proposes that the knowledge individually constructed is not subject to creational norms. Consequently, constructivism can easily run stuck in a morass of subjectivism and relativism. Christian educators need to be continually critically discerning.

Chapter 15

1. Does cooperative learning *really* work, even when carefully and correctly structured? Or will it always end up as a picture of "pooled ignorance"? Studies increasingly confirm the effectiveness of cooperative learning. Students learn faster and retain longer than in traditional classrooms. Cooperative learning decreases discipline problems and improves time on task, helps students to enjoy their learning tasks, and enhances self-esteem. It develops the skills of cooperation, acceptance

of differences, and respect for others. Meanwhile, the research is continuing. Among the studies supporting the benefits of cooperative learning are the following: David W. Johnson, G. Maruyama, Roger T. Johnson, & D. Nelson, "Effects of Cooperative, Competitive, and Individualistic Goal Structures on Achievement: A Meta-analysis" in *Psychological Bulletin*, Vol. 89, No. 1, 1981, pp. 47-62; David W. Johnson and Roger T. Johnson, *Cooperation and Competition: Theory and Research* (Edina, MN: Interaction Book Co., 1989); Robert E. Slavin, *Cooperative Learning: Theory, Research, and Practice* (Englewood Cliffs, NJ: Prentice-Hall, 1990); Robert E. Slavin, "Synthesis of Research on Cooperative Learning" in *Educational Leadership*, Vol. 48, No. 5, 1991, pp. 71-82; D. Solomon, M. Watson, E. Schaps, V. Battistich, & J. Solomon, "Cooperative Learning as Part of a Comprehensive Classroom Program Designed to Promote Prosocial Development" in *Cooperative Learning: Theory and Research*, S. Sharon, ed. (New York: Praeger, 1990), pp. 231-260.

2. For research on this point, see E. G. Cohen, "Restructuring the Classroom: Conditions for Productive Small Groups" in *Review of Educational Research*, Vol. 64, No. 1, 1994, pp. 1-35.

3. Donald W. Johnson & Roger T. Johnson, *Learning Together and Alone* (Englewood Cliffs, NJ: Prentice Hall, 1991).

4. John Van Dyk, "Cooperative Learning in Christian Perspective: Opening the Dialogue" in *Humans Being: Essays Dedicated to Stuart Fowler,* Doug Blomberg, ed. (Melbourne, Australia: Association for Christian Scholarship; Sydney: National Institute for Christian Education, 1996), pp. 335-353.

5. For a discussion of cooperative learning as a fad, see Robert E. Slavin, "Here to Stay or Gone Tomorrow," guest editorial in *Educational Leadership*, Vol. 47, No. 4, 1989, p. 3, and D. B. Struthers, "Cooperative Learning: Fad or Foundation for Learning?" in *Phi Delta Kappan*, Vol. 72, No. 2, 1990, pp. 158-162.

6. Romans 12:16; I Corinthians 1:10.

7. David W. and Robert T. Johnson, "Conflict in the Classroom: Controversy and Learning" in *Review of Educational Research*, Vol. 49, 1979, pp. 51-61; *Teaching Students to Be Peacemakers* (Edina, MN: Interaction Book Co., 1995); "Teaching Students to Be Peacemakers: Results of Five Years of Research" in *Peace and Conflict: Journal of Peace Psychology,* Vol. 1, No. 4, 1995, pp. 417-438; "Conflict Resolution and Peer Mediation Programs in Elementary and Secondary Schools: A Review of the Research" in *Review of Educational*

Research, Vol. 66, No. 4, 1996, pp. 459-506; "The Three C's of School and Classroom Management" in *Beyond Behaviorism: Changing the Classroom Management Paradigm*, H. Jerome Freiberg, ed. (Boston: Allyn & Bacon, 1999), pp. 119-144.

8. In his second edition of *Walking with God in the Classroom*, Harro Van Brummelen includes a brief discussion of dispute and conflict resolution. He provides a summary of steps based on otherwise unidentified sources. See *Walking with God in the Classroom* (Seattle: Alta Vista College Press, 1998), pp. 73-75.

9. M. Sapon-Shevin & N. Schniedewind, "Selling Cooperative Learning Without Selling It Short" in *Educational Leadership*, Vol. 47, No. 4, Dec./Jan., 1990, pp. 63-64.

Chapter 16

1. In his first edition of *Walking With God in the Classroom*, Harro Van Brummelen makes a significant distinction between "individualized learning" and "personalized learning." "Individualized learning (e.g., through computer-based instruction)," he says, "does not necessarily meet the learning needs of the person, nor does its exclusive use prepare persons to live in *community*. Individualized learning, while effective for learning some basic concepts and skills, is often based on a deterministic, behavioristic view of the person. . . . What is a Biblical view of personalized learning? First, personalized learning means that teachers treat students with care and concern, and allow them to exercise the abilities that are part of their personhood. Second, the learning is structured to involve tasks and methods that, as much as possible, meet the needs of all persons in the classroom. Third, learners are encouraged, when appropriate, to make choices about their learning, act on them, and bear a measure of responsibility for their own learning decisions." *Walking With God in the Classroom* (Burlington, Ontario: Welch Publishing Co.), 1984, p. 80.

2. John Van Dyk, "Kids in the Middle: Winners or Losers?" Two articles in *Christian Educators Journal*, Vol. 34, No. 3, February, 1995, pp. 2-4; and Vol. 34, No. 4, April, 1995, pp. 11-12.

3. Romans 12.

4. The term "multifunctional" may be cumbersome. Currently the word is "differentiated" or "diverse." Nevertheless, I continue to think of "multifunctional" as suggestive of a more wholistic classroom situation than does "differentiated." An excellent book, full of practical ideas speaking directly to the sort of classroom I am promoting in this

chapter, is Carol Ann Tomlinson's *The Differentiated Classroom: Responding to the Needs of All Learners* (Alexandria, VA: ASCD, 1999). The book forms a fine resource for staff development programs.

5. Matthew 5:9; James 3:16-18.

6. Job 30:25; Romans 12:15; Romans 15:1-2; Galatians 6:2; Colossians 3:12-16; Hebrews 13:3; I John 3-4.

7. Ephesians 4:12.

8. I Corinthians 13.

9. For a wealth of ideas, see Tomlinson's *The Differentiated Classroom*, note 4 above.

10. Howard Gardner's theory of multiple intelligences is probably one of the most influential (and successful) theories to enter the educational world in recent years. For his latest thinking, see *The Disciplined Mind: What All Students Should Understand* (New York: Simon & Schuster, 1999) and *Intelligence Reframed* (New York: Basic Books, 1999).

11. A. H. Maslow, *Motivation and Personality* (New York: Harper & Row, 1954). Maslow proposed a "hierarchy of needs" ranging from physiological to self-actualization needs.

12. William Glasser, *The Quality School* (New York: Harper & Row), 1990.

13. For a sample of the literature, see David Kolb, *Learning Style Inventory* (Boston: McBer & Co., 1976); Bernice McCarthy, *The 4MAT System: Teaching to Learning Styles* (Barrington, IL: Excel, 1981); Anthony Gregorc, *An Adult's Guide to Style* (Maynard, MA: Gabriel Systems, 1982) and *Inside Styles* (Maynard, MA: Gabriel Systems, 1987).

14. Rita & Kenneth Dunn, *Teaching Students Through Their Individual Learning Styles: a Practical Approach* (Reston, VA: Reston Publishing Co., 1978); "Teaching Students Through Their Individual Learning Styles: A Research Report" in *Student Learning Styles and Brain Behavior* (Reston, VA: National Association of Secondary School Principals, 1982), pp. 142-151.

15. See footnote 10 above.

16. Harro Van Brummelen, *Walking With God in the Classroom* (Burlington, Ontario: Welch Publishing Co.), 1984, pp. 80-81.

17. See Carol Ann Tomlinson, "Mapping a Route Toward Differentiated Instruction" in *Educational Leadership*, Vol. 57, No. 1, September 1999, pp. 12-16.

Chapter 17

1. E.g., Donald R. Cruickshank, D. L. Bainer, and Kim Metcalf list nearly 100 entries in the reference section to their chapter on classroom
management in *The Act of Teaching* (New York: McGraw-Hill, 1999),
pp. 394-397.

2. Cruickshank and others, *The Act of Teaching*, pp. 361-362. Alfie Kohn
vigorously opposes the distinction. See especially the first five chapters
of his book *Beyond Discipline: From Compliance to Community*
(Alexandria, VA: ASCD, 1996).

3. Harro Van Brummelen, *Walking with God in the Classroom* (Seattle:
Alta Vista College Press, 1998), pp. 75-79.

4. Donald C. Orlich and others, *Teaching Strategies: A Guide to Better
Instruction* (Lexington, MA: D. C. Heath and Co., 1994), pp. 351-367.

5. Alfie Kohn, *Beyond Discipline*, pp. xiv-xv.

6. Donald R. Cruickshank and others, *The Act of Teaching*, pp. 387-388.
Also see Alfie Kohn, *Beyond Discipline,* pp. 24-32.

7. Matthew 5:38-42.

8. Ephesians 6:4.

9. Alfie Kohn, *Beyond Discipline*, p. 121.

10. For helpful descriptions, see H. Jerome Freiberg, ed., *Beyond
Behaviorism: Changing the Classroom Management Paradigm*
(Needham Heights, MA: Allyn and Bacon, 1999).

Chapter 18

1. Since everyone is short of time, popular books on time management
sell well. For literature specifically concerned with the time problems
experienced by teachers, consult the following: J. Applegate, "Time" in
Donald R. Cruickshank & Associates, *Teaching Is Tough* (Englewood
Cliffs, NJ: Prentice-Hall, 1980), pp. 257-302; C. Collins, *Time
Management for Teachers* (West Nyack, NY: Parker, 1987). For helpful
suggestions, also see chapter 4, "The Effective Use of Time" in
H. Jerome Freiberg and Amy Driscoll's *Universal Teaching Strategies*
(Needham Heights, MA: Allyn and Bacon, 1996).

2. For interesting insights into the "inner landscape of a teacher's life," see
Parker J. Palmer, *The Courage to Teach* (San Francisco: Jossey-Bass
Publishers, 1998).

3. Dr. Stuart Fowler of Antithesis Educational Services, Melbourne,
Victoria, Australia, personal comment.

4. Matthew 10:16.

NAMES

Index of Names   279

SUBJECTS

Inductive inquiry, 166-168, 271
Information processing, 268-269
In loco parentis, 48-49
Intellectualism, 61, 65, 94, 106, 176,
    252-257
Integrated curriculum, 122, 211, 228
Interests, 35-37, 39, 48, 226
Inventory work, 131-137, 225-226,
    229, 232
Invitation to teach, 34-39, 47, 51, 89
ITIP, 161

Jigsaw, 197, 213-214
Journey *See* Teaching Christianly

Kids in the middle, 220
Kingdom of God, 32-41, 51-53, 69,
    105, 115, 160, 251, 254, 260
Knowledge *See also* Wisdom
    as cognition, 61-65
    as content, 117
    as goal of discussion and shared
        praxis, 192-193, 198
    biblical view of, 23, 65, 88, 106
    constructivist view of, 255
    knowledge-how, 64
    knowledge-that, 64
    to be unfolded, 104-105

Learning activities
    as aspect of a teaching strategy,
        145-149, 158, 164
    as mere suggestions, 11, 143
    in relation to devotional activity,
        52, 102
    in relation to service projects, 24
    result of planning, 93
    practicality of, 143-144
Learning centers, 167, 228
Learning outcomes, 60, 104, 144-149,
    158, 187, 231, 269
Learning styles
    and egalitarianism, 220, 257

diversity of, 92, 123, 180
in direct instruction, 163
in multifunctional classroom,
    223-229
theories of, 116, 227
Learning theory, 12-13, 79, 116, 151,
    198, 255, 273
Lecturing, 9, 25, 147-153, 157, 161-
    166, 195
Lesson plans
    affected by sin and redemption,
        33
    aimed at goals, 57-59, 67-69
    and teaching strategies, 150-
        152, 168, 186-188, 194
    as service, 50-52
    authority over, 49
    questions in, 175-176, 181
    to be appropriately designed,
        91-93
Letterhead approach to questioning,
    180-181

Mass instruction/teaching
    See Whole-class instruction
Master teachers, 76, 159
Mastery learning, 268
Materialism, 250-251
Math anxiety, 107
Math manipulatives, 27, 33, 107
Math-Their-Way, 198
Memorization, 26, 51, 58-61, 161-
    166, 255, 269
Metaphors of teaching *See* Teaching
Mission statements, 19, 57-58, 113
Mnemonics, 268
Modeling
    as definition of teaching
        Christianly, 21-22
    as direct instruction, 160
    as a guiding function, 100-102,
        106
    in cooperative learning, 206

in questioning, 178
of discipleship skills and various
habits, 66-68, 93-94, 124
research in, 265-266
Models of teaching *See* Teaching
Monitoring, 207
Motivation, 101, 151-161, 185, 233-
237, 241
Multidimensional, 88-95
Multifunctional classroom, 222-232
Multiple intelligences, 116, 226-227,
266
Mutual checking, 195, 209, 214

Needs *See* Gifts
Neomarxism, 192
Neutrality of teaching methods, 20-
22, 147-150, 174
New Age philosophy, 20, 210-211
Nondirective teaching, 268
Nonparticipatory discussion, 188-189
Normative response, 66, 89-95, 109,
255-256

Objectives *See* Goals
Objective testing, 172
Office, 38-53, 115, 124, 153, 186,
255
Office consciousness, 41-54, 115,
255
Open classroom, 57, 165, 187
Ordering/organizing classroom, 77,
93, 103-104, 145-146

Pacing, 91-92
Parables *See* Story telling
Participatory discussion, 188-192
Participatory teaching, 152-154, 165-
168, 174, 183-199
Passive learning, 25, 131, 152, 164
Peace education, 215
Pedagogical content knowledge, 79
Pedagogy *See* Teaching

Perennialism, 17, 76-77, 87-88, 106,
159, 228, 253
Performance objectives
See Goals/objectives
Personality of teacher.*See* Teacher
Personalized learning, 219, 230, 267,
275
Perspectivalism, 23-24, 105
Perspective
and view of giftedness, 226
as basis for evaluation, 79
as defining teaching Christianly,
23-24
as unwanted influence, 51
function in teaching strategies,
146-149, 176
holistic, 61-62, 65, 250
on subject matter, 105-106
shared, 18
Philosophy of education
and classroom arrangement, 228
and curriculum, 117
and metaphors of teaching, 76-79
and questioning, 176
and teaching, 11, 87-88
in Christian educational literature,
1, 6
influence of, 114
unrecognized, 10, 17, 51, 108-109
Phonics, 27, 151
Plummet-right-in approach, 130-131,
134
Popularity syndrome, 4
Positive interdependence, 206-207
Positive reinforcement, 238
Positivism, 61, 252-253
Postmodernism, 212, 252, 270
Power *See* Authority
Practical tips *See* Teaching
Pragmatism, 10-12, 17, 144, 232, 254
Privatization of teaching, 9-10, 28
Problem-based learning (PBL), 271
Problem-posing pedagogy, 271

Shock of the familiar, 3, 261
Simply group work, 119-121
Simply teaching, 20, 86, 90
Simulation *See* Drama
Sin
    and classroom management, 242
    and constructivism, 255-256
    and cooperative learning, 208
    and first-step approach, 137-138
    and Kingdom of God, 52
    and multifunctional classroom, 224
    and progressivism, 255
    and servanthood, 66
    and subject matter, 117
    battle with, 75, 100
    scope of, 33, 88, 105, 176
Skills *See also* Critical thinking and
    Discipleship skills
    as gifts or needs, 133, 228
    and direct instruction, 158, 162
    and unfolding, 104-107
    drill in, 96
    in definitions of teaching, 85
    in goal taxonomies, 60-69
Special education, 220
Sphere sovereignty, 48-49
Spirituality, 20-21
Standardized tests, 52, 108, 257
Stewardship, 66, 91-92, 105
Story telling, 26, 77, 96, 153, 159, 167
Stress, 53, 249-250
Structuring for learning, 103-104,
    146, 186, 242, 266
Student-teacher relationship
    ability to establish, 38-39
    and authority, 45-46
    and Kingdom of God, 52-53
    and military metaphors, 75
    and modeling, 100, 124
    as a problem, 4
    by contracts, 231
    in first-step approach, 135

    in multifunctional classroom,
      224
    in shared praxis, 199
    trust and fairness, 90
Subjectivism, 256, 273
Subject matter *See* Content
Suchman's inquiry model, 269
Synectics, 268, 269

Talents *See* Gifts
Task *See* Teaching Christianly
Taxonomy
    Bloom's, 60-63
    goals, 60-69
    teaching strategies, 153-154
    three c's, 63
Teachable moment, 59, 111, 186, 188
Teacher
    aides, 220
    born, not made, 7-8
    gifts
      and calling, 32, 35-39
      and sphere sovereignty, 48
      as prerequisites, 7-8
      for lecturing, 164
      for teaching Christianly, 79,
        114-115
    personality, 36-39, 48, 79, 115,
      130
    responsibility
      See Responsibility of teachers
Teaching *See also* Teaching Christianly
    as art, 8-9, 91
    as bag of tricks/practical tips/
      recipes, 11, 143, 147, 153,
      185, 238-240
    as craft, 52, 77-82, 91, 148, 161
    as a personal/private matter, 9-10
    Christianly
      See Teaching Christianly
    definitions of, 85-88, 145-150,
      153, 163
    direct *See* Direct instruction

BIBLE PASSAGES

Breinigsville, PA USA
29 March 2011
258683BV00001B/2/A